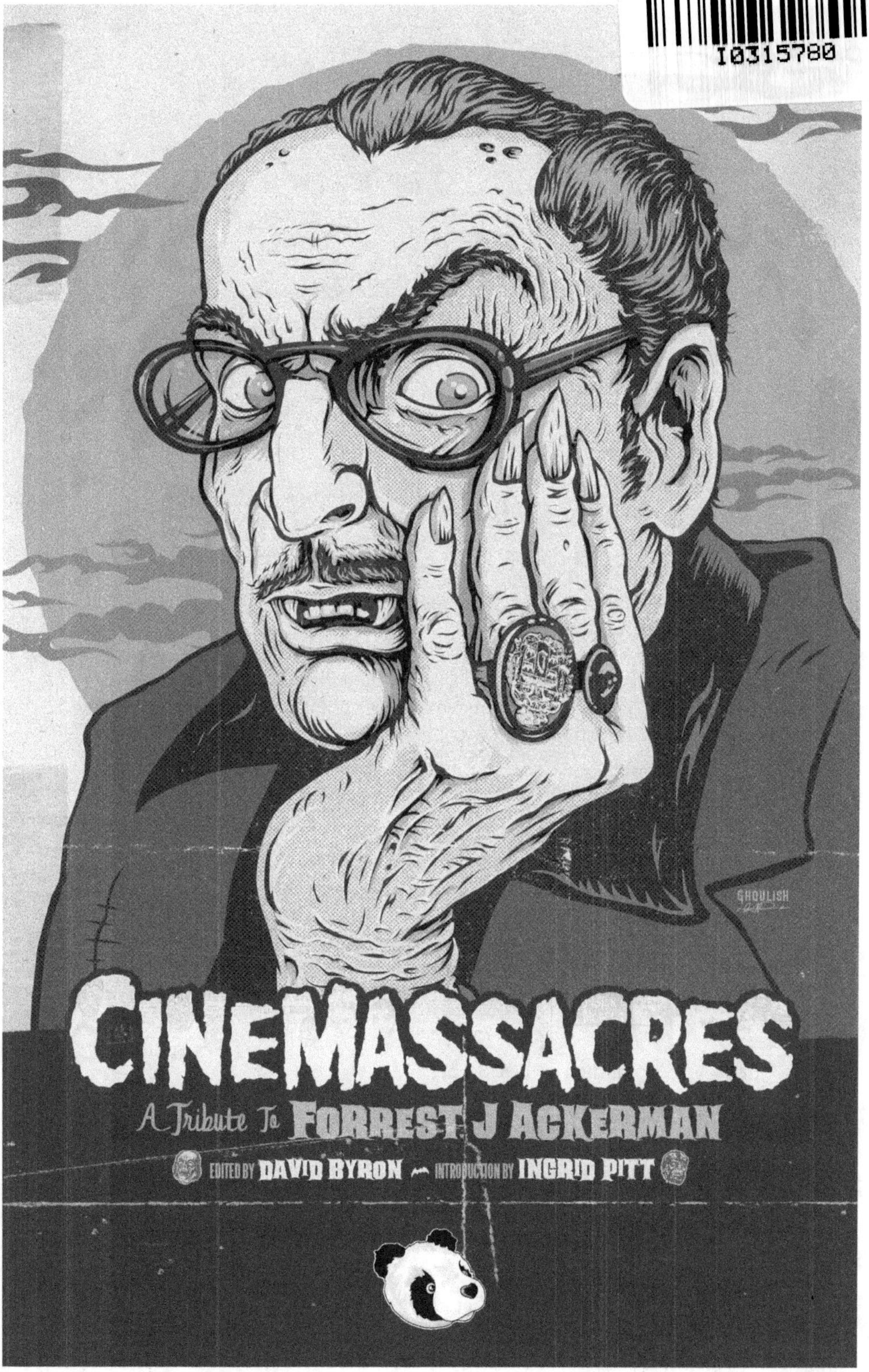
GHOULISH
CINEMASSACRES
A Tribute To FORREST J ACKERMAN
EDITED BY DAVID BYRON
INTRODUCTION BY INGRID PITT

Cinemassacres: A Tribute to Forrest J Ackerman
© 2010 David Byron. All Rights Reserved.

No part of this book may be reproduced in any form or by any means, electronic, mechanical, digital, photocopying or recording, except for the inclusion in a review, without permission in writing from the publisher.

All interviews and images used by permission.

All interviews are original to this book excepting for:
The Chet Williamson interview first appeared in *Horror Prodigies & Legends,* © 2010 LOH Press. The Joe R. Lansdale interview first appeared in *NVH Magazine,* © 2009.

Cover art design by "Ghoulish" Gary Pullin/Artwork by Gary Pullin. First published in *Rue Morgue Magazine* #83. © Copyright Marrs Media Inc. Used with permission. Dr. Mangor photo/artwork by Bethalynne Bajema — based on a photo by Robyn Van Swank.

Published in the USA by:
BearManor Media
PO Box 1129
Duncan, Oklahoma 73534-1129
www.bearmanormedia.com

ISBN 978-1-59393-544-3

Printed in the United States of America
Book design by Brian Pearce | Red Jacket Press

Acknowledgements

A big thanks go all of the featured guests, without whom this book wouldn't exist; thanks to Michael McCarty, for his insight and advice; to Ingrid Pitt, for her heart-felt introduction, to Ben Ohmart of BearManor Media for his patience, and last, but not least, to all of my readers at the former *NVF Magazine,* for all of their support when the fiction magazine folded. Your patronage will not be forgotten.

Table of Contents

Introduction by Ingrid Pitt 7
Kind Comments 11

INTERVIEWS 15

Michael McCarty (Author, *Modern Mythmakers*) 17
Frank Dietz (Artist) 27
Joe Moe (Multi-Media Artist and Forry's "best pal") 33
Michael Mallory (Author, *Universal Studios Monsters: A Legacy Of Horror*) 39
John Dimes (Actor/Artist/Author of *The Rites of Pretending Tribe*) 45
Brian Walker (Creator of *Brian's Drive-In Theatre*) 51
Robert Leininger (Producer, *The Undying Monsters*) 57
Dick Dyszel (Count Gore Devol, host of *Creature Feature*) 63
Jim McDermott (Artist) 69
Lucy Hell (*Mystery Island Publications*) 73
"Ghoulish" Gary Pullin (Art Director, *Rue Morgue Magazine*) 77

SPECIAL GUEST PHOTOS 81

Courtlandt Hull (Creator of "The Witch's Dungeon"
Museum in Bristol, CT.) 93
Kevin Sean Michaels (Director, *Vampira: The Movie*).... 99
Frank Winspur (Creator, *Moebius Models*) 105
Dr. Mangor (Antimator, Photographer,
Creator of *Suicidal Suzi* comic) 109
Pam Keesey (Editor, *Scifi-Womanthology*) 115

SPECIAL GUEST INTERVIEWS 119

Joe R. Lansdale: East Texas Gothic 121
Chet Williamson (Author, *Gandhi At The Bat*) 131
Don Calfa (Star of *Return of the Living Dead*) 137
Fred Olen Ray (Director, *Scalps*) 143
Muse Watson (Star of *NCIS*) 153
Jason Paul Collum (Author, *Assault of the Killer Bs*) 165
John Kenneth Muir
(Author, *Horror Films of the 1980s*) 177
Christopher Golden (Author, *Strangewood*) 181
Jim O'Rear (genre Actor/Stuntman/Screenwriter) 189
Sara Karloff (Daughter of horror icon Boris Karloff) 195
Iron Dave (Author, *Cinemassacres*) 199
John Everson (Author, *Covenant* and *The 13th*).......... 209
The Amazing Kreskin 215
Count Gregula... 231
Jim Wynorksi (Director, *Chopping Mall*) 235

Echoes.. 243
Anonymous Posthumous Cheers from Forry's Fans...... 257
Afterword 261
About the Author.. 263

Introduction

First time I met Forry was way back in November 1975 at the *Famous Monsters of Filmland* Convention in New Year City. I nearly didn't make it. I was filming in Tres Arroyes, a little town about 200 miles south of Buenos Aires. The film was called *El Lobo* and was about a virgin and a wolf that was a devil in disguise. Type casting, I thought. Things hadn't been going so well on the set. Argentina wasn't exactly the most stable country to be working in and the producer was having a bad time both financially and politically, so when I received a telegram from my agent reminding me that I was due to be at the convention in New York in three days time I sensed he was relieved to get me off his hands for a few days.

When I arrived at the Convention I was given a bodyguard/guide named Jerry Arden. I was told that Jerry was there *for me*. I soon found that I could hardly set foot outside my room without Jerry being *there for me*. Flattering at first, but a bit inhibiting. Jerry was guiding me through the hotel on the morning after I arrived when this tall, interestingly dressed man threw himself down on one knee in front of me and pledged undying love and declared he wanted to marry me. I gave him a weak smile and tried to walk around him but he wouldn't let me pass. I didn't want to make a scene so I painted on a smile and broke the news that I had married Tonio only a few weeks before. The man claimed he was devastated and would wait for me forever.

Jerry came to the rescue.

"How's the wife, Forry?" he asked.

The man climbed to his feet and gave me a broad smile. "Well it was worth a try," he said.

Jerry introduced him as Forry Ackerman. It still didn't press any buttons, but Jerry made a date with him for lunch so I guessed it was all right.

Jerry filled me in on Forry's background. Forry could rightly claim the title of "Mr. Sci-Fi." He loved the genre and spent his entire life surrounded by like-minded fans of alternative worlds and ways of life. His friends were the people who made the genre live. He was the editor of the long running magazine *Famous Monsters of Filmland* and was still talking about bringing it back to life until his death on December 6, 2008. He was also the owner of the *Vampirella* comic book franchise. But Forry was much more than a workman in the field of the future: Forry made it happen.

He was born in 1916. At the age of ten he read a magazine that generated his life's obsession for the remote and unbelievable. The magazine, *Amazing Stories*, was the slightly dodgy Hugo Gernsback's vehicle to get his stories published without the inconvenience of having to find an editor who shared his enthusiasm.

As the Sci-Fi genre began to take hold, Forry was there astride the leading rocket. He gathered together others who were enchanted by the fast growing medium and did everything he could to foster their talents. His enthusiasm was so catching that he soon had a coterie of budding writers who were to become the greatest names in the business.

The home-away-from-home of the American Sci-Fi writers of the day was Clifton's Cafeteria. There you would find the fledgling Robert Heinlein, Henry Kuttner, Leigh Brackett and many other writers discussing other worlds and parallel Universes. Forry was a great life-long fan of Ray Bradbury. When Ray wanted to start a magazine for the futurists called *Futuria Fantasy* it was Forry who scraped together the funds to get it into print. Before long, Forry had turned his passion into a business and was agent for such luminaries as Isaac Asimov, A.E Van Vogt, Curt Siodmak, L. Ron Hubbard and, of course, Ray Bradbury.

Forry's house in Lincoln Park in Los Angeles, dubbed Acker Mansion, was a magnet for all fans of a Sci-Fi or Horror persuasion. He had somehow managed to inveigle his way into more than 50 films and had taken home souvenirs from most of them. Friends and grateful fans had donated others. There was hardly an inch of space in the whole house that didn't tell a story. And Forry was there to tell 'em. Even the toilet was papered with posters and magazine covers. On most Saturdays he would throw open the door and greet the fans lining up outside. He would then spend the day taking his visitors around the exhibits giving well-honed stories on any of the pieces in which the fans showed an interest. I was invited to visit the Acker Mansion when I was in Los Angeles in 1997 for the Festival to celebrate the hundredth anniversary of the publication of *Bram Stoker's Dracula*. Forry picked me up from the hotel and took me to his home. On the way we picked up another Horror icon, Bob Quarry. Bob was America's answer to Christopher Lee. On the way to Forry's place he told me that in one of his films, I've forgotten which, there is a scene from either *Countess Dracula* or *Vampire Lovers*. Unfortunately I can't even remember the name of the film. Forry was still declaring undying love and promising to marry me but the fun had gone out of it a little. His wife Wendayne was ill and Forry was obviously worried about her. But he gallantly did the tour for me and at the end did me the honor of asking, not for my hand in marriage, but for my signature on the flyleaf of his first addition of the Stoker masterpiece. I really felt privileged to be among such giants of the Horror scene as Bela Lugosi, John Carradine, Christopher Lee, Peter Cushing, Bob Quarry, Elsa Lancaster and many others.

I suppose it was a bit childish carrying on the 'courtship' performance for so many years, but we both enjoyed it. I'll miss him next time I go to America. The last time I saw him was at a convention in Baltimore: approaching his nineties, he retained all the enthusiasm and chutzpah that he had all those years ago in New York. He gave me a copy of his book. *Forrest Ackerman's World of Science Fiction*. On the flyleaf he wrote, in various coloured inks:

'For Ingrid the Rapturous, Captor of the Heart
of your Eternal Fan and Friend.
With Ardent Affection — Forry.'

You can't have it better than that!

Ingrid Pitt
December 2009

Kind Comments

"Forry was a hero and inspiration to thousands of genre filmmakers and fans. He certainly inspired me. I grew up on Famous Monsters of Filmland, and I have many cherished memories of meeting the man over the years, both at his home and at conventions. I also enjoyed publishing his words in Fangoria, *especially for our 100th issue. Most of all, Forry is partially responsible for where I am today; he bought or helped sell several articles of mine when I was first starting out, for* Enterprise Incidents *and* Monsterland. *During his final days, I'm glad that I got to say goodbye to the man in person and tell him how much he meant to me."*

Anthony Timpone
Editor, FANGORIA

"Thanks, Uncle Forry — you caught me just at the right age with FM # 5 and set my feet on that dark path forever after. Rest in peace, Mister Monster..."

Chet Williamson

"Like any horror fan who grew up in the mid to later half of the 20th century, you knew Forry Ackerman was a legend. Without him and Famous Monsters of Filmland *there would have been no* Fangoria, Rue Morgue, HorrorHound, Gorezone, Femme Fatales, Cinefantastique, HorrorShow, Alternative Cinema, Scarlet Street, *et al. Now in a time where hard copied publications are becoming extinct and horror fans gleam all of their information from the often nameless glow of website screens, it seems there are fewer "Uncle Forry's" to look up to...to put upon some minor form of idol worship. Forry made reading fun, brought our favorite movie monsters and those who created them to life in our minds, and fed our all-consuming passions for the genre we love. He is an icon and an original who will be truly missed."*

Jason Paul Collum
director of Something to Scream About

"Forrest J. Ackerman was a walking encyclopedia of science fiction and horror. As the well-known editor of "Famous Monsters Of Filmland" for twenty years (and over 200 issues), he had personally known such legends as Boris Karloff, Bela Lugosi, Lon Chaney Jr., Peter Lorre, Christopher Lee and Vincent Price.

After twenty years and 191 Mr. Ackerman resigned as editor of "Famous Monsters" — his two-decade tenure had influenced generations of horror fans, including Academy Award-winning director Steven Spielberg and author Stephen King — who sent his first story to the magazine. There was also George Lucas, Rick Baker the monster-maker, John Landis, Joe Dante — all were readers who grew up and made an impression on the world.

If it wasn't for Forry Ackerman and Famous Monsters Of Filmland, I doubt I would have ended up a speculative fiction writer in the first place.

I started collecting Famous Monsters in 1973. My mom actually bought my first copy of the magazine, issue #107 with West World's cowboy robot Yul Brynner on the cover. I read the magazine from cover to cover, fascinated with the black-and-white stills of monster movies and the pun-filled humor, courtesy of Mr. Ackerman.

The first time met Forry at a science fiction in Iowa City. Shortly after that, I did an interview with him for my first book called Giants Of The Genre (2003, Wildside Press).

The second time I met Forry was in 2003, at the World Horror Convention. I sat next to him at a signing and we talked and shared plenty of laughs.

Over the years, we exchanged, mail, email, Christmas cards and of course, more interviews. I interviewed him for Modern Mythmakers (McFarland & Company, 2008) and dedicated the book to him and again in Esoteria-Land (BearManor Media, 2009,) again dedicating the book to him.

He was truly a giant and gentleman of the genre and will be sorely missed."

Michael McCarty

Interviews

Michael McCarty

Michael McCarty has been a professional writer since 1983 and is the author of 10 books (fiction and nonfiction) and several hundred articles, short stories, poems, etc. He is the 2008 David R. Collins' Literary Achievement Award winner from the Midwest Writing Center. In 2005 was a Bram Stoker *Finalist for the Nonfiction Book Of The Year with* More Giants Of The Genre. *He lives in Rock Island, Illinois and was a former stand-up comedian, musician and managing editor of a music magazine and is currently is a staff writer for "Science Fiction Weekly" the official website of the* SCI FI Channel. *His novel* Monster Behind the Wheel, *co-written with Mark McLaughlin (Delirium Books/Corrosion Press) was published in the summer of 2008, the vampire satire* Liquid Diet *(Black Death/Demonic Clown Books) and the novella* Monster Hunter *(Skullvines Press) and the science fiction novel* Out Of Time, *was co-written with Connie Corcoran Wilson (Lachesis Publishing). Mike's short story collections include* Dark Duets *(Wildside Press, 2005),* All Things Dark and Hideous, *co-written with Mark McLaughlin and published in England (Rainfall Books, 2008) and* Little Creatures *(Sam's Dot Publishing, 2008). He also co-wrote the poetry collection* Attack of the Two-Headed Poetry Monster, *with Mark McLaughlin (Skullvines Press, 2008). His nonfiction books include* Giants of the Genre *(Wildside Press, 2003),* Modern Mythmakers *(McFarland & Company, 2008) and* Ghostly Tales of Route 66, *co-written Connie Corcoran Wilson (Quixote Press, 2008).*

His websites are: www.myspace.com/monsterbook, www.myspace.com/lovein2025, www.myspace.com/route66ghosts *and* www.myspace.com/ottochurch.

ID: Greetings and salutations, Mike. Been keeping busy? Or is that an understatement?

MM: Busy, busy and more busy — I'm too busy to schedule a nervous breakdown *(laughs).* As the saying goes, "No rest for the wicked" — so I must be extremely wicked.

ID: I have recently finished reading your book with Mark McLaughlin, Monster Behind the Wheel, and I must say, it is a regular horror tour-de-force. Your title character, Jeremy Carmichael, is one of the most memorable characters I've ever seen in horror fiction. Where did the idea for Jeremy come from? Or...should I fear to ask?

MM: Thank you for your kind words. Jeremy was a truly organic character that sprang to life quickly. When I was going to college, I had this idea of the "Land of the Dead" — a Purgatory-type place where the dead wait and wait until their time and fate is decided. I also had the idea of someone speaking to character through car speakers.

When I started *Monster Behind the Wheel*, I originally wanted the book to be a collaboration with Mark McLaughlin and myself. He looked at my outline and storyline and character development sheets and said, "I think this is much too personal of a book for me to be involved in." So I planned on writing the book on my own, after finishing up a different novel, a vampire book called *Liquid Diet*.

For *Monster*, I had the idea of an average person taking on the Goliath-like insurance companies and lawyers. I was influenced by Richard Laymon's everyday-type characters who are thrown into weird situations as in such books as *Night in the Lonesome October, Bite* and *The Traveling Vampire Show*.

At that time, I was also working on which would become my first published book, *Giants of the Genre* — a collection of interviews. What I decided to do was interview my fictional character, Jeremy Carmichael. I asked a series of questions and wrote down his answers. Believe it not, I still have that Q&A in my file cabinet. Anyway, that was the beginning of *Monster Behind the Wheel*. I showed this to Mark and he read it and said, "If you can do the same thing with the villain, Frank Edmondson, than you have the beginnings of a great novel." Good advice!

I integrated some of my own personal experiences into Jeremy's history — we both were pizza delivery drivers in college (and both went to a community college), we both have been involved in a major automobile accident (his was worse), and we both had to fight insurance companies.

Mark was doing a bit of editing on *Liquid Diet,* so as we worked together more, he soon changed his mind and agreed to become my co-author for *Monster Behind the Wheel*. As he became more and more involved in writing the book, he made Jeremy even more likeable. He added a lot of humor to the character (which was sadly missing). Being a former stand-up comedian, I couldn't let him get all the laughs, so I had to start writing funny passages, too — which is the reason I think the book turned out great. Mark started his work on the end chapters, since I'd already done a lot of work on the beginning, and we sort of met in the middle!

Jeremy's voice as a character was a voice I really enjoyed writing and eventually Mark and I will write a sequel — or two!

ID: It seems that you — like me — have a genuine love for the horror genre, which, of course, always helps when you write within the same genre. What first prompted your interest in the macabre?

MM: Two events that happened around the same time during my childhood: my mom bought me a copy of *Famous Monsters of Filmland Magazine* (issue No. 107 with *West World* on the cover) and I discovered *Acri Creature Feature* on Saturday nights. I remember the first one I saw, the '60s black-and-white thriller, *Carnival of Souls*.

I had been reading science fiction long before horror. The first horror books I read were by Stephen King and Dean Koontz, both whom I still enjoy reading after all these years.

ID: To me, your book, Modern Mythmakers, *is like a template for writing the perfect interview book. It takes a real talent to know how to talk to people the way you do. Who was the first person you interviewed? Were you nervous?*

MM: My first interview was in the sixth grade with my fifth grade teacher, Mrs. Stonebraker — I had the biggest crush on her (I mention the crush, and the interview, in *Modern Mythmakers*). Strangely, I wasn't nervous, because I had a job to do — the interview for the school newspaper. I had a defined role, so it kept me focused.

My first genre interview was in 1989, right after I graduated from college. I'd moved up to Chicago and, at one point, interviewed science fiction legend Frederik Pohl at his home. I even sat in his office, where he let me hold his one of Hugo Awards in my hands — that was a thrill. I sold the interview to *Starlog Magazine* and became a nationally published freelance writer overnight.

ID: My first interview was with Herschell Gordon Lewis, and he couldn't have been a nicer guy; not at all like you would picture someone who (proudly) bears the moniker "The Godfather of Gore." You've interviewed him, too. What was your first impression of him?

MM: Your first interview was with H.G. Lewis? Cool.

He was the final interview I did for *Modern Mythmakers*. He is a busy guy and when Mark McLaughlin and I interviewed him, he was in his early nineties. Because he was a former public relations man and in show business for such a long time, it was an easy and fun interview to do, and he's a nice guy to boot.

ID: How did you meet scream queen Linnea Quigley?
MM: I interviewed Linnea Quigley for my book, *More Giants of the Genre*. Shortly after that, the *Cemetery Dance* anthology *Midnight Premiere* featured short fiction by horror actors and actresses. I'm not a horror performer, but Linnea Quigley is — she has appeared in such films as *Return of the Living Dead, Hollywood Chainsaw Hookers, Night of the Demons, Sorority Babes in the Slimeball Bowl-A-Rama*, and *Silent Night, Deadly Night* (I have a warm spot in my heart, or elsewhere, for her Best Impaled-on-Antlers Performance in that film).

I met Linnea while she was filming the movie *Unaware* in Gelena, Illinois, and hit her up with a story idea. She gave me a lot of innovative input and later we bounced more thoughts back and forth over the phone and emails. The resulting story, "The Wizard of Ooze," was published in *Midnight Premiere* and was also reprinted in *Little Creatures*. I am interviewing Linnea again for my upcoming book, *Masters of Imagination* for BearManor Media.

ID: Back to you, now. You are apparently an avid reader — when you can find the time, that is — and I was just curious: what kind of books would I find on your bookshelf? I mean, you never can tell. I write horror myself, but, sometimes I read Dave Barry or Elmore Leonard.
MM: Oh, I read Dave Barry and Elmore Leonard, too. I have eclectic tastes. I like reading science fiction, horror, mysteries and even — *gasp!* — the classics (the horror! The horror!).

In college, I read Shakespeare, Hemingway, Twain and lots of other literary dead guys. I managed to cram those classics in my brain between trying to score with coeds and getting drunk until I puked — until one day, unbeknownst to me, I earned a Bachelor of Arts in English and Journalism. All that effort, so I could someday write books about haunted muscle cars, rock stars going back in time to save the world and horny vampires. My family is so proud (laughs).

For non-genre writers, I really like Carl Hiaasen, Tom Robbins, Steve Martin ("Well, excuuuuuuuuse me!"), Leslie Langtry (her books mix mystery, romance and humor and are always a great read), Cormac McCarthy (his book *The Road* has been influential on the sci-fi novel Mark McLaughlin and I are currently writing), Vicki Hendricks (she writes hot mysteries), Jane Smiley (been a fan of hers for a long time), Alice Sebold (I've liked everything she has written so far), and occasionally if I have time, Dickens, Poe or Melville — because I still love the classics.

ID: I have always enjoyed your literary collaborations with Terrie Leigh Relf. You two work well together. How did you two meet up?

MM: I really enjoy writing with Terrie Leigh Relf. She is such a fun person to write with. Terrie is the editor of *Hungur*, a vampire magazine published by Sam's Dot Publishing. We met a couple years ago, when I submitted the story "Lucania" (which was co-written with Sandy DeLuca and is going to be reprinted in *A Little Help From My Fiends*). Terrie and I hit it off right away. So far, I have been published in *Hungur* about five times and once in *Drabbler* (which Terrie also edits).

Terrie and I wrote the haunted love story "Rhiannon" for *Little Creatures*. We've written three collaborations for *A Little Help From My Fiends*: "Moved To Mars — No Forwarding Address," "The Hunter's Moon" and "Help Wanted."

Terrie and I are batting around the idea of working on a novel. We both are extremely busy people with crazy work schedules, but we have a lot of fun writing together, so it still might happen someday.

ID: I know this question may cover a lot of ground, but here goes: Just how many collaborations have you been involved in? Should I break out the coffee and cigarettes for this one?

MM: I think I might be a literary slut, because I write with so many people (laughs).

For books, I have only written with Mark McLaughlin and Connie Corcoran Wilson. Currently I am working on a YA science fiction book Sherry Decker...so that's three. I am also thinking of working on future projects with Michael Louis Calvillo, Terrie Leigh Relf and Cindy Hulting.

For the story collections, there are a lot:

For *Dark Duets,* I worked with P.D. Cacek, Michael Romkey, Charlee Jacob, Jeffrey Thomas, Mark McLaughlin, Cindy Hulting, Teri Jacobs, R.L. Fox, Cristopher DeRose and Sandy DeLuca.

For *Little Creatures,* I worked with Mark McLaughlin, Linnea Quigley, Sherry Decker, Cindy Hulting, Terrie Leigh Relf, Scott Morschhauser, Sandy DeLuca, Connie Corcoran Wilson, Teri Jacobs and R.L. Fox.

For *A Little Help From My Fiends,* I worked with Mark McLaughlin, Sandy DeLuca, Cindy Hulting, Sherry Decker, Michael Louis Calvillo, Terrie Leigh Relf, Benjamin Szumskyj, Charlee Jacob, R.L. Fox, Ken Lillie-Paetz, Dave Miller, Jason Tanamor and Cristopher DeRose.

I should add, Mark and I also wrote a chapbook of collaborative stories, *All Things Dark and Hideous,* for Rainfall Books in England.

I work with a lot of the same people — we're all close friends, so it is like one demented extended family.

ID: Ok, here's another one that may take awhile: What is your favorite film or book? Should I break out the java and smokes again?

MM: There just isn't enough room to answer that question (laughs). For example, covering the '70s only, Connie Corcoran Wilson and I wrote *It Came From the '70s* which is almost 300 pages long. My list would be endless, but I have interviewed many great people in horror and science fiction in my books, so pick up copies of *Giants of the Genre, More Giants of the Genre, Modern Mythmakers, Estoteria-Land, It Came From the '70s* and *Masters of Imagination* (when that book comes out).

ID: How about your good friend and collaborator, Mark McLaughlin? How did you two meet up? You two are like the Stephen King and Peter Straub of the small press.

MM: Thank you for the kind words again. Mark and I are from the same area, so eventually we'd run into each other and it was inevitable that we would become friends. I used to write for Mark's old magazine, *The Urbanite* — I think I appeared in two or three issues. I once interviewed Mark at a local writers' conference for *Scavenger's Newsletter,* a writers' market magazine that used to specialize in genre publications.

After we became friends, I asked Mark to edit my book *Liquid Diet*. Then we wrote some short stories together. Then I convinced Mark to collaborate with me on *Monster Behind the Wheel* — which was the best thing that has happened to me in my 25 years as a professional writer.

ID: What is on the horizon for Mike right now? Other than taking a well-deserved vacation, that is.

MM: In 2008 I was fortunate to have numerous publishers release my work. The end results were this: *All Things Dark & Hideous,* a short story collection, co-written with Mark McLaughlin and published by Rainfall Books, U.K.; *Little Creatures,* a short story collection from Sam's Dot Publishing; *Modern Mythmakers,* an interview book from McFarland; *Ghostly Tales of Route 66,* true ghost stories co-written with Connie Corcoran Wilson, from Quixote Press; *Monster Behind the Wheel,* a novel from Corrosion Press/Delirium Books, co-written with Mark McLaughlin; *Out of Time,* a novel from Lachesis Publishing, Canada, co-written with

Connie Corcoran Wilson; and *Attack of the Two-Headed Poetry Monster*, a poetry collection co-written with Mark McLaughlin, from Skullvines Press. Whew! I'm tired just saying all those titles. I knew that in 2008, I'd spend my time editing and promoting those books and doing signings, interviews, yadda, yadda, yadda! What I wasn't planning on, was that in 2008, I'd also write another five books and they are: *Liquid Diet*, a vampire satire novel from Black Death/Demonic Clown Books; *Monster Hunter*, a novella from Skullvines Press (which is my tribute to Richard Laymon); *A Little Help From My Fiends*, a short story collection from Sam's Dot Publishing; *It Came From the '70s*, a book of movie reviews, interviews and trivia, co-written with Connie Corcoran Wilson, from BearManor Media, and *Esoteria-Land*, a book of interviews, reviews and articles — over 75 of them — for BearManor Media.

The major difference between the lists for 2008 and 2009 is collaborations: I did more in 2008 and less in 2009. In 2009, I plan to write only two books for 2010 — so I will be taking sort of a vacation...or maybe I'm just slowing down in my old age *(laughs)*.

ID: Anything to say before you leave us?
MM: Buy my books — I have over 15 to choice from! I'd like to leave you with this excerpt from *Monster Hunter:*

> *They stood outside a side entrance of the Freak Tent, the floodlight making monsters out of people's shadows. One light had been aimed directly at the hand-drawn poster of a werewolf, crimson blood dripping from yellow fangs and claws, the caption shimmering in the glare:*
> REAL-LIFE WEREWOLF!
>
> Paula shook her head. She thought, did I let Tommy see me naked for this?
>
> *Not fair.*
>
> A passionless barker stood on an upturned bucket next to the opening of the tent, a microphone in hand, trying to entice the gawking crowd. "Come one! Come all! Come see the real-life werewolf. More frightening than the beast in An American Werewolf in London *or* in Paris *too. More scary than all seven* Howling *movies combined!"* Yawn. "Show starts in a few minutes. Tickets are going fast! Get yours now!"
>
> Paula looked at the werewolf's painted eyes and tugged Tommy's arm. "Let's go inside."
>
> "I don't know," Tommy said, shifting from side to side nervously. "It's probably some flea-bitten mutt or something."

The barker turned and smiled. "Ain't no dog in there, boy. Come on, now. Take the little lady to the show." His voice boomed through the speakers. "You ain't scared already, are you?"

"Scared of a fake werewolf? Hell, no!" Tommy answered quickly. "Come on." But Paula was already standing next to the barker, dancing lightly on her toes.

Frank Dietz

Inspired at age five by a viewing of Abbott & Costello Meet Frankenstein, *Frank Dietz has found success in the film industry as a writer, producer, director, actor and animator. As one of the new wave of classic monster illustrators, he was inspired by the work of artists like Basil Gogos, Frank Frazetta, Jack Davis and Mort Drucker. Frank pays tribute to his heroes through oils, charcoal, pastel, watercolor and pencil.*

Frank grew up on Long Island, NY, and then attended the State University at Oswego, where he majored in theatre and art. He starred in a series of now-cult low-budget horror films like Zombie Nightmare, Rock N' Roll Nightmare, Black Roses *and* The Jitters. *Bitten by the film bug, Frank then moved to Los Angeles, where his screenwriting career began. He wrote the scripts for many independent features, including* Naked Souls, Cold Harvest *and the* Magic in The Mirror *series.*

In 1996, Frank returned to his artistic roots and joined Walt Disney Feature Animation as an animation artist. His work can be seen in such films as Hercules, Mulan, Tarzan, Fantasia 2000, Atlantis — The Lost Empire, Treasure Planet *and* Home On The Range.

During this period, Frank created the Sketchy Things *series of classic monster sketchbooks, which became extremely popular with genre fans. This led to years of commissions for horror and fantasy books, magazines and convention appearances. In October 2006 he was invited to host a solo Gallery Show of his oil paintings and sketches in Burbank, CA.*

In both 2006 and 2007, Frank was awarded the Rondo Hatton Classic Horror Award for "Artist of the Year." Frank returned to acting with a role in Larry Blamire's The Lost Skeleton Returns Again, *set for a July 2010 release.*

Frank's website is www.sketchythings.com *and his art blog is* http://sketchythings.blogspot.com.

ID: Greetings, Frank. How was your Christmas holiday?

FD: This past year I working pretty regularly, so I really enjoyed having a bit of time to work on my own artwork. I finished an oil painting of Lon

Chaney that I had started over four months earlier! That was a Christmas gift to myself!

ID: Sounds like a great present! I see you were born in Long Island, NY, but now reside in Burbank, CA. Was the change in atmosphere quite a culture shock for you?

FD: I had been working in Manhattan, and decided to make the move to Southern California at the end of 1990. By February 1991, while my east coast friends were trampling through three feet of snow and slush, I was wearing shorts and grilling steaks on the porch. That wasn't such a difficult adjustment!

ID: I understand you had a long lasting acquaintance with Forry Ackerman. How did you two meet up?

FD: Well, I should point out that I wasn't as close to Forry as a great many of my friends. But my acquaintance with him dates back over 30 years, to the first time I met him at the *Famous Monsters Convention* in New York. When I visited Los Angeles to determine if I wanted to move there, Forry opened up his house for me, even though it was closed to the regular Saturday morning "tours." Once I made the move, I would see him on a more regular basis. We were often guests at local conventions. I lunched with him at the Smorgasbord restaurant, attended his 85th birthday party at The Friar's Club. But my favorite memory was one of the last. Forry attended my gallery show in October 2006, where every piece was a classic monster character. There was a sparkle in his eyes as he looked over each painting. I felt like I had given something back, for all the years he had inspired me.

ID: And what an inspiration he was. The man a lot of people refer to fondly as "Uncle Forry" will be sadly missed. What do you think were some of the keys to his longevity, both in health and in business?

FD: I don't know if I can accurately address the business end of it, but as far his sticking around so long, I believe it had a lot to do with his lust for life. I used to joke that every time the Grim Reaper showed up at the Ackermuseum door, Forry would just start telling the story of the first time he saw *Metropolis*, and how he met Ray Bradbury, and would talk the Reaper's ear off until the spectre simply threw up his bony hands and gave up. Forry never lost the sense of wonder that so many others lose after childhood. He clung to it with a passion, and I think that kept him going.

ID: You know, I was looking through some old VHS tapes awhile back, and guess what I found? An old recording of Zombie Nightmare. *I really enjoy the old 80s horror films, and they seem like a breath of fresh air compared to the films being released today. Was that your first film role?*

FD: Yes, and it seems it will be with me forever! It was a big thrill to be acting alongside my childhood hero, Adam West, but I couldn't have imagined that people would still be talking about it 25 years later! Of course, *Mystery Science Theater 3000* had a lot to do with that. Their version of *Zombie Nightmare* is considered by many to be one of their best episodes. I just recently did a full-length audio commentary for an upcoming DVD release of the original film. I sometimes wonder, considering all the terrific films I've worked on, if *that* is the movie I'll be remembered for!

ID: What a memory! What was it exactly that prompted your interest in becoming an artist? Any early influences?

FD: Certainly *Famous Monsters* had a strong influence. Those Basil Gogos covers that just jumped off the paper and grabbed you. The James Bama *Aurora* model kit box covers, also. And my caricature work is definitely inspired by the great *MAD* magazine artists, particularly Mort Drucker.

ID: I've seen examples of your artwork, and I must say, you've created some really classic images of the famous Universal monsters. Have you ever captured Forry on canvas?

FD: Quite a few times! I've actually had people commission sketches of Forry for magazines. My favorite is the final one. I did it only a few weeks before he passed, and I asked Joe Moe to make sure he saw it. It was of the elderly Forry, and I decided to render it in the medium I would have used when I first became aware of *Famous Monsters* — I used Crayola crayons! I was really happy with the results, because I felt I had captured the "rascally" aspect of his persona.

ID: And capture it you did! I see you became hooked on scary films after seeing Abbott & Costello Meet Frankenstein. *Do you still prefer the older, B/W classics?*

FD: I'm a monster fan, and I enjoy the Hammer movies, the Harryhausen movies, the *Planet of the Apes* movies, the Romero zombie films, and so on. But there will always be a soft spot in my heart for the classic Universal films. I never grow tired of drawing them, either.

ID: What's it like working for Disney? Did you ever get to meet Walt in person?

FD: Oh my gosh, Walt was a little before my time! I was only a kid when *The Jungle Book* was released, and that was his last film before his passing. I started at Disney Feature Animation as an artist on *Hercules* in the mid-1990's. I stayed for almost eight years, and really enjoyed my time there. My favorite film to work on was *Tarzan*, because it had roots in my childhood, reading Gold Key comics and watching Ron Ely play him on television.

ID: What's on the horizon for Frank right now?

FD: I continue to work as an animation artist and as a screenwriter. I recently returned to acting also, with a great part in Larry Blamire's *The Lost Skeleton Returns Again*, the sequel to his 2004 cult hit. I've been working with an animation company on developing some projects that I think genre fans will enjoy. And I'll continue to appear at conventions, to share my love of classic monsters with the wonderful fans of my work.

ID: Any last words before you go?

FD: The ongoing achievement throughout Forry's life was helping keep the memory of classic films and characters alive for younger generations to enjoy. I'd like to think that I've followed his example, and in my own way contributed to the preservation of those movies. As he was an inspiration to me, I hope that some kids will be inspired by what I've done, so the legacy of Uncle Forry Ackerman will continue.

Thanks, Iron Dave!

Joe Moe

Joe Moe is an authentic renaissance artist: a third generation Polynesian entertainer, studio vocalist (look for his solo CD, Mainland*), screenwriter, FX artist and designer of dark-rides for international theme parks. Random trivia: Joe sculpted a monster mask for Don Post Studios* (Schizoid), *once operated the front half of beloved Muppet, Snuffleupagus, and swam with a 7-foot Tiger Shark (not intentionally)! Joe lived for many years in "Horrorwood, Karloffornia" where he cared for the late 92-year-old genre legend Forrest J Ackerman in the Ackerminimansion of Sci-Fi, Fantasy & Horror movie memorabilia. Joe Moe's day job is as Creative Director for 3Mac Studios where he's gleefully occupied in development, writing, design and direction of intriguing movies like* Red Velvet, Wasted Space *and other existing and "coming soon!" Indie-gems. Drop in and say Aloha!*

ID: *Aloha, Joe! How goes it way over yonder in Hawaii?*

JM: Mahalo, Dave! While my heart is always wading in the warm waters of Waikiki Beach, my ol' body is firmly planted here in Hollywood, California. I haven't lived in Hawaii for over 20 years but that's where it all started for me. That's also the unlikely place that I discovered my love of movies in general and monsters in particular. Oahu, Hawaii's where I was born and raised and where I read my first *Famous Monsters of Filmland* magazine. Like many of my generation, the pages of *FM* are where I learned how monsters were actually made and met the artists that make them. Forry, Jim Warren and their magazine turned the fantasy of horror movies into a reality of craft that we kids of that era could aspire to.

ID: *Let me say, in all sincerity, that this book wouldn't have been the same without you. When did you and Forry first meet up?*

JM: I'm grateful to participate in this project. Any offspring of Forry's is a Monster-Cousin of mine! I met Forry around 1980-82. I made the trek to the Ackermansion up on Glendower Ave., like droves of fans before me over the decades. One look around that Mecca of Monster-bilia and

I was mesmerized. A second look and I could see that Forry needed help maintaining the place. It was teetering on the precipice. It could easily have fallen into dilapidation. I offered to help clean up and sort out and Forry snatched me up like a rare movie prop on eBay! Soon after my friendship with Forry was established, his wife Wendayne's health began to decline. It was then that Forry and I truly bonded. I was one of a few close friends in his inner support circle. He really grew to depend on me. Losing Wendy was quite a blow.

ID: I think it was a wonderful gesture on your part to have been a caregiver for Forry when he really needed someone. Not to be intrusive, but what was Forry like over the last few years of his life? I would hate to think of him having suffered much.

JM: People often thank me for looking after Forry all those years. It always makes me a little sheepish. I so appreciate the support from fandom, but I never looked upon my relationship with Forry as a "choice." It just happened because it needed to be. For both of us. I was so grateful for his oblivious mentorship over the years and had so much fun in his company, naturally, when he needed me I took responsibility for his well-being. He was family to me. In Hawaii "O'hana" (or "family" for those of you who didn't watch *Lilo & Stitch*) is all-important. Not just blood relatives. All the people who matter in your life. People you love. Well, you go to the ends of the earth for them — without question. And Forry was ever appreciative of my presence. Who really took care of whom? I mean, without Forry I would never have seen the things I've seen. Met the heroes I've met. Learned the lessons I've learned to help me be a better artist and person. I, like all of you, are so sad it had to end. But I'm happy to say that Forry's mind never diminished up until the moment of his death. He was sharp and punning all the way. Slower as the years piled up, but never lacking his wit or charm. And with that ever-present, encyclopedic knowledge and memory of the genre. Forry never suffered. He was in control of his own destiny right to his last breath. Truth be told, he was fed up with being weak and tired and unable to taste food. He never wanted to see another hospital. His joy for life was gone. He was ready to rest.

ID: And may he rest in peace, and God-speed. I understand you took care of his museum, too. Did you handle the tours as well?

JM: Forry was the curator of the museum. So perhaps I was a custodian? Most of the joy of a visit to the Ackermuseum was not in the "stuff" but in Forry himself, so I would never presume to overstep my boundaries when it came to the tours or the collection. I was there to make sure everything was maintained, preserved and presentable. Also, to make sure the attention was directed toward the monster-maestro. Finally, I was present to ensure that nothing went missing. Other than unscrupulous trades, which Forry was known to make on occasion, I'm happy to say nothing was stolen on my watch. I'm also happy to say that I restored (along with a handful of close friends) the Ackermansion to its ultimate glory and luster, which lasted up until the time we moved down the hill to the Acker-mini-mansion on Russell Ave. There on Russell, we were able to replicate a smaller version of the museum, which fans continued to visit up until mere days before Forry's death.

ID: Someone as close to Forry as you were must have had some fascinating conversations with him. Are there any chats that stand out in your mind? Any amusing anecdotes?

JM: After many years of hearing Forry-stories and getting to know him, my conversations with Forry tended to run off the beaten path. I am a very open person and Forry was a very, VERY shy one. He never conquered his fear of public speaking even though he spoke publicly so often. My nature is to express feelings very candidly. As a result, Forry was exposed to my tragedies and triumphs on a daily basis. After a few years, he automatically opened up to me. We would talk about our dreams and disappointments. Forry was never a complainer but we did often reflect on his early days and his relationship with his family. The loss of his brother Alden in the Battle of the Bulge and such. Forry and I talked about things that he didn't share with the public. Nothing scandalous. Actually, surprisingly mundane things. Not Sci-Fi or Monster-y at all. Often after one of these conversations he'd remark, "OK, Dr. Moe. You can send me a bill." Now, I know you're itching for me to follow up with the content of some of these conversations… nope. Mine. All mine.

ID: I don't blame you — I'd keep them for myself, too. Your career has been an interesting and colorful one to say the least: writer, musical artist, and majored in theater. What first prompted your interest in the horror genre?

JM: Coming from a show-biz family and not being that interested (at the time) in pursuing my parents' and grandparents' path as Hawaiian entertainers, I loved movies. I wanted to be a part of that world in any way I could. There was boundless opportunity for imagination and creativity in the horror genre. It affected me more than other genres or themes. I fell in love with the concept of the sympathetic creature. I found the struggle of monsters so profound and urgent, it delighted and frightened me at once. My Dad took me to see every movie he could. The day he brought home my first issue of *Famous Monsters* magazine I'd been begging for (the 1968 *Fearbook*) my fate was sealed. I started out dabbling in makeup, which my mom supported by sacrificing carpet and kitchen counter, and ultimately moved into writing. As a sideline I've been a studio singer for over 20 years having performed on many tracks for *Disney* and others. My solo CD, *Mainland*, is out and features my best pals and fellow musicians Ogre of *Skinny Puppy* (in a piece that was a fun departure for him) and my musical mentor Van Dyke Parks.

ID: I see you have a piece in the book Anthology of the Living Dead, *that has been praised highly. How did your participation in the book come about?*

JM: Writer J. Travis Grundon was a friend I met on tour while promoting my first horror feature (as writer, producer, designer) *Red Velvet* — which, by the way, features Forry's last cameo. J. Trav really appreciated my work on *RV* so when the opportunity to solicit submissions for a zombie anthology came about, I got the call. It was the last work of mine that Forry ever read and he loved it so much he asked if he could help support the project by lending his name to it. Of course I said no! But after laughing at his bewildered expression for a few minutes I gratefully accepted his endorsement and passed it on to J. Trav and our publisher, Nicholas Grabowski of Black Bed Sheet Books. The anthology has been making the rounds and I am so pleased that my story has gotten such a terrific reception. J. Trav and I have more projects in the works at the time of this writing.

ID: And a Rue Morgue *and* Scarlet *magazines contributor! Is it fiction, columns? I am a nosy little bugger, aren't I? (Laughs)*

JM: While I'm not a regular contributor, I'm proud to have participated in those mags. They are our horror-future and I am thrilled to report that our Monster Grandkids are representing themselves extremely well! *Rue Morgue* and *Scarlet* in particular do a great job of pushing the contemporary, bloody envelope while maintaining a strong foothold in the classic horror milieu — I think that's French for old-school spooky world! (laughs hard). Add to that list my pal "Uncle Creepy" (Steve Barton) at *DreadCentral.com* where I do a regular on-line Forry-column and beloved Horror Hosts like Spooky Dan Walker who keeps the flame burning — for the monsters, NOT the villagers' torches! We continue to enjoy a community of exceptionally talented, big-hearted horror friends and fans.

ID: In closing, let me ask this: if you could speak to Forry one more time, what would you say to him? What would be the last words spoken between you?

JM: I am happy to be able to tell you that I said every word I wanted to say, right to Forry's face, before he left us. I told him I loved him. I told him how much he had shaped my life. I promised there'd be many of us who would carry on for him. I asked him every question I needed answered in order to feel sure he felt satisfied with his life and legacy and that he had no fear of dying. He reminded me that, even though he was an atheist, if he discovered he was mistaken, he'd take time out from visiting with Wendayne, Lon, Boris and Bela in Heaven to drop in and say, "Hello." I wait eagerly for that visit.

ID: What's on the horizon for you right now?

JM: I'm scheduled to direct my first feature in 2010 (*depending on when you're reading this, did that come true?*). I'm also developing a couple of stage musicals and a children's TV show. I've always got irons in some fire or another. In Forry's tradition, I support my fellow horror-makers with every fiber of my being. It's been tricky transitioning in the minds of my peers from an Ygor to an actual artist of any consequence, but I've always been up to a good challenge. The priceless years I spent looking after the Ackermonster did, by necessity, take me away from more self-centered pursuits. Now I'm making up for lost time trying to prove my talents and make inroads toward the career I've dreamt of since I was that little boy in Hawaii. Monster-siblings! Please support my work. You know can count on me to continue supporting yours! You can see what I'm up to at: www.gojoemoe.com

ID: Any last words of wisdom before you leave us?

JM: Only these: FORREST J ACKERMAN SHALL NOT DIE!

Michael Mallory

Michael Mallory is an author and journalist living in Southern California. His books include Universal Studios Monsters: A Legacy of Horror *and* Marvel: The Expanding Universe Wall Chart. *Mike's four-hundred plus articles have appeared everywhere from* Newsday *to* Fox Kids Magazine, *and his published fiction includes a novel and more than 100 short stories.*

ID: Good morning, Michael. How was the holiday season for you?
MM: Very good, thank you...except for a case of food poisoning. Don't ask.

ID: Ok, I won't ask! First of all, let me ask you about the first time you ever picked up a copy of Famous Monsters of Filmland. *Were you captivated?*
MM: Absolutely. I was given a copy by a friend when I was, oh, about ten, and was entranced. Obviously, I'd never seen anything like it. I think I wore it out reading it and then started looking for it on the newsstands.

ID: In your honest opinion, do you think that Forry Ackerman paved the way for the rest of the horror-themed magazines that clutter the book store shelves today?
MM: Absolutely. There was nothing like *FM* before it came out, but there have been countless derivations since. And his influence is not limited to horror-themed publications, either. Just about every film-related magazine out there, regardless of genre, owes a debt to Forry. Even those promotional fan magazines — *Doctor Who, Harry Potter*, et al — are simply copying the format Forry created.

ID: I totally agree. I see you wrote a book called Universal Studio Monsters: A Legacy of Horror. *Were you always a big fan of the older, B/W monster flicks?*
MM: Oh, yes, from the time I was very young. In the 1960s the films showed up very often on television, and while this might be hard for today's

kids to understand, television back then was largely black and white until the late 1960s, so watching a black-and-white movie was nothing unusual. When I was putting the book together, I used memories of reading *FM* as a guide to looking for photos, because Forry would publish pictures that nobody had ever seen before, many of which haven't been seen since (and no, I didn't seek Forry out for photos, because there was simply no time, given the publication schedule; I went through a photo archive). One of my guilty pleasures from the old Universal films is the *Paula the Ape Woman* series, which is largely unknown, even today. I first learned about them through *Famous Monsters*, and over the years became a fan of them, and told my publisher, who was then in talks with Universal about the book, that if I couldn't include Paula, I didn't want to do it. But having said all that, I also greatly enjoy the color Hammer horror films of the 50s and 60s.

ID: I see you are a big pop culture fan. Was this one reason for your interest in Marvel comics?

MM: I was a comic book geek as well as monster geek, and in a sense, what Stan Lee did with Marvel Comics in the 1960s was similar to what Forry did with *FM:* he made his readers feel like they were friends and part of an exclusive club that not everyone was privy to. Looking back, I have to say that the 1960s, for all its other peccadilloes, was probably the greatest single decade of the century in terms of pop culture, so it was a good time to be an imaginative kid.

ID: And...experience in animation as well! What films have you worked on?

MM: I'm not an animator, but I write about animation. I've written a few books on the subject — the most recent of which is *Iwao Takamoto: My Life with a Thousand Characters*, the autobiography of the man who designed *Scooby-Doo* (and a thousand others), which I co-authored with him — and I've written literally hundreds of magazine and newspaper articles on the animation business. It's another longtime fascination of mine. I attempted to make an animated cartoon one time, in college, but the results weren't good. I do a little bit of print cartooning, but only to illustrate my own kid's stories.

ID: And...an actor, too! What was it like having a role in Mad Men*? Honestly? I have never quite figured out the general plot of that show.*

MM: Me either. I'm not even sure what the plot of the episode I appeared in was! Part of it was set in Italy, and my part in some upstate

New York town. When I moved to California, the goal was to break into acting, and I did, at least in a small way. I did a lot of soap operas and a few commercials, some TV films, things like that. But in my spare time (of which there was quite a bit) I started writing, and that eventually took over. I've only gotten back into acting this past year, because I'm now more of "type" than I used to be. We'll see what happens with that.

ID: What has been your favorite line of work during the course of your career? Writing? Acting?

MM: I'd have to say writing. Acting is a hoot, because you get to be different people, but you also have to wait until somebody tells you it's all right to ply your trade. When you're a writer, you can sit down and ply your trade any time you want to, without someone else's permission.

ID: Any amusing anecdotes from your career to share with us?

MM: The incident I absolutely love happened about ten years ago at a mystery writers' conference in L.A. I write murder mysteries in addition to everything else. During the course of the event this woman came up to me and she was absolutely shaking, quivering like she was nervous. She said: "Oh, Michael, I have to tell you, I'm such a huge fan of yours!" I was rather startled, but any time you meet a fan, it's great. I thanked her and she kept going on and on about having read everything I've ever written — which at that time was a chore, since most of it was in the realm of short stories — and then delivered the punch line: "Harry Bosch is absolutely my favorite character!" Now, Harry Bosch, as you may know, is the series character of Michael Connelly, who of course is a major bestselling author, and was also at the event. So I turned slightly so she could see my name tag read "Michael MALLORY" not "Michael CONNELLY." She stared at it for a moment, then said, "Oh," and spun on her heel and marched away without another word. I saw Connelly again a couple months ago and told him the story, and without batting an eye he said, "Oh, yeah, that was my mother!"

ID: What's on the horizon for you right now?

MM: I've just signed with a new agent, so hopefully I'll be doing more TV, but for the most part it's finishing my latest novel and pitching more nonfiction books.

ID: Any last words before you leave us?

MM: Just that I'm delighted to talk about Forry Ackerman, since he was one of the key influences on my childhood, and in a sense, on my life, since

I continue to have the same interests now that I did when I was that kid reading *Famous Monsters*. Forry not only gave young people permission to dream and follow their dreams, he encouraged it, and the results speak for themselves: Steven Spielberg, Rick Baker, Joe Dante, John Landis, Stephen King, and countless others. I never got to know Forry all that well, but went to the Ackermansion a few times and saw him in what might have been his last public appearance, along with "The Two Rays" — Harryhausen and Bradbury. Forry was truly unique.

John Dimes

I'm an INFP according to the Keirsey Character Profile test (not the Kinsey Test, which I score somewhere in the middle, but only depending upon my mood), which means I'm an introvert, surprisingly enough. Which is rather odd, since I have a great many talents that would do well for an extrovert. Sigh...I'm on TV sometimes www.thespookymovie.com, *as Doctor Sarcofiguy. Sarcofiguy makes a lot of appearances on* Monster Madhouse Live! *I've got a couple of books published (*Coincidissonance, The White Corpse Hustle: A Guide For The Fledgling Vampire, Intracations *And* The Rites of Pretending Tribe)*!*

And I've some graphic novel or comic book work coming out too (Spiky Particulars, Omega Comics Presents, *and* 13 Hosts)*!*

AND I've appeared in several documentaries (Every Other Day is Halloween, American Scary, *and* Virginia Creepers)*!*

ID: Greetings, John. I trust you are well?

JD: You can trust that. I trust that. It's always good to trust. One should never be skittish around people, I says. God, you must've seen that tired response coming, right? Heh!

ID: I saw it coming! First of all, how did your alter-ego Dr. Sarcofiguy come into being?

JD: Hmm...I believe it came about when I was doing this other show, *Tales That Make You Say Goodness!,* back in '94 or '95. Something like that. Anyway, we wanted to do a horror show, sort of in homage to our childhood hero, a horror host of our mutual acquaintance, One Count Gore Devol, on WDCA Channel 20! So, I quickly came up with a name, and a voice, and the rest was pure nonsensical "ham-iness."

ID: How does it feel to be the first — and still only — African American TV horror host? Wait...that was a dumb question, wasn't it?

JD: That's not a dumb question at all! These days I liken myself to a Barack Obama for the horror host set! I'M ONE OF A KIND, BAYBEEE!!! And actually, I'm not really black. I'm more of a burnt sienna. Or cocoa. That's how I fill out most of my job applications. I check "other," then I insert the word "cocoa."

ID: I see you are also an illustrator and writer, with a graphic novel under your belt. Tell me all about it! I love graphic novels!

JD: Well, I got into all of graphic novel/comic book stuff, simply because I'm an avid fan of comic books, horror, sci-fi. All of that. So, when I was a kid, naturally I wanted to draw comics. When I started realizing that I was a bit of a surrealist, I knew that my illustrative work wouldn't fly right away. So, I decided to write. So, writing I have. I've been elated by all the support I've gotten for my brand of Lynchian storytelling. Only within the last few years have I been able to get my graphic/illustrative work the notice I've been wanting.

ID: An actor, too? Tell me about your role in The Blair Bitch Project.

JD: HAHAHAHAHAHAH! I play somebody that gets lost mid-way through, then found again. Riot!

ID: And I most definitely want to hear about your "mockumentary" White Corpse Hustle.

JD: Well, that. The Genesis of that was based on the simple concept, "Where do vampire's clothes disappear to when they transform?" And I ran with that. I did all of the "diagrams" myself. There's this picture of a vampire butt *nekkid* in there, after transformation! It's been favorably compared to Doug Adam's *Hitchhiker's Guide To The Galaxy,* which for me is the highest praise I could ever get for anything, I says! That guy was a comedic genius. I especially loved his Dirk Gently stuff. I wish they'd do movies about that character. I'd love to play him, actually. I have a sequel to *The White Corpse Hustle*. It's entitled *Size 666: The Monster Men's Catalogue!* I'm just trying to find the right publisher for it.

ID: What type of films and literature do you prefer? I ask because sometimes folks who write horror don't often read or watch it. A friend of mine caught me reading Danielle Steele once, and almost fainted. Hahaha!

JD: AHAHAHAHAHAAH! That's brilliant. Danielle Steele. Barbara Steele. It's all the same, right?

Actually, I love "genre" stuff. I avoid Stephen King, because he has WAAAY too much stuff out there. I can't keep up with him. Can't afford him. But, I find myself meandering to my book shelf and picking up my Neil Gaiman stuff. *Coraline* is brilliant. The audio book for *Anansi Boys* as read by Lenny Henry, equally brilliant. Douglas Adams' stuff, I've already mentioned. Other of my favorites: *Perfume* by Patrick Suskind; *Einstein's Dream* by Alan Lightman; *It Could Be Verse* by Victor Buono; *Instant Lives* by Howard Moss (with illustrations by Edward Gorey!), *Beloved* by Toni Morrison, and *Douglas Adams' The Starship Titanic* by Terry Jones (of Monty Python!).

The rest of my collection centers on "comic" writers. Grant Morrison. Alan Moore. Folks like that.

My favorite movies (not even naming a few!): *Angel Heart; Blue Velvet; Brazil; Intacto; Uzamaki: The Spiral; Prospero's Books; The Cook, The Thief, His Wife and Her Lover; Gothic; Lair of the White Worm; Mirrormask; Dune* (the David Lynch version, of course!)*; Phantom Museum: The Short Films of the Brothers Quay; The Piano Tuner of Earthquakes; The Dark Crystal; Legend, Alien, Bladerunner (*see the Ridley Scott theme running here?*), Hellraiser 1 & 2, Hellboy(s)*. OH! *Pan's Labyrinth!!!!*

And when there's enough time in the day, I love all the *Lord of The Rings* stuff. There are only a few movies that I just don't like. Unlike some, I go to movies to enjoy them, not critique them. If I'm entertained, then I'm entertained. Usually when people ask me what I thought of a movie, my usual preamble is "Well *I* liked it, but...."

ID: Here's a good one for you: if you could open your own drive-in theatre, what is the first film you'd premiere?

JD: Hmm...that's difficult. I'm torn. My first thought would be to premiere Roger Corman's *The Masque of the Red Death*, with Vinnie Price. Also on that bill would be my other favorite: *Torture Garden,* starring Burgess Meredith and Jack Palance. Still, I so desperately want to have a Blaxplotation night. You know, have a triple feature — *Blacula,* followed by *Scream Blacula Scream,* then *Abby,* the black version of *The Exorcist*!

ID: Anything exciting on the horizon?

JD: Thank God, I've got loads of stuff coming out this year! There's another documentary that I'll be in soon! And I've got graphic novel/comic book works coming out as well: *Spiky Particulars (Crossing Chaos Enigmatic Ink)*, which is an assortment of illustrated "metaphysical comedies," *a la* Edward Gorey, that I published years ago, which are collected for the first time in one stunning volume.

Also, I'm proud to be a part of two fun comic book anthologies, one is *Omega Comics Presents (Pop Goes The Icon)*, which features a Chaplinesque cipher of undetermined gender competing against a superhero, and the other anthology is

13 Host (Monkey Goat Boy) which features various and sundry horror hosts from across the country. *13 Host* features a rather special comic debut of one Dr. Sarcofiguy, written and drawn with my own wittle paws, yeeees!

ID: Any last words before you leave us?

JD: Well, lemme express a pet peeve. Never use the word "weird" around me. I like the word "unusual." That is so less of an indictment against one's character, I think. Thank you, and good day!!!!

ID: Same to you, man!

Brian Walker
of *Brian's Drive-In Theatre*

ID: Greetings and salutations, Brian. How is college life treating you?
BW: Pretty well, actually, but it's a hectic career! My main function at West Virginia University is heading the Commuter Student Program effort. Although I love my job, in a sense it is much like a horror film, in that there are hours of anticipation and moments of sheer terror!

ID: I feel very lucky to have stumbled upon your website, Brian's Drive-In Theater. I, too, loved the drive-in era, and wish it was still around. What prompted your interest in creating the website? Just a genuine love for the genre?
BW: I suppose my generation (I am 43 years old) was probably the last that grew up at the drive-in. I have such fond memories of piling into my mother's Buick and heading to the drive-in, which in the late 1960s and early 1970s were very kid-friendly. And since these were the days before HBO, we went to the movies *a lot*, at least twice a week. One of my favorites was the Isle of View Drive-In in Panama City, Florida: the drive-in had a huge fountain as you drove into the theater, which was pretty spectacular for the time. Many drive-ins had small playgrounds at the very front, close to the screen, where all the kids would play until the cartoon began to roll. That's when we would all made mad dashes back to our parents' cars.

On the other hand, neither my mother nor my father had any patience for children's films, so we saw mostly horror films, the occasional blockbuster disaster movie, and pretty much anything that starred Charles Bronson or Clint Eastwood. I still vividly remember seeing *The Exorcist* in its initial run at a drive-in, a film that terrified me for days! Mostly, however, we went to see B movies, anything with Vincent Price, such as *Theatre of Blood*, the *Dr. Phibes* films, in addition to action films like *Electra Glide in Blue*, *Vanishing Point*, and *Dirty Mary, Crazy Larry*. I was very fortunate in that my parents loved horror, action, and western films, and they did not shy away from extreme violence or movies with an MPAA R rating. They even took me to the drive-in to see Hitchcock's *Frenzy* and Peckinpah's *Straw Dogs*, two of the most violent films from the early 1970s! Ultimately, I didn't miss anything by not seeing all those Disney movies, and I was the envy of many of my friends, whose parents would not take them to see anything more shocking than *Mary Poppins*.

When I was about six years old, I begged my mother to take me to see *Blood Suckers*, primarily because the local radio stations were playing these incredibly exaggerated spots hyping the film. In reality, the radio spots were far more frightening that the film! I have to say I was somewhat disappointed when we saw it, because it's a rather tepid British horror flick with little blood-sucking but lots of talk — not a great deal to keep a six-year-old riveted to the screen. Oddly enough, I find it an enjoyable movie these days. The hoopla was such a part of the experience, and perhaps that what I really miss most about B movies.

ID: If you owned your own drive-in theater, what movies would you show? I think I'd show The Texas Chainsaw Massacre *for sure.*

BW: *Texas Chainsaw*! My mother took me to see that in a filthy grindhouse with sticky floors and a scary men's rest room when I was about nine or ten years old, and we both loved it the film, as it was so unlike anything else that was out at the time. This was in the days before mall cinema megaplexes, and if you wanted to see a low-budget film, you either went to the drive-in or an old downtown theater that was in disrepair.

As for my top picks for my own drive-in, I'd have to start out with *The Abominable Dr. Phibes*, the original *Night of the Living Dead, Attack of the 50-Foot Woman, Blood Feast, Two Thousand Maniacs!, Strait-Jacket, Day of the Triffids, Black Sunday, Carnival of Souls*, and maybe something campy and fun, such as *Dr. Goldfoot and the Bikini Machine*.

ID: I think it is a pity the drive-in era is long since past. Horror cinema, in general, has somewhat changed for the worse, too. It seems filmmakers — and no offense intended toward anyone — have lost grasp on what key elements make for a good horror film. Now films are full of cardboard killers, rubber reality, and CGI effects. Do you miss the classics as well?

BW: Home video effectively killed the drive-in era. Yet there are still some thriving drive-ins in existence, at least in the Pittsburgh area, where I currently live.

What is missing most in contemporary horror are the actors who were in those classic old horror films, because they were the ones who really delivered the chills without the assistance of CGI or gallons of stage blood. There is no one today like Boris Karloff, Vincent Price, or Bela Lugosi, to name just three actors whose names alone guaranteed an audience. And they always delivered the best performances possible, which in hindsight must have been difficult given the short production schedules and lack of budget for most of their films. Big-name talent aside, watch the old films of horror directors such as Ray Dennis Steckler, George Romero, and Herschell Gordon Lewis. Despite the lack of budget and talented actors, their films clearly illustrate that these directors really loved the horror genre. I don't feel that same sense of enjoyment from current horror flicks. From the standpoint of producers, making a horror flick is like money in the bank, as these films have a built-in audience. This has been the case for decades. In addition, you don't need an "A" list star to sell a horror flick; you merely need an actor on the way up the ladder, or an actor whose best years are behind him or her. And horror is generally fantastically cheap to produce. However, many current producers have no artistic intentions — they're just out to make a fast buck. And I get the sense that most contemporary actors have the same mercenary intentions as producers, in the sense that they do a horror film as a springboard to something "better." For example, I'm not a fan of James Wan's *Saw* or its innumerable sequels. The *Saw* films aren't actually horror films; instead, they're merely 90-minute autopsies that are relentless and painful to watch and, ultimately, do not engage the audience. Nothing is left to the imagination, and twenty minutes into *Saw*, you're already desensitized to the violence and it becomes boring. One bright spot, at least in my estimation, is Rob Zombie. I love his films, especially *House of 1000 Corpses*, and his remake of *Halloween* is fabulous. Graphically, Zombie's films are way over the top, but when you watch them, it's readily apparent that he loves old horror movies and relies on talented actors, such as Karen Black and Sid Haig, to terrify audiences. The performances, not the gore, provide the thrills.

ID: I even miss the old Godzilla films, among other "creature features." I loved the way Forry Ackerman showcased the classic monster films in his magazine, Famous Monsters of Filmland. *Did you ever read the mag, or have a chance to meet him? Forry Ackerman had a very profound effect on the horror cinema genre, yet his magazine ceased to exist, being replaced by mags full of blood, gore, and semi-nudity. Wouldn't you like to see the older classic magazines come back?*

BW: The Japanese *Godzilla* movies are great fun, but let's face it — they never scared anyone. I'm a huge fan of Italian horror from the 1960's, particularly Mario Bava. Regrettably, I never met the great Forrest J. Ackerman, but I'm appreciative of his work and how much he did to promote the genre. But times and tastes change, and everything eventually outlives its usefulness. As with the drive-in, the home video market ultimately brought about the demise of the original *Famous Monsters of Filmland*, as horror aficionados no longer needed to buy a magazine to be reminded of horror classics. *Famous Monsters* ceased production in 1983, just at the time when many people were buying their first VCRs. Home video can also be blamed for the demise of local TV horror hosts, such as "Chilly Billy" Cardille from Pittsburgh's WPXI's *Chiller Theatre*. Honestly, though, there is absolutely no hope of the old horror magazines making a comeback. That train has definitely left the station! Few people read printed magazines these days, because so much information is on the Internet, right at your fingertips. Besides, with publication costs spiraling upward, even if you did create a magazine in the spirit of the original *Famous Monsters*, you would have to sell at least 60 percent of it as ad space just to break even. And the creature era in horror films is done. Today's generation of horror fans aren't frightened by monsters. They are afraid of other human beings, and rightfully so, particularly for those folks who are well-informed about current world and national events.

ID: Here's a good one: what is your favorite horror film? I love to ask this question, because more often than not, the other party is stumped for an answer!

BW: My all-time favorite horror film has to be the 1932 version of *The Mummy*. Boris Karloff's performance is chilling! It's one movie that I could probably watch every day and never get tired of.

ID: Where do you think the horror genre is headed? Do you think it will continue to flourish, or eventually just fade out?

BW: I think there will always be movie audiences who love to be frightened and will seek out horror films. I believe technology will play an important role in keeping the genre alive — CGI is merely scratching the surface — especially any technology that encourages greater audience involvement in films. Horror film fans aren't as passive as fans of other genres and seek a greater attachment to the actual film. They are also an intensely loyal fan base, which is why you see so many sequels in modern horror films.

ID: What's on the horizon for Brian? Will you keep Brian's Drive-In Theater alive and kicking?

BW: I would love to see Brian's Drive-In Theater stay on the Internet long after I'm gone! And I'll do everything I can to keep the site going. My future plans for the Drive-In include more video streaming and a complete redesign, to make the site more interactive and less static. Eventually, when the technologies surrounding the World Wide Web and television fully merge, I think that will usher in a "golden age" of sorts for entertainment, where anyone with a laptop and a little know-how can be a media mogul. I think you will see more of a localization of entertainment, particularly with horror films, whereby someone with a digital camera, a laptop, and a few friends can create effective films. And you'll see the big media giants become more fragmented, with many falling by the wayside. That's exactly what I would love to see happen.

ID: Any last words before you leave us?

BW: I would like to thank everyone for the interest in Brian's Drive-In Theater. I've had such a great time creating the website, and I am amazed at the overwhelmingly positive response I have received over the years from site visitors. Not bad for a middle-aged guy who lives 2,500 miles from Hollywood, huh?

ID: Nope...not bad at all!

Robert Leininger

I was born and raised in Los Angeles. I was brought up on monsters and horror by my uncle who is a voice over actor named Mark Silverman. He is the voice of Rod Serling in the Twilight Zone Tower of Terror *at Walt Disney World and* Disneyland. *I graduated from California State University, Northridge, in 2006 with a degree in Cinema and Television Production. My senior project was the documentary* The Undying Monsters, *which won an award at the Broadcast Education Association for best student short. It was also nominated for a Rondo Award for best independent production. I have worked on several other shorts as well as a music video. Currently I am an editor for a production company creating trailers and behind the scenes footage for Pay-Per-View.*

ID: *First of all, tell me a little about your documentary,* The Undying Monsters. *It sounds like something that would be right up my alley.*

RL: The Undying Monsters is a documentary that looks at classic horror films and the people that love them. It is separated into three sections. The first asks the interview subjects what their favorite horror films are. The second discusses why people collect monster memorabilia, and the third discusses Forrest J Ackerman. It was extremely exciting to make this documentary because of my love of classic horror films and to just talk to different people about the subject is quite thrilling. The documentary was my senior project at California State University, Northridge, and it won an award for the best project in the Television department, an award for best student short at the Broadcast Education Association, and it was nominated for a Rondo Award. I also flew to Idaho for a film festival called

Spudfest, which is run by Dawn Wells of *Gilligan's Island* fame. At the film festival, we screened *The Undying Monsters* and followed it by a Q&A session with many kids from the local high schools.

This is a little synopsis that I wrote about the documentary:

Dracula, Frankenstein, King Kong, *and* The Wolf Man. *These are only a few of the classic characters that brought terror to people in cinemas around the world.* The Undying Monsters *explores why characters in these such fright films are beloved by so many. You will encounter a monster movie historian, true monster movie fans, and a person who has influenced the genre more than any known man. These most unusual people will take you to a world where corpses 3,500 years dead walk again, where vampires are on the hunt for blood, and where werewolves prowl under the full of the moon. This is the fang-tastic world of* The Undying Monsters!

ID: Sounds great! I see your two big heroes are Forry Ackerman and Walt Disney. Great choices! You know, I've always been told the Pinocchio *story had an "underlying" horror theme. Do you think there is any truth to that?*

RL: *Pinocchio* definitely has an underlying horror theme. *Pinocchio* is my favorite Disney film of all time and the horror of it is a big reason why. The villains in *Pinocchio* are both frightening and very intriguing. The most horrifying image to me would have to be when Stromboli threatens to chop Pinocchio into firewood. After saying this, Stromboli throws an axe at an old wooden puppet. The image of that puppet with the axe through his chest is perhaps the most horrific thing *Disney* has ever produced. *Pinocchio* is not the only example of horror in a *Disney* production, however. Almost every *Disney* film has elements of horror in it, whether it is the old hag from *Snow White and the Seven Dwarfs* or the Night on Bald Mountain sequence from *Fantasia*. By the way, Bela Lugosi was supposedly hired by Walt Disney to act out scenes of the Night on Bald Mountain demon. Animators would then base their animation on his movements. There is a nice article in an old issue of *Famous Monsters* about a time when Forry met Walt Disney and asked him about Lugosi being in *Fantasia*. But when it comes to the most frightening things in a *Disney* film, *Pinocchio* stands alone thanks to the likes of Stromboli, The Coachman, Honest John, Gideon, Lampwick, and Monstro the Whale.

ID: A regular Walt Disney scholar! Your taste in film proceeds you; 70s horror films and the Universal monster flicks. You have listed one of your favorites as Bride of Frankenstein. *How do you feel about the later versions of the* Frankenstein *legend? I found some of them to be less than appealing.*

RL: Bride of Frankenstein is my favorite movie of all time, but I have not been crazy about non-Universal *Frankenstein* films. The only non-Universal *Frankenstein* film I really enjoy is *The Monster Squad*, which I wouldn't really call a *Frankenstein* film. There are some versions of *Frankenstein* that have some good things in it like *Frankenstein: The True Story* or *The Bride*, but when comparing them to Universal's *Frankenstein* films, they don't even come close. Boris Karloff is the definitive *Frankenstein* Monster and no one can come close. In *Bride of Frankenstein*, Karloff's acting performance was Oscar worthy. Growing up with *Bride of Frankenstein*, a child can really relate to the Monster. As kids start school and try to find their place in the world, they feel like outcasts. Kids have difficulties finding who they really are, establishing good friendships, and basically just growing up. The Monster in *Frankenstein* and *Bride of Frankenstein* deals with these same issues. That is why kids can relate to the Monster and that is certainly why I did. Karloff pulled off a performance that hits a subconscious nerve of relation that no other actor could have done.

ID: How true. I was checking out your movie ratings, and see you gave John Carpenter's Halloween *five stars, and gave Spielberg's* Crystal Skull *only three stars. Was it because you didn't feel it stood up the previous installments, or because it wasn't a horror film?*
RL: Well, *Halloween* and the original *Indiana Jones* trilogy are a few of my favorite films of all time. *Halloween* is a perfect horror film as it scares the hell out of you and you really care for Jamie Lee Curtis' character. It is also one of the most important films in the realm of horror. It really started the "slasher" generation.

Now while I love the original Indy films, *Crystal Skull* just doesn't hold up. There are some things I like in the film though. I like the opening warehouse scene and I like Cate Blanchett as Irene Spalko. I didn't really like the story of the inter-dimensional beings. True, the other Indy films have fantastic things in it, but I just felt like the alien storyline was weak. Even Spielberg didn't like the alien story line. If you watch the features on the *Crystal Skull* DVD, Spielberg talks about how Lucas kept coming to him with this idea of Indy vs. aliens and Spielberg kept saying no. So Lucas said he would change them to inter-dimensional beings. Spielberg finally agreed. It seemed like Lucas was not going to budge and Spielberg just gave in to the idea. I can't help but compare *Crystal Skull* to the previous Indy films and it is nowhere near as great. Even John Williams' musical score was weak in *Crystal Skull*. Each Indy film has its own musical theme and each one is very memorable. The theme in *Crystal Skull* was just ordinary and very forgettable. Another thing that was a let down was the usual Indy "gross out" scene. Each film has a gross out scene. *Raiders* has its snake scene, *Temple of Doom* has the bug scene, and *Last Crusade* has the rat scene. *Crystal Skull* has an ant scene, which doesn't work for me. The ants were all CGI and they didn't look very good. I didn't get the creepy feeling that every other Indy film had. When I saw the scorpion crawling on Shia LaBeouf earlier in the film, I thought *Crystal Skull* would have a bunch of scorpions as their "gross out" scene. Unfortunately, it wasn't the case.

ID: I totally agree once again. Having been raised in L.A., one would think you would have had the perfect venue for an aspiring filmmaker. Has so-called "progress" caught up with L.A.? Has the filmmaking industry changed for the better or the worse?

RL: I believe filmmaking has changed a lot. I am only 25 so I don't know any other world of filmmaking than what was told to me, but it seemed like things were much easier back in the day. There are so many people that want to be filmmakers now and many of them have connections through friends and family. It seems to me that connections are more important than talent these days. So many people working in the industry have jobs just because they know someone. It's not about pure talent anymore. People with talent, but not as many resources are not making it. It is a very frustrating thing, but at least in this age, the filmmakers without the resources can still make their own film. It is just up to a viewer to make a search for these original independent filmmakers.

In terms of technology, I think most things are changing for the worst. I think CGI works best when used with a mixture of real-life animatronic creatures like in *Jurassic Park*. Relying only on CGI is not a good thing in my opinion. It is much more realistic and personable to combine the best of both worlds. I believe this technique has to be done more often instead of usually only CGI. But then again, I really liked Peter Jackson's *King Kong*, which was all CGI. What is really important is that a good film is made. I can like an all CGI film if it has a good story. It just depends on the talent of the writers and directors.

ID: Here's one just for fun: if you could have cast Forry in your own horror film, what role would you have cast him in? And...who would have been his leading lady?

RL: If I had to cast Forry in my own horror film, I think I would cast him as a kindly old grandfather type in a sort of remake of Peter Cushing's role as Grimsdyke in *Tales From the Crypt*. Instead of making toys for the children, he writes monster magazines! If I had to cast a leading lady, I think I would choose Carla Laemmle. It would be a nice cameo to have both of them together.

ID: *What's on the horizon for you right now? Any more documentaries coming up?*

RL: Right now I am working as a video editor for a production company. I would like to continue *The Undying Monsters* documentary one day and make it feature length. Hopefully the time will come. For personal projects, currently I am writing some things for future productions and I have a couple of blogs that I update daily: My film review blog is *www.aweekahead.blogspot.com* and my classic movie monster blog is *www.classicmoviemonsters.blogspot.com*.

ID: *Any last words before you leave us?*

RL: Well I just wanted to say a few things about Forry. The first time I met Forry was in the mid 1990s when I was about 10 years old. I had just gotten the book *Graven Images* by Ronald V. Borst and Forry wrote a section of the book. I brought the book to the Ackermansion so Forry could sign it. Forry took the book and I remember being very impressed that he knew exactly where his chapter started. He flipped the book right to that page and signed it for me. He then gave a tour of his Ackermansion and it was such a thrill. I saw Forry a few more times in the following years, but then we lost touch with him. I wasn't sure if he was doing his Ackermansion tours anymore. Well when my documentary came up, Ron Borst gave me Forry's phone number. So I came by and visited him in the mini Ackermansion. It was so great to see him and talk to him about monsters. Speaking with Forry put me at such ease. It was as if I was talking to someone of my own family that I had known my entire life. That year, when we were making our documentary, Forry invited me to his 90th birthday party and it was a wonderful time. At the party I met Joe Dante, Ann Robinson, and Ray Bradbury, just to name a few. But the real treat was seeing Forry and just being around him. Even though I only knew Forry for a small amount of his lifetime, he really made an impact on mine. Not a day goes by where I don't think about Mr. Sci-Fi: Forrest J. Ackerman.

Count Gore Devol

With the crack of lightning, the rumble of thunder and the strains of a Bach fugue reverberating through his dank castle, viewers around the world know it's time for Count Gore De Vol! The Count provides them with a dose of horror, a dash of humor, and some of Hollywood's worst public domain horror films, as well as an ever-growing number of new independent releases! Thanks to his weekly web program, viewers get this and much more, including book, video, music and movie reviews, contests, extensive listings of horror history, convention listings, and the list goes on.

But who is the dark figure and self-proclaimed sex symbol to the world? The story started in Paducah, Kentucky, where in 1971, he began his horror host career under the pseudonym of M.T. Graves. Eighteen months later he became the horror host to the nation's capital as Count Gore De Vol. For 15 years on WDCA-TV, he made Saturday nights a guilty pleasure for thousands of viewers, many times surpassing Saturday Night Live *in the ratings! But with a change of ownership, Gore slipped out of view in 1987. Then in 1998, everything changed as he became the first horror host of the Internet with* Creature Feature *the Weekly Web Program! For almost twelve years, this program has grown and expanded to incorporate a number of contributors from around the country, including several other horror hosts. He has interviewed and worked with such horror celebrities as Bruce Campbell, Forrest J. Ackerman, Dee Wallace Stone, Sid Haig, Reggie Bannister and Don Coscarelli. Thanks to the Internet, Gore is no longer limited to a single market or country. Some of his reviews have even been quoted on the covers of video releases in the UK! The Count is also a regular at several major conventions, including Cinema Wasteland, Balticon, and Horrorfind.*

Count Gore is played by actor Dick Dyszel, who also produces the program. The video segments are shot in his own high definition studio in suburban Virginia. In addition to portraying The Count, Dyszel produced and hosted several award winning children's programs for WDCA-TV and has appeared in several feature films including The Alien Factor, Nightbeast, Galaxy Invader, Cremains, Countess Dracula's Orgy of Blood, *and the soon to be released* Every Other Day is Halloween, *a feature-length documentary about his amazing career that premiered at the American Film Institute in 2009.*

ID: Greetings and salutations, Count. Are we feeling...thirsty, this morning?
CGD: Actually I fed very well last night...a fine vintage Type AB+.

ID: I see you originally hailed from Washington, D.C. How did your show go over in our nation's capitol?
CGD: It almost took an Act of Congress! I had been hired to produce children's shows for WDCA-TV, but my true desire was to host horror movies as I had done at WDXR in Paducah, Kentucky. After getting the kid's stuff successfully on the air, I lobbied for *Creature Feature*, but the general manager was reluctant. It seems that one of the local VHF stations had tried to run a syndicated version of *Sir Graves Ghastly* with limited success. He felt that we would do no better. I finally talked our program director into letting me do a pilot. He liked it and backed my request. The last stumbling block was a new name. The GM wasted something with "gore" in it and we finally decided on Count Gore De Vol. The rest, as they say, is history!

ID: I see you were also the first TV host to broadcast an unedited version of Night of the Living Dead. *I bet you received "mixed reactions" on that one. LOL!*
CGD: The program had been on the air for a couple of years with great ratings. We were schedule to show *NOTLD* in a few weeks and my program director asked me if I would like to show the theatrical print, rather than the TV print. I really think that we got the wrong print by mistake and he didn't want to mess with getting a replacement. But whatever the reason, I said "YES!"

Not only did we show it in the home of the FCC, but I promoted the hell out of it and got very good ratings...and surprisingly, no complaints! But then, this was the wild and crazy mid-1970s!! Sex, drugs and eating intestines...or something like that.

ID: And...the first TV horror host to host a show on the Internet. A man full of surprises! What film did you show the first time?
CGD: Let us not forget the first horror host to broadcast in stereo (May 25, 1986..*Zardoz*). And there are a few other firsts I just don't remember. Actually the first edition of *Creature Feature* the Weekly Web Program, which hit the Internet on July 11, 1998, did not have a movie. At that time

most people were using either 28.8 or 56K dial-up and you just couldn't stream video. So, I brought the audience some written interviews, some streaming audio interviews, a contest, some book reviews, movie reviews and other stuff. I got into streaming movies as quickly as possible and that was probably later that year. I honestly can't remember what public domain film it was, but the picture was very small.

ID: Not to be nosy, but ...what's this about Penthouse *Pets on your show? Bold, aren't we? Don't get me wrong; I admire boldness!*
CGD: Bold, sexy, hot...my favorite words! Actually the sales department was responsible for my good fortune. *Penthouse* had their Pets on regular tour and whenever they came to DC they called all the stations and we were the only one that had the "balls" to put them on. Most of the time we did either short interviews or just had them do promos for the show. But once, we had Dominique Maure, the Pet of the Year, on the show and she was a good enough actress that we had her do a whole show with me. It was one of my favorites. Ironically, one of her prizes from *Penthouse* was a couple weeks stay at the Club Med in Tahiti the following year. Unbeknownst to me, she was there the same week I was. Unfortunately, she brought her boyfriend and several chaperones. I also had to pay for *my* trip.

ID: I see you are acquainted with Dr. Sarcofiguy and Karlos Borloff, both really great guys. How did you meet up with them?
CGD: I met the good doctor through a mutual friend who also produced his show in Falls Church, Virginia. We very quickly hit it off and really enjoy working together. I met the man who plays Karlos Borloff in 2005 when he appeared on my show as a building contractor. He got bitten by the hosting bug...mutations occurred...and soon *The Monster Madhouse* was born. He also was big fan of my TV show.

ID: Did you ever get a chance to meet up with any of the other big names in the 70s and 80s? Like...Elvira?
CGD: The funny thing is that prior to the Internet, horror hosts didn't talk with each other. We were all very isolated and protective of our own markets. I had only heard about Elvira when she started doing the *Coors* commercials and didn't see any of her work until she hosted the annual horror host segment on Dick Clark's *TV's Bloopers and Practical Jokes*, which included some of my work. I've still have not met her in person, but we are *MySpace* friends.

I did meet Dr. Shock from Philly in the 80s and since then I've had the pleasure of meeting and sharing horror stories with many famous horror hosts.

ID: Do you still hope to be entertaining us, say, ten years from now? Is the horror biz "in your blood"?

CGD: For an immortal, what's ten years? Hosting horror films and the associated craziness is part of my being. If I didn't do it, what else am I good for...the all-night greeter at WalMart? No, assuming no one takes a stake to me or my program, I'll most certainly be around.

ID: Any last words before you go?

CGD: I want to thank you for this interview and I invite all your readers to get their weekly dose of bad hosted horror movies on *Creature Feature* the Weekly Web Program at *www.countgore.com*. I look forward to meeting you and your readers at the various conventions I do. And lastly...

May all your blood be warm!

Jim McDermott

ID: Happy New Year, Jim. How was your holiday season?
JM: To paraphrase Burl Ives, it was a holly jolly folly.

ID: Wonderful! I see you graduated from Boston's New England School of Art, and then moved to California. Why do all artists move to California? Do they enjoy suffering a total culture shock? (laughs)
JM: The day I graduated from art school, my father bought me a one-way ticket to California, and gave me a bag full of peanut butter and jelly sandwiches. Heading west, many get their kicks on Route 66. To quote Carl Sagan, a glorious dawn awaits.

ID: I've seen one of your Forry Ackerman pieces, and I must say, you really captured him well on canvas. Did he pose for that one, or did you use a photo for reference?
JM: I looked at quite a few photos of Forry, but I did go meet him with my sister when I was living on the West Coast. He invited us into his home to look at his collection. Forry was very friendly and even had us stay for lunch.

ID: Were you always a big fan of Famous Monsters *magazine?*
JM: I read *Famous Monsters, Creepy, Eerie*...all the Warren Publications. I loved them all. The Warren magazines left an impression on me like *EC* did to an earlier generation.

ID: You have an impressive client list: Apple Computers, IBM, Fruit of the Loom. What kind of design did you create for Fruit of the Loom? Or... should I fear to ask? (laughs)
JM: To paraphrase Franklin Delano Roosevelt, the only thing we have to fear is underwear itself. I worked for Salem Sportswear, a division of Fruit of the Loom, doing illustrations of major sports figures for their T-Shirt line.

ID: What's this about a character design for Ghostbusters?

JM: No, I did character design for the DIC animated series, *The Real Ghostbusters*. Also did designs of props and backgrounds. It was seasonal, so I did freelance between seasons.

ID: Out of all of your cartoons, paintings and illustrations, which would you say has been your favorite subject?

JM: It's a tie between Boris Karloff and Lon Chaney.

ID: Good choices! How about early influences? I was partial to Frank Miller and Max Brooks.

JM: Jack Davis, Franklin Booth, Haddon Sundblom, Bob Peak, N.C. Wyeth, J. Allen St. John and a little known artist, Steve Fiorilla.

ID: Have you ever considered doing a graphic novel?

JM: Not really, but graphic novel cover illustrations would be cool.

ID: What's on the horizon for you right now?

JM: Doing covers for *Vincent Price Presents* and other titles published by Bluewater Productions.

ID: Any last words before you leave us?

JM: Tune in tomorrow!

Lucy Hell

ID: Good morning, Lucy. Mystery Island *been keeping you busy?*

LH: Good morning. There is actually never a dull moment on *Mystery Island*. We just interviewed Eric Burdon of The Animals and we're working on a *Lucy Hell, Devilgirl* graphic novel!

ID: Speaking of them, how did you and them meet up?

LH: Bradley Mason Hamlin created *Mystery Island* in 1998, initially as a publishing imprint, to house the various "metaphysical crime fighters" he created to form the adventure series *The Secret Society*. Over the years I really fell in love with his mix of horror, science-fiction, and mystery — mixed with a down-to-Earth literary realism and lots of humor. In 2006 I started modeling the Devilgirl character for the *Intoxicated Detective* line of digest adventure books and in *American Strip* and finally Devilgirl got her own comic book, written by Bradley and drawn by Mort Todd.

ID: How did you first meet up with Forry Ackerman?

LH: Via the magic on the wicked world wide web. He liked our online adventure strip at mysteryisland.net called *American Strip*, featuring Devilgirl and the rest of *The Secret Society*, and I know he was excited about the comic book. He thought the story of *Lucy Hell, Devilgirl* would make a great movie — and he was right!

I only wish I had connected with Forry earlier in his life. We were going to do an interview but he became ill and it never came to be, but he will always be remembered on *Mystery Island*.

ID: In your honest opinion, would you consider Uncle Forry the original "pioneer" of the scifi genre for the twentieth century?

LH: Honestly, I don't think there is anyone else in the world that is so synonymous with science-fiction — in terms of the love of the genre and helping to create a dynamic fan-base. If I were to pick a writer, I would say Ray Bradbury — or for film, I would say Roger Corman, but Forrest

J. Ackerman was one of us, someone who loved the genre as a whole and lived his life honoring that passion.

ID: Being an avid fan of pop culture, who have been your favorite interview subjects?
LH: Well, I work primarily on the musical side of the Island, so I love to interview all the great punk bands like The Angry Samoans, The Dead Kennedys, The Dickies, and Dinah Cancer of 45 Grave, but it was also great to interview Mort Todd (former editor of *Cracked Magazine*) to get to know each other before working on the *Lucy Hell, Devilgirl* comic book.

ID: In my opinion, the pop culture movement — especially that of the 60s and 70s — had a profound effect on the comics, pulps, and films we read and watch today, don't you?
LH: Especially the 1960s — the explosion of creativity in comics, movies, and music is undeniable, but for pulps and books, I think you have to at least go back to the 1950s when books started being mass-produced in paperback editions. For instance, Mickey Spillane's *Mike Hammer* series was so popular it literally inspired the whole direct-to-paperback market in order to fulfill the demand for great genre books at a reasonable cost. Along with comic books, the pulp paperbacks were the direct inheritors of the pulp magazines. And who could live without *Ace Double* science-fiction paperbacks?
B.T.W.: My current favorite series to read is the Ed McBain *87th Precinct* books.

ID: Why the moniker "Lucy Hell"? Is there some special significance there for you?
LH: I am a Devilgirl, *hello!*
For the full "secret origin" you must read the comic book, and yes, there is a special significance.

ID: Just for fun, what would you say your favorite scary movie?
LH: Well, growing up in the '80s, having girly sleepovers and girl/girl pillow-fights and eating popcorn, the scary movie of the time was *Poltergeist*, but I'm not a big fan of that one. I don't necessarily like the really scary stuff, and I definitely don't like the gross slasher films.
I like suspense. I would say my very favorite "scary" film is *The Birds*, directed of course by Alfred Hitchcock. It frightens me, but it's so well done.

ID: If you could speak to Forry one more time, what would you say to him?
LH: Well, to be honest, I don't think we've lost the ability to speak to Forry. He's one great ghost who will haunt us eternally.

ID: Any last words before you leave us?
LH: I wish this was 1942 and I could just say: *Buy War Bonds!*
How 'bout: *Beware the Mushroom Man!*
Or: *Life is short, don't mess it up.*
Thank you so much for honoring Forrest J. Ackerman.

Ghoulish Gary Pullin

Possessed with a true affinity of classic horror, gore-soaked films of the 1980s and hailing from Toronto, Canada, "Ghoulish" Gary Pullin has been Rue Morgue's *art director since 2001. Since that time, Gary has been the creative lead behind virtually all design aspects of* Rue Morgue, *including layout and illustration for the covers, event posters, merchandise, and the magazine's now infamous logo. Gary has worked on cover concepts with genre notables such as Clive Barker,* Hellboy *creator Mike Mignola and more recently, the legendary monster artist Basil Gogos. Heading into its thirteenth year,* Rue Morgue *swept the Rondo Awards last year, winning for best magazine, best article, best radio pod cast and best cover art (featuring Gogo's portrait of Forrest J. Ackerman).* Rue Morgue *is distributed internationally and has quickly become the industry's leading magazine for horror in culture and entertainment.*

On the little time he has off, Gary is a regular contributor to the popular heavy metal magazine Revolver *and* Royal Flush Magazine, *a publication dedicated to music, art and comics. His love of music has landed him work designing gig posters, t-shirts and album art for bands such as The Misfits, Tiger Army, Electric Frankenstein and The Creepshow.*

In December of 2008, Gary hosted "I Remember Halloween" at the historical Gladstone Hotel in Toronto, a one night only solo art show that was featured on Space TV, Canada's science fiction channel.

Gary is currently working on a few new projects, revamping his website, ghoulishgary.com, and trying to stay clear of the moors.

ID: Greetings, Gary. Has Rue Morgue *been keeping you busy?*
GG: Definitely. We're heading into our thirteenth year now.

ID: *I want to pay you a big thanks for doing this interview, and I'm sure Forry would have appreciated it, too. How did you two meet up?*
GG: Thanks for asking me. I've only had the pleasure to meet Forrest once at a *Chiller Theater* convention in New Jersey. He was sitting in the

hotel lobby by himself watching all of the horror fans. I walked over and introduced myself as the art director for *Rue Morgue Magazine*. His eyes lit up, and much to my surprise he said, "You have a wonderful magazine!" He had some nice things to say about the layout and design, so of course, I took that as a massive compliment! He was very warm and inviting. I felt like I had met a cool relative.

Most of us from the magazine went to L.A. last February to attend the memorial for him and it was an honor to be there. It was a very moving... I don't want to say service, because that sounds too formal. It was a very moving event. He was loved and respected by so many. I hadn't been around that much horror "royalty" before so it was kind of surreal!

ID: I bet it was. I see you hail from Toronto. Was Canada a good venue for an aspiring horror artist? I know David Cronenberg sure helped to put Canadian horror films on the map.

GG: Yes, thanks to cable TV. I was exposed to a wide range of horror films and if it wasn't on Saturday afternoons or late night TV, I rented it. At the same time I found mags like *Famous Monsters, Fango*, Balun's *Deep Red* and down the rabbit hole I went. It was all available here — you just had to look harder to find it. Cronenberg certainly helped but there are tons of great films from Canada: *The Changeling, My Bloody Valentine, Black Christmas, Deathdream, Rituals,* the list goes on. More recent films like *Ginger Snaps, Fido* and *Pontypool* are very good. Anyone with even a passing interest should check out the book *They Came From Within: A History of Canadian Horror Cinema* by Caelum Vatnsdal. It's a great read. I think the amount of good stuff that was shot or made here would surprise some people.

ID: Guillermo del Toro sure praises you highly. Have you ever worked with him on any art-related projects?

GG: No, but of course I wouldn't turn it down if given the opportunity! But that was another shock. Guillermo came to *Rue Morgue* one evening and we all got to spend some time with him. He too had some nice things to say about the magazine. He was extremely encouraging. So, much later on I was promoting an art show and I asked him for a quote. I wasn't really expecting a response but then a few days later I got an email and he took the time to look at my website and sent me a few to use. He's one of the most down to earth people in our industry I've ever met. He's a genius in every sense of the word.

ID: I see you moonlighted for Rue Morgue *for awhile before you became full-time. Were you welcomed with open arms? It seems to me that most of the time, the horror community is a very friendly and helpful group of people.*

GG: Yeah, Rodrigo and I hit it off right from the start. You have to understand that in the beginning Rodrigo was writing almost the entire magazine himself and doing the layout, distribution, subscriptions. He was dying for a layout guy! He wanted to focus on editorial. So when we met, we really clicked on where the direction of the mag should go. From that day on, he was shooting me as much work as I could handle like the *Rue Morgue* logo, covers, illustrations, title treatments, house ads...it was tough back then. Working full time for a major design firm during the day and then working on *Rue Morgue* stuff in the evenings and weekends. I was a young and hungry artist, driven and dedicated. About three years after we met, as the company grew, he hired me officially, full time, so I quit my design gig. And yes, it's a big community here in Toronto. I always say Toronto is a horror town. There are a lot of talented filmmakers, writers and artists here. We all sort of help each other out to attain our goals.

ID: With your genuine love for the horror genre, you most definitely fit into Rue Morgue's *subject matter. I see you like '80s slashers. Do you think the '80s slasher would have made for good subject matter for your artwork?*

GG: I grew up in the '80s so I guess there's some of that stuff in there. I love the artwork on those old VHS covers. I used to just stare at them. And I love a lot of films that came out of the '80s, not just the slasher stuff.

ID: Have you ever considered doing a graphic novel?

GG: It's something that's always been in the back of my mind, for sure. I'm a big fan of them and collect them. I love Charles Burns' *Black Hole* series and Vincent Locke's *A History of Violence.*

ID: What exactly is involved in being a "director of art"?

GG: Well, basically I oversee and approve all of the artwork that comes out of *Rue Morgue.* For the mag, I make decisions, with Dave, on how something should look or what direction the covers should take. I delegate the tasks that need doing and I'm lucky to have a very talented right-hand man Justin Erickson in the art department. He's a hard working guy and he brings his own ideas to the table. He's done a couple of covers that have been excellent and I know I can give him a big job and it's going to look great. We're not just a magazine anymore so there's a constant need for artwork. The company has grown so the duties have tripled. We're a website, a weekly radio station and an annual convention. We throw parties and events. We design all of our own merchandise. Now, Rodrigo is making films, so there's stuff that needs to be done for that. We're always busy, but we love doing it.

ID: What's on the horizon for you right now?
GG: We're just coming off of our Christmas break and about to start another year at *Rue Morgue*. I hope the readers like what we have planned. We're coming up to our 100th issue and we're having meetings now about how we can do something special, so that's exciting. On a personal side, I'm redesigning my website and working on some really cool things I can't announce at the moment, that I'm really excited about.

ID: Any last words before you go?
GG: Readers have said they see bit of all their favorite horror magazines in *RM*, especially *Famous Monsters*, and I'm really proud of that. Forrest has been an amazing inspiration to me over the years. His influence reached us monster kids up North too!

Special Guest Photos

Above: Ingrid Pitt as Countess Dracula.

Right: Forry's autograph for Ingrid.

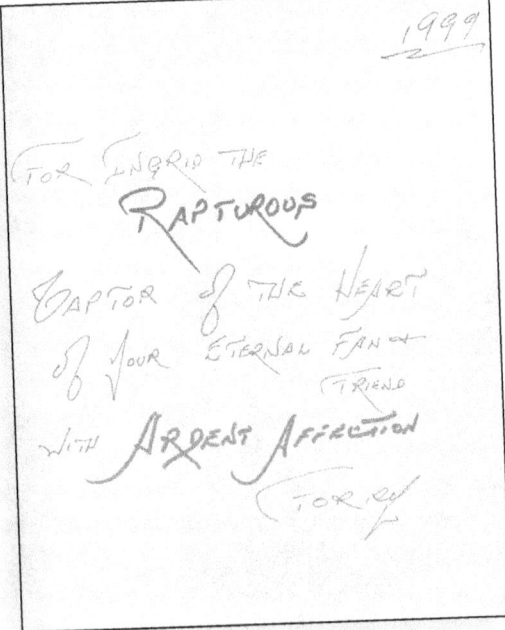

Basil Gogos, Zacherley, Forry, and Courtlandt Hull.

Frank Dietz, Forry, and Terry Pace.

Portrait of Forry by Jim McDermott.

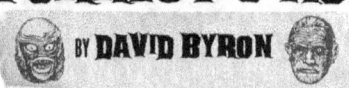

Cinemassacres logo by Gary Pullin.

Harry Walton survived Forry Ackerman's 65th Birthday party!

Forry and his monsters.

Kevin Sean Micheals and Forry.

Forry and Steven Speilberg.

Forry at The Ackermuseum.

The Amazing Kreskin and Mike Huckabee.

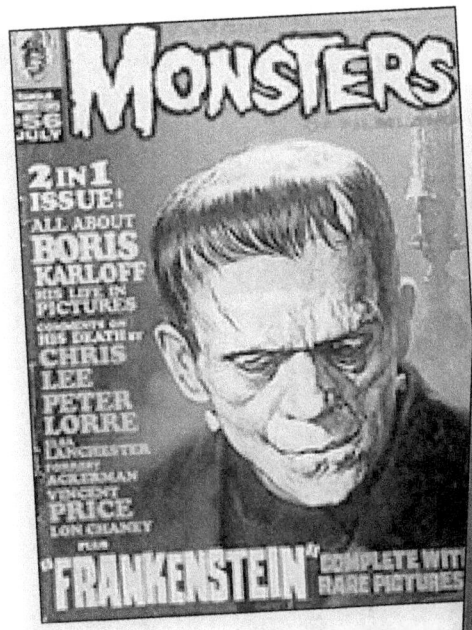

Courtlandt Hull

Cortlandt Hull, artist and film historian, began The Witch's Dungeon Classic Movie Museum when just 13. It is now considered the longest running tribute to the makeup artists and actors from classic horror films. The museum features accurate life-size figures of Boris Karloff, Vincent Price, Lon Chaney, Bela Lugosi, and many others in 13 scenes or dioramas based on the vintage movie chillers. Many of the figures are made from the actual life casts of the actor's faces, and some original costumes or props are featured in the sets. Guiding you through the tour are special voice tracks by Vincent Price, Mark Hamill, John Agar and voice actress June Foray as your hostess, "Zenobia The Gypsy Witch."

As you prepare to enter The Witch's Dungeon, outside, the "Graveyard of Classic Ghouls" sets the atmosphere, in memory of those famous monsters. During its fall season, rare original movie props are often on display, plus classic silent horror films are shown on a large outdoor screen, while eager visitors wait in line. Occasionally, a celebrity guest will host the evening. The museum has been continuously open every October for over 40 years, since 1966. For details, go to the "Dates" page of the museum website: www.preserevhollywood.org

Cortlandt and co-director, Dennis Vincent, have produced documentaries on the history of classic horror and fantasy films. Actor Henry Hull (Werewolf of London) *was Cortlandt's great uncle, and Josephine Hull* (Arsenic and Old Lace) *was his great aunt, so fantasy and horror is "in the blood"!*

ID: Happy holidays, Cortlandt. How was your Christmas?

CH: Very busy! Dennis Vincent and I were filming introductions for our new documentary, *The Aurora Monsters.* These segments are hosted by John Zacherle (Zacherley The Cool Ghoul), on very elaborate sets, which we filmed at Bill Diamond Studios. Zach gave us a great performance, which we believe fans will love, bringing them back to the "Monster Craze" of the 1960s.

ID: It's a pleasure to make the acquaintance of such a "connoisseur" of classic films.
Did Forry ever get a chance to see your museum?

CH: Yes, Forry and his wife Wendy visited for several days in 1971, not only taking a tour of my "Witch's Dungeon," but a marathon of classic silent horror films, from my 16mm film collection, long before video! I had previously provided Forry with frame blow-ups and other material for *Famous Monsters*, since Forry and I first met in 1966. A very special reward was given to me by Forry and Wendy a few years later: a casting of the Lugosi *Dracula* Ring, made directly from his original, identical to the ring he gave Christopher Lee, which Lee wore in his later *Dracula* films for Hammer. A prize I will always treasure.

ID: I understand you actually started the museum at the age of 13. What was the first piece you put on display?

CH: The first was my own creation, "Zenobia The Gypsy Witch," whose voice is done by June Foray, known for her cartoon voices in Warner Bros. Jay Ward and Disney cartoons! Five of the classic movie monsters joined "Zenobia" for the opening night of "The Witch's Dungeon" in October of 1966. Of course, in my early teens, it was a bit crude, but I was constantly improving it. I still am. I was inspired by the colorful Basil Gogos covers for *Famous Monsters* magazine, and the intricate cover art on the Aurora monster kits by James Bama. Forry was always very supportive of my museum, and introduced me to Don Post, Sr., and makeup artists Verne Langdon and John Chambers. I learned more from them, and later Dick Smith, than my years at the University of Hartford Art School!

ID: Your museum features life-like figures of Boris Karloff, Bela Lugosi, and Vincent Price, among others. Which ones were made from actual face-casts?

CH: At one point, most all the figures were based on life casts of the actors. But life casts can be expression-less: they need re-sculpting, as well as opening the eyes, as so much life comes from the eye area. I was fortunate to know make-up artists John Chambers, Dick Smith and Arnold Gargiulo, who provided me with castings of the actors' faces to work from. As mentioned, "Zenobia the Gypsy Witch" is totally my own creation.

One of my favorites, Dr. Phibes, was totally my sculpture, not even using Vincent Price's life-cast, just studying many photos. Vincent Price was a dear friend, and very supportive of the museum, doing special voice tracks for it, and donating his formal suit from *House of Wax* for our figure. Both my sculpts of *Dracula* and *Kharis the Mummy*, I have re-worked over the years. Lugosi is one of the most difficult to get a good likeness; the eye area on him is crucial!

ID: I see the actor Henry Hull was your Great-Uncle. Did he ever get a chance to visit your museum?

CH: Yes, we got to know each other best in his latter years. He was not only a versatile actor, but a talented makeup artist. Most early stage actors did all their own character makeup, like Lon Chaney, Sr. One of Henry's best, and most elaborate make-ups, was that of Edgar Allan Poe on the Broadway stage in 1936. Of course, he is best remembered as the first movie wolfman in the 1936 Universal classic, *Werewolf of London*. As Henry said, "You have the dubious honor of claiming your uncle was a werewolf!" I asked Henry so many questions about that film. He finally said, "You know I made at least 70 other films, could we talk about those sometime?" Josephine Hull was Henry's sister-in-law: she was one of the murderous but lovable Brewster sisters in *Arsenic and Old Lace*.

So, my great uncle was a werewolf and my great aunt a murderess — it's in the blood!

ID: What a bloodline! Have any celebrities ever dropped by to visit?

CH: Among the celebrities that have hosted, and greeted fans to "The Witch's Dungeon" are Oscar winning makeup artist Dick Smith, Sara Karloff, Ron Chaney and Bela Lugosi, Jr.

ID: Have you added an '80s slasher section yet?

CH: No, that is not an area of horror I am interested in. I think what has set "The Witch's Dungeon" apart from the Halloween "haunted houses" is that we specialize in accurate re-creations of the classic chillers of Karloff, Chaney, Lugosi and others. We hope to expand the museum to include the Hammer Horrors of Chrisopher Lee and Peter Cushing. I believe our museum is unique, as it appeals to all ages, film students and especially families. It is a reprieve from the blood and gore, making "The Witch's Dungeon" the longest running Halloween attraction in the country.

ID: Do you do all the sculpting yourself?

CH: Most of the figures I have sculpted over the years, although some heads have been done by Dick Smith, Henry Alvarez, Kelly Mann, Paul Clemens and others. But I do all the painting and insert the glass eyes, plus making the bodies, costuming, set and prop design. The incredible hair work is done by Dante Renta.

ID: If you could have met your favorite character from the museum, who would it have been?

CH: Well, either the *Werewolf of London*, but safer in his "Dr. Glendon" form, or the Chaney *Phantom Of The Opera*, but I guess I should keep my hand up, to avoid the Phantom's Punjab hangman's noose! The Chaney "Phantom" I find the most interesting of the monsters, as he is artistic, as well as an Edgar Allan Poe-style inventor! That's why I enjoy the horrors from the 1930s into the 1970s, the makeup and character backgrounds had a fantasy and fun element to them, plus an element of pathos to them.

ID: What's on the horizon for you right now?

CH: Dennis Vincent and myself are co-directing a series of documentaries called *Legends Of Film & Fantasy*. The first of our new series, "*The Aurora Monsters,*" centers not only on the *Aurora* monster kits, but the "Monster Craze" of the 1960s, which includes Forry and *Famous Monsters*, as well as the horror hosts, and much more. Other documentaries to follow include movie makeup, the early years of Hollywood fantasy films, and additional subjects related to fantasy films.

ID: Any last words before you go?

CH: In the 1960s, the great horror hosts, such as Zacherley and Vampira made horror movies "kid friendly." In the days of *Famous Monsters*, there were no DVDs on the secrets of movie making, no books devoted to makeup and effects. It was

Forry Ackerman who brought this to several generations, and opened up a whole world of imagination for us! If not for Forry, there may never have been a "Witch's Dungeon," plus many of our top makeup artists and effects people may not have developed a career in the fantasy field! We all owe a lot to our "Uncle Forry"!

Kevin Sean Michaels

Kevin Sean Michaels was born and raised in New York City. He started making films at age thirteen with a Super 8 home movie camera in the style of silent movies. Michaels was the Art Director for Troma Entertainment for three and a half years, working closely with filmmaker Lloyd Kaufman on Troma's film Poultrygeist! Night of the Chicken Dead, *as well as numerous DVD extras. He founded his own production company, Vamp Productions in 2005. Michaels is known for his documentaries:* Vampira: The Movie *was his first documentar,y released on Alpha Video in 2008. Since then, he has produced* The Wild World of Ted V. Mikels, *about the grind-house filmmaker, due in stores March 2010, also on Alpha Video.*

In 2008, Michaels met David Lynch and is producing a documentary, Beyond The Noise, *about a teenager's journey learning Trancendental Meditation. He is working on a project with horror legend Ingrid Pitt on an animated short on her experiences in the Holocaust.*

ID: How goes it over at Vamp Productions?

KSM: It couldn't be a more exciting time. I feel like the Octo-Mom, trying to produce eight baby projects at once. It's frustrating because there are so many mouths to feed and how can you send them off to college?

ID: Yeah, I've been there, done that. You are obviously a big fan of '60s and '70s pop culture, including the horror and sci-fi genres. Were you one of the many who cited Forry Ackerman as a major influence?

KSM: *Famous Monsters* was a great publishing dynasty. Forry was a great networker. His love of the genre bubbled out of the pages. He was Mr.Sci-Fi, of course. You never got the feeling that he or his magazine had anything but love for the horror and sci-fi films it covered. I wanted to be an editor for a magazine myself and I eventually became a writer and editor myself before going into film.

ID: How did you meet Forry?

KSM: On April 23, 2005, I made my first visit to what is referred to as the "Son of Ackermansion" at 4511 Russell Avenue, in Hollywood, CA. The address is well known to movie fans as Forry has (or used to have) open-houses in which to visit with him. I was amazed when I got there. Everywhere I looked at was more amazing than the last. Spry as ever, Forry popped up as an ersatz tour guide. "Go ahead and try it on," Forry said, handing me a mysterious beaver-skin top hat. Right as I am obliging him, he added, "That was used by Lon Chaney." "*London After Midnight*?" I gasped, quickly putting it down as if I angered the gods of movie land history. "No, put it back on," he urged. That is Forry in a nutshell. We sat down in Forry's living room and set up a camera and lights to record the interview. Over by the window, I discover Bela Lugosi's original *Dracula* cape and a large wooden coffin next to it.

"Maybe we should shoot the interview in the coffin?" Forry suggested. "Really?" I said. As we ponder that possibility, Forry's assistant Joe Moe ran in the room. He explained to Forry that the coffin was full of junk and would take time to clean out and that he meant to get to it sooner. Disappointed, Forry took to his Archie Bunker chair as second choice. The subject of the interview was Maila Nurmi, known in the 1950s as *Vampira* on Los Angeles TV station KABC and played the wandering ghoul girl in Edward D. Wood's *Plan 9 From Outer Space*. Forry knew Maila Nurmi since 1944. Forry stayed friends with Maila for over sixty years. They attended conventions, screenings and ceremonies together. I'm sad that they are both gone now.

ID: I see you were employed at Troma Films as art director at one time. As a former "insider" would you say that Lloyd Kaufman's films could have been classified as "exploitation" films?

KSM: "Exploitation" is a silly term, as every film is exploited. It only ever meant that. I believe that the term was put out there by jealous corporate mega-studios to belittle independents. Naturally, Lloyd exploits his films — what else would he do to keep the electric in the studio on? I designed over 150 DVD covers for Lloyd. You soon realize that you are not competing with big studios, even though you are. For example: you have to be saying with your art that this thing called Troma is a secret society. Not too secret, though, you still want to sell a few DVDs. But I mean in the way that a certain amount of people will get what you are saying with your art. So then you are not part of the mainstream, because you don't want to be, rather than feeling blacklisted. That said, you feel like you are not looking over your shoulder. I learned that from Lloyd: Say 'screw you' to the industry and take the lumps. There is nothing exploitive in that, it's just doing your art, your way, and being true to yourself.

ID: As somewhat of a scholar of film, would you say that Ted V. Mikels' films would have fit into that category as well? Other terms I've heard used were "drive-in" movies and "grindhouse" films.

KSM: Ted never liked those categories, as he discusses in my documentary, *The Wild World of Ted V. Mikels*, which John Waters narrated for us. Again, where do these labels come from? I never heard that they originated from fans. Same with "cult." Honestly, no filmmaker trying to make a living wants to reach a niche audience, sell a few thousand copies, yet they are forced to (due to lack of money) only be able to reach a small market. They simply don't have the nickels to make a big splash. With 100 million dollars, Ted could make 200 movies (laughs). So it's funny for me to hear about filmmakers now trying to copy the films made in the 1970s that used $500,000 budgets with their $100 million dollar budgets.

ID: As an obvious David Lynch fan, how would you "classify" his films? David Cronenberg would be another filmmaker that would be hard to place on any certain category.

KSM: That's true. This "classify" thing. Not to sound like the great George Carlin, but who makes these rules? I'm glad to see that finally we don't need to "classify" music anymore. But films still need to be put into ticky-tacky little boxes. Lynch and Cronenberg don't worry about their films being neatly filed, that's why there is so little commercial success. But, as Herschell Gordon Lewis says, if you stick around long enough you become legitimate. That's why I love their films. You can dream in those spaces. You are not told to laugh or cry or are required to do anything but watch.

ID: What was the inspiration for the film Vampira: The Movie? *I mean, other than the obvious? (laughs).*

KSM: Believe or not, it all started with loving *Elvira: Mistress of the Dark*. That was my "horror host" growing up. I was always fascinated by Vampira in *Plan 9 From Outer Space*, but didn't know until much later that she started the whole hosting thing. I never in my wildest dreams (wildest nightmares?) thought that Maila Nurmi would enter my life, but it just happened and I credit Forry for nudging me along. He thought Elvira and Vampira were two separate entities and he liked them both. Forry was not involved in their feud. I didn't want to be either. I like them both, but there are fans out there that don't like when I say that. It's either you are a tea drinker or a coffee drinker — you can't be both. So I was inspired by both women. If I said something favorable to Maila about Elvira, she would freak out, so I stayed off the topic. When the movie was done, Maila saw Elvira's name on the credits. She said, "At least you did your homework."

ID: What's this project with Ingrid Pitt all about? It sounds fascinating.
KSM: I approached Ingrid Pitt about doing a documentary based on her autobiography. Since she doesn't travel to the U.S., I had to go to the U.K. to film her. She is the most delightful human being. She has been through so much in her life. Her experience in a Nazi death camp really shook me. I was in her home and she told me about her childhood. I was worried about how worked up she got. We were going to shoot the next day and I felt that all the questions about Vampire movies I had prepared seems trivial in comparison. We shot an entire day at Twickenham Studios, where The Beatles filmed *A Hard Day's Night*. Just amazing. Ingrid, ever the trooper, was very professional and shooting came off without a hitch. We covered all the questions, which touched on the chapters in her autobiography. I am attempting to produce a short animated film on her time in the Holocaust that will stand alone, but will eventually be part of a greater documentary on her life and career.

ID: Tell me a little bit about your own film career, as an actor.
KSM: I really love acting and want to do more of it. I think about how Hitchcock felt that actors where cattle and that somehow the director is a supreme being. What an odd idea. But it is so much fun to do both and I don't feel I can one day be a great director without being in the hot seat in front of the camera.

ID: As a producer, actor, visual artist, and filmmaker, it's probably rare when you get some down time, get to chill out. What's on your agenda for the near future?
KSM: I started doing Trancendental Meditation. Lynch talks about it all the time. It's really helping me with stress. After all, I used to work for Troma. Even Howard Stern does it. I recommend that people try it out. "You can still be edgy and make dark films, but be joyful inside," says Lynch. Werner Herzog told me that I am being ridiculous doing TM. I hope I can work with Werner someday.

This year, I have been thinking about friends I've lost, which includes Maila and Forry. My goal is to start paying attention to my life and my work and make it meaningful. Sappy, I know.

ID: No, not sappy: very good outlook, actually. Any last words before you go?

KSM: Do what you love, have love and bring love to your art. That will transfer to others. I think that was Forry's legacy. Be the lightning rod. Forry said, "Whatever I do, I'm still a fan." Me, too.

Frank Winspur

Born in Connecticut in 1961, Frank Winspur was a classic monster kid. The era provided so much to encourage a young model fan: it's no wonder the course his life has taken! A long time builder and collector of kits, toys, and books, Frank was greatly influenced by Famous Monsters, *and the late, great,* Monster Times. *Forry and Basil's role in his life wouldn't come complete until the start of Moebius Models in 2007. Influenced by the undying love of plastic kits and monsters, Frank and Moebius began by putting out a classic kit never before re-issued, Aurora's* Dr Jekyll and Mr Hyde. *From there, it hasn't found its end yet. Other great re-releases include Monster Scenes, and the classic Gigantic Frankenstein. New monster kits such as Invisible Man, The Mummy, and Frankenstein are also on their way, hopefully to start a new generation of monster kids! Operating now out of Florida, Frank is determined to see monsters and models keep its tradition of entertaining the masses. New fans will be exposed to Basil Gogos by the use of his art for the upcoming Mummy kit release.*

NVF: Greetings, Frank. How are you today?
FW: Not too bad, pretty cold here in Florida. Eighteen degrees last night here!

NVF: I think what you are doing is great. Re-releasing the old model kits. I used to have a collection of them as a kid. What made you take the plunge?
FW: At the time, Polar Lights was sold to RC2, and they stopped re-releasing them. There was so much interest still, I had to keep it going some way. Moebius is the result.

NVF: So you were greatly influenced by Forry Ackerman's magazine, Famous Monsters. *Me too! Did you ever get a chance to meet him?*
FW: I never did. Every time I went to California I made plans to stop by, but something always changed my schedule. Definitely a huge regret.

NVF: I met Doug Bradley once — Pinhead in the Hellraiser *films — and he was a really nice guy. Have you ever met any celebs in your line of work?*

FW: I have met plenty at the different shows. I have three favorites. I hate to say that, but they were so nice in person I just have to mention them: Linda Hamilton, Kelly Hu, and Alessandra Ambrosio. I was just shocked to see how great they were with the fans, signing pictures and answering questions.

NVF: Do you plan to expand, carry more models as time goes by, or just specialize in one certain line?

FW: With Moebius, we're going to expand into other types of kits and products at some point. For now, we're just trying to keep as many fans as happy as we can with our choices. The Irwin Allen kits we produce have been great sellers so far, and we plan on continuing that line as long as we can.

NVF: Do you remember the old Johnny West and GI Joe dolls?

FW: Those were real quality items in those days. Those things took a beating! Great stuff, not much like it anymore. I guess if they were still made us old guys would buy them, and not the kids!

NVF: As an obvious connoisseur of horror, what magazines would you say are some of your all time favorites? Other than mine, that is. LOL!

FW: Famous Monsters, of course, is the first one that comes to mind. Growing up, I really loved *Monster Times*. I hear it may be coming back in some form, but nothing will replace that original old newspaper type mag. Fun stuff. Today, if it has a monster in it I'll grab it. Can never get enough of it!

NVF: What would say is on the horizon for Frank? Your own model empire?

FW: Not sure I'd say empire, but were getting there. Twelve kits out in 2008, looks like we'll have 12 more in 2009. We'll start to branch off into other products soon though, keep watching!

NVF: Any last words before you leave us?

FW: I'd just like to say thanks again to Forry for all he did for everyone in the hobby. He really was a legend to many of us, and will be missed dearly.

Dr. Mangor

Dr. Mangor is a somewhat suspicious character of unknown age and quite frankly, unknown intentions, or perhaps it should be said that he is made of intentions you'd rather not know of. Some say he's simply a very clever brain that has been body snatching for well over several decades: his ultimate ruse to blend into the everyday just long enough further his occultist studies until that uncertain day that he unleashes the Blind Squid upon the world and enslaves the masses. But until that point he simply adds more of the foolish to the Kult of the Blind Squid and works at fitting into society through character animation and his own brand of eccentric comics, artwork and photography. In the past he's worked on everything from South Park *to high end films like* I, Robot *and just recently finished animating on a short film by director Spike Jones called* I'm Here. *With this done he is currently finishing up his* Suicidal Suzi *comic, planning your doom and drinking tea as often as possible.*

ID: Good day, Dr. Mangor. Been performing any strange and dangerous experiments lately?

Dr. M: Greetings, sir. Amazed this machine actually got me here in one piece in this rain, so to say. Experiments? Quite a few. I have stopped self-experimentation and started on more deserving patients. Subject #67 and I just had tea the other evening. It...er...*she* is doing well, except for that terrible dribble I must fix up sooner than later.

ID: Wow...when you are finished, will you set me up with her? But for now, allow me to jump right in and be nosy: when did you first meet up with Uncle Forry?

Dr. M: Once upon an LA time, I was invited by a friend to tour the "Ackermansion," which was Forry's residence and sci-fi museum all rolled up into one splendid, surreal chateau up in the hills of Los Feliz. Friends and fans of Forry's would gather for a party-slash-tour-slash-storytelling-hour of sorts at his mansion. On my first visit, I was thrilled when Forry himself guided us through his museum of bizarre artifacts, props, film memorabilia, and random paraphernalia. Like ghost-hungry kids around a campfire god we gathered in a circle on Forry's acid-green shag carpet as he sat in an overstuffed armchair throne and regaled us with tales of twisted and fascinating Hollywood history, from run-ins with Barbara Leigh from *Vampirella* to meeting Bela Lugosi on set and acquiring his cape (which he would then proceed to show off). Now, at this time I knew of Forry's *Famous Monsters of Film-land* but little of the editor himself. So at first I was taken aback by this extremely animated and theatrical older man, acting out past events as if they had occurred just yesterday. I had the pleasure of attending a few of these tours before being invited to more personal shindigs such as Forry's birthdays and other random events organized by Joe, his caretaker at the time. I met the most amazing host of characters at these parties: ohGr from Skinny Puppy, Richard Metzger from DisInformation, just to name a few, and the list goes on. Yes, this was Hollywood and to be expected yet some of these people I had looked up to since I was young. It was quite intimidating at first until realizing we were all on the same level of horror and sci-fi geekdom, and were drawn to the phenomenon of Forry. I met some stellar people and made lifelong friends. It was also a great time to fondle the relic from *Indiana Jones* and ogle original Ray Harryhausen models!

ID: I bet you have some wonderful memories of him regardless. Any amusing anecdotes from your conversations with him?

Dr. M: For one, you might not want to have a conversation with him if there was a pretty lady about. His attention would be fixated on her, charming her shoes off. He seemed to thrive off being the ultimate dashing and relentless charmer, *a la* Vincent Price. He also thrived on entertaining guests with his special tours, and the best part was the outside trek downstairs to Ackermansion's dungeonesque basement. Forry had transformed the crawlspace into a haunted house of latex corpses (many of them rotting into even creepier forms) all screaming, yawning or creeping from the depths of the shadows. All sorts of dark props, monsters, and creatures from horror film sets of yore made for a genuinely disturbing experience. Forry would warn us to pause while he went ahead and entered the dungeon, then freaked us all out by pretending to be attacked by something horrible and screeching. You had to listen closely for there was a story behind EVERY prop/art/item in the house (and in the depths below).

One thing that struck me about Forry was his undying love for his wife, and I wish I'd had the chance to meet them together when she was still alive. However, one couldn't help but feel like she was still around in one form or another: in his kitchen Forry had a wall-size photo of her; in the bathroom there was her portrait; in fact in almost every room and hallway, she stared back. When he talked about her his eyes would tear up...he surrounded himself with her ghost. But I wouldn't expect any less from a true aficionado of the afterlife.

Sadly the last time I saw him he was in a new house, and not doing too well physically. But despite this he was still just as alive and energetic with his conversations.

ID: Just out of curiosity, does being a "doctor of unknown age and unknown reasons" place you into the same category as Hannibal Lecter?

Dr. M: Now I do believe what my dear Hannibal did was quite unbecoming yet one must admire his twisted sense of humor, cunning, and perhaps, tastes? I've finally quit the human meats myself yet I have no qualm about human experimentation. If I must, I prefer small kittens or children of a bitty age for they tend to heal quicker than the elderly. Now if it's in the name of science or winning a war, well, the victor will be morally right and the defeated will be wrong. Lecter was caught, yet made a Houdini-like escape...well I guess you could place this dear doctor in that category.

(Pauses)

You don't plan on turning me in, do you Dave?

ID: Never! I find the world much more interesting with you in it...your "personal interests" list includes amputations, absinthe, biting flesh, and zombie porn, just to name a few. Are these interests "practiced" in any certain order?
(laughs)

Dr. M: (Stares at Dave's arm.)

ID: Why are you staring at my arm?

Dr. M: Excuse me? Sorry I haven't eaten my meal today. *(Reaches into doctor's bag)*

ID: Uh...hold on just a few minutes, and I will run down to the local Hardees and grab you something.

Dr. M: Oh...alright. *(Puts bag away)*

ID: Thank you. Have any of your brain transfers been successful? I've been thinking of getting a new one...

Dr. M: OF COURSE! I've been body snatching, as it were, for over decades. Out with the old flesh and in with the new! Now, though, if you need a new brain...well I've not found a way to transfer the soul nor the memories to a new one. If you would like to contract me to experiment on this, well we can talk more after a few drinks of my "special" tonic.

ID: All joking aside, what exactly does Dr. Mangor's Surveillance and Photographia services consist of? What is your "specialty"?
Dr. M: Surveillance consists of a collection of my photography throughout my life. Some are planned shoots while some are right from life of people and nature. I'm very attracted to abandoned places and currently am working on a series of photos I took in Berlin, Germany, last year of an abandoned children's hospital. This put the Linda Vista asylum in Los Angeles to shame. Add to this, someone had a horrid accident and blood was literally sprayed on the walls in one of the rooms.

My specialty though, to blend into society? Well I would say character animation pays the bills. In the past I've worked on projects stepping from *South Park* to high end films like *I, Robot*. I just finished animating on a short film by director Spike Jonze called *I'm Here*. When I'm not animating for studios or freelancing on multimedia I'm working on my own comics, artwork and photography.

ID: Back to Forry for a moment. Here is a question I've been tossing around to mixed reaction lately: If you could see Forry one more time, what would you say to him?
Dr. M: I would thank him for having such a positive impact on my creativity and inspiring me to do greater things with my life. He also put me at ease about aging gracefully and maintaining an entertaining life — that one never need give up on having a fantastic time with friends and throwing endless parties. You see, his house was a physical manifestation of his mind: full of so many amazing tales, experiences, and strange adventures, it would take years, if not decades, to listen to them all.

And I would thank him for being the light in the dark that is Forrest Ackerman.

ID: Amen. What's on the horizon for the good doctor right now? A lobotomy? The defilement of an innocent victim's flesh?
Dr. M: I am working on a new *Suicidal Suzi* comic that really is ripe and almost ready to be printed! Other experiments include re-animation of dead puppets and giant squids if the thing we call money falls into the doctor's jars anytime soon. Well, now that you mention it, a lobotomy of a wealthy banker may be a wondrous idea. Defilement of his flesh would

come next if he didn't comply...but those loathsome creatures are far from being innocent!!!
(Pauses)
Sir, Is it time for a tonic break?

ID: Yes, you may drink your tonic.

Pam Keesey

ID: Good morning, Pam. Has the publishing business been keeping you on your toes?

PK: It certainly has! Especially with the resurgence of the popularity of vampires in mainstream. It seems you can't keep a good (or even a not-so-good) vampire down.

ID: How true! You have a very solid reputation for writing about women in horror, including lesbian horror. In your honest opinion, what exactly is it that women in horror REALLY want?

PK: The same thing anyone wants in a good story, especially a good horror story: something that captures the imagination and stays with you long after the story has been told.

ID: I see you co-edited a Scifi Womanthology *with Forry Ackerman, too. I, unfortunately, never got a chance to meet him in person. What was it like to know him personally? To work with him?*

PK: How to begin? Knowing Forry was a gift. He was such a good friend, and such a dear man. I feel very lucky to have known him, and to have become such close friends with him. He was one of my earliest influences and one of my dearest companions. The genre is what it is in part because of Forry: Stephen King submitted his very first horror story to Forry; John Landis, Joe Dante, and Rick Baker were childhood readers of *Famous Monsters of Filmland*.

Sci-Fi Womanthology was the only project he and I ever collaborated on. It was a dream of his to collect some of his favorite stories by women from the pulp science fiction magazines, and bring them to a whole new audience. Many of them I heard of for the first time when I was helping to select stories for the anthology.

It's really quite amazing how prevalent women were among the authors of short science fiction stories in the early years of the genre, and how few of them found success in the book publishing industry. Of course, quite a few of the great authors of science fiction were women, but wrote under male or gender neutral pseudonyms: James Tiptree, Jr. and Andre Norton, for example. It was fascinating to me how many women were writing in the pulp magazines, and were using their own names, not male pseudonyms. Forry introduced me to a lot of great writers I'd never heard of before through our collaboration on *Sci-Fi Womanthology*. It was a great experience.

ID: I understand he let you try on a pair of shoes once owned by Marlene Dietrich. How did it feel to "walk in her shoes" for a little while?
PK: Oh, what a pleasure it was! When Forry and I were first getting to know each other, we discovered that we both not only loved the Universal horror classics, but many of the same great classic movies and great classic movie stars. Marlene Dietrich was one. When I first went to his house in Hollywood, the Ackermansion, he said that he had something that he wanted to show me, and brought out a pair of gold high-heeled sandals. That's when he told me that they had once belonged to Marlene Dietrich, and asked me if I would like try them on. "Really?" I asked him in disbelief. "Of course," he said, and he handed them to me.

It wasn't just that the shoes belonged to Marlene, or that Forry had once met her, but that he was as passionate about the experience as I was. Forry had a way of making Hollywood, and certainly making science fiction and horror, whether film or fiction, come alive for each and every person who came to see him and to view his collection.

ID: Tell me about your publication, MonsterZine. *Do I detect a tribute to Forry in the title?*
PK: It's certainly a tribute to Forry in the sense that he helped nurture, directly by way of *Famous Monsters of Filmland*, and indirectly through his influence on the horror industry and the various ways in which horror was marketed to children in the '60s and '70s, my own love of horror. For me, *MonsterZine* is about exploring the aspects of horror as it imbues and reflects the social issues of the day, about celebrating the art and artistry of horror filmmaking, and celebrating those films we loved as kids, and the films we love today.

ID: Did your days as a technical editor and news editor help prepare you for your career within the horror field?
PK: Actually, I think the question is whether my career in the horror field prepared me for my career as a technical writer. I got into technical

writing through doing web development for my online horror movie magazine, *MonsterZine*. The technical writing came later. Much later.

ID: In all honesty, considering the horror genre is such a maligned genre as it is, do you feel it is still going strong? I've noticed film and book sales have dropped over the last couple of years, and some critics claim it isn't because of our economy, either.

PK: I think it is still going strong, perhaps even stronger now than it has in the last decade. Sales have dropped, but the industry is also changing, and changing dramatically, so sales figures aren't the only measure of popularity anymore. For example, there's a plethora of horror movie sites online: web sites, forums, chat rooms. There are even horror dating sites. Clearly, marketers think that horror fans are a significant target market. The question is, what are people selling, and how and where are people finding it? I think that it's not the usual suspects — mainstream publishers and movie studios.

I think it's significant that most of the successful horror films around right now are actually less successful remakes of really great foreign horror films. I suspect that the decline in sales has more to do with what American publishers and American studios assume is the kind of horror that will attract an audience than what horror fans are actually spending their hard-earned time and money on.

ID: You strike me as the type to really enjoy the older, classic films, like the Universal monster flicks. Do you feel that the older films are better than the ones produced now? I mean, you have to admit, a lot of the newer films are pretty clichéd, and the endless onslaught of sequels and remakes of classic horror films is getting old fast.

PK: I think it really depends on what you're thinking of as the "newer" films.

First, I should say that you're absolutely right. I am a fan of classic horror: the Universal monster movies, James Whale, Val Lewton, and — I'm bridging decades and genres here — Robert Wise. There's not a lot of what people think of as contemporary horror that I like, but there are certainly many contemporary horror films that are among my favorites. Admittedly, they have more in common with the classics than with what most people think of as genre horror films, but they are really fantastic films. And not just fantastic films, but fantastic horror films. *Shadow of the Vampire* comes to mind, as does *The Devil's Backbone* and *Pan's Labyrinth*. I thought the Hong Kong film *Jian Gui* was fantastic, but the American remake (*The Eye*) was a complete disappointment. *Let the Right One In* is another fantastic film, much better than the book, in my opinion, and one that is slated for what is likely to be a lesser quality American remake.

ID: Fair enough. What's on the horizon for Pam right now?

PK: There's so much going on at the moment that it's hard to pinpoint any one project. At least nothing that's ready to be publicly announced. I've been on an extended hiatus, and needed that time to focus on other things. It's exciting to be creating again, to be in the midst of what seems to be a revival in the horror genre and a renewed interest in the classics. Of course, with the deluge of social networking apps out there, it's much easier to keep in touch with people than ever before, so people are more than welcome to come find my online on *MySpace, Facebook, Twitter,* and, of course, my personal blog.

ID: Any last words before you leave us?

PK: I find myself thinking about Guillermo del Toro, one of my favorite directors of contemporary horror films, and something that he said at a tribute to Forry in March 2009, celebrating Forry's life and his work. What he said is, "There are places inside of us that are only touched by monsters. Good places."

I think he's right. And through *Famous Monster of Filmland,* Forry helped many of us find those good places.

Special Guest Interviews

Joe R. Lansdale

Introduction by Chet Williamson

My buddy David Byron asked me if I'd be interested in doing an interview with my ole pard Joe Lansdale for NVF, *but I declined, since I'd already conducted a lengthy palaver with Joe a year or so ago for* Weird Tales. *Still, I offered to write a very brief intro to the interview if David conducted it.*

Joe does a lot of interviews, but in every one you'll find his distinctive voice saying pretty wise things, and this one is no different. David's tone is more conversational and jocular than mine had been (I always tend to interview "for the ages"), and Joe loosens up nicely here. Reading it gives the flavor of sitting in a quiet room with a friend, sharing stories and swapping yarns, and there isn't a better guy to do that with than Joe. Read on, and feel the mojo!

ID: **Howdy Joe! How's the weather in Texas? It's so cold here, the brass monkeys are wearing thermal undies.**

JRL: It's cool and wet here, but pretty pleasant, though according to the weather guessers, that's about to change and it's about to turn cold and nasty.

ID: **Sounds fun! I just picked up a book the other day entitled** Horror Writers on Horror Film, **and lo and behold, you were in there! I knew there was good reason I bought that book. I got the impression from your article that you grew up really enjoying the old drive-in theaters. Me, too. Was your love for that era — and its films — an inspiration for your book** The Drive-In?

JRL: I don't even remember writing that article unless it's the one called *A Hard On For Horror*. That was about my love for low budget horror films. I don't like them straight across the board; it depends on the film. But, yes, that grew out of my love for drive-ins and drive-in movies and all the fun I had there, and the fact that there were certain types of movies that showed there that showed nowhere else, as well as some that did, and some second run movies from what Joe Bob Briggs used to call hardtop theaters. Truth is — I don't quite have the passion I used to have for low budget horror films because now there are a lot of better made, better budget films than there were before. Still, some are so good, or so goddamn bad, that they are still on my list of favorites.

ID: Yeah, I hear ya. I've always enjoyed your Hap and Pine novels, too, one of my favorites being The Two Bear Mambo. *Could Hap and Pine possibly be based on real-life characters?*

JRL: They are a mixture of people, though Hap is primarily me if I hadn't met my wife and had had a mid life crisis — I didn't have time or need for one — and I had made slightly different choices. All this would have been without all the shooting and the like, I think, but I could have ended up a lot like him. Hell, in many ways, I am a lot like him. I get older though, and I've stopped aging him and Leonard as I wait sometimes years between their adventures. I have a new one, *Vanilla Ride*, about them, coming out summer of 2009, and another will follow in 2010, plus I have a partial, *Blue To The Bone*, and another that has yet to be finished and find a home. One of them may turn out to just be a long short story. I like the guys, though, and one reason there's been a delay is they were with Warner — now Grand Central — and my new publisher didn't want to publish novels about them when the back list was owned by someone else. Now, all the back list of the Hap and Leonard series, plus audios of their adventures, and possibly a film--been close several times before--is forthcoming, with me writing the screenplay. The current book that may be a film is the first in the series — *Savage Season*.

ID: I understand you are a Burn Notice *fan. Me too! That Bruce Campbell is real hoot, isn't he? You had a funny story you told me once, about you and your family and Bruce going out to dinner, and a waitress recognized him. Tell me that one again.*

JRL: Yeah, I really like *Burn Notice*. I watched it because I like Bruce, and then I got hooked for a lot of other reasons. I wish it would get on a slightly more regular schedule. The martial arts in it are very good. The story is Don Coscarelli, Bruce, my wife and daughter and myself went to dinner here in Nacogdoches, and a waiter came over and told Bruce he looked like that guy in *Army Of Darkness*, and Bruce told him, "Yeah, I get that a lot."

We would have left it at that, but my daughter and wife couldn't keep their mouth shut. They told him. Said it was him.

ID: Poor old Bruce...he is going to have to start wearing a mask to go out and eat. Speaking of Bruce, were you happy with the job Don Coscarelli did on the film Bruce was in, Bubba Ho Tep? *I really enjoyed it, myself. I believe that was adapted from one of your stories?*

JRL: I adored *Bubba Hotep*. I think it's Don and Bruce's best film, hands down. Ossie Davis is one of my favorites, so I was really happy he was in it.

ID: I totally agree. You often mix horror and humor into the same story, as in the tale The Night They Missed the Horror Show. *Do you think that some writers use this as an escape? Sort of a creative outlet for their own fears?*

JRL: An escape. A way to make a statement. A way to work out demons. A way to deal with fears. That story actually has a number of true and "told for true" events I heard about. I linked them together for that story and made a lot of stuff up too, but the tone and the feel is right for where I grew up, the attitudes then. *Night They Missed The Horror Show* is my favorite of all my stories, and for lots of reasons. It changed my life as a writer, it became somewhat famous and has resold over the years, and it was a story where I felt I had learned how to write about the things I wanted to write about in the way I wanted to write about them.

ID: And a grand job you did of it, too. I understand you are acquainted with Chet Williamson. He seems like a real nice guy. What do you think a literary collaboration between you and him would be like? I think it could prove to be very interesting...

JRL: Chet and I are very good friends. I met him at a convention many years ago, and I really wanted to meet him because I was a fan of his work. I'm especially fond of his short stories, and wrote the intro to his short story collection, and it is so good. As for how a collaboration would be...I don't know. We've edge around that with film scripts and comics, but it never quite happened. Most of the time, I think writers do their best work alone, at least in books and short stories. We are very different kinds of writers, so I don't know how we would blend. I'm a poor planner. I never know what's going to happen from one day to the next, except in a few rare cases where a story came to me in a flash, or it built in my head over time. I'm more of an idea and emotion writer than a big planner. I like a compass, not a map.

ID: Ok, here is one for fun: If you could trade places just for one day, with one of your favorite characters from one of your favorite books, who would it be?

JRL: None of them. I like my life too much.

ID: I don't blame you there. OK, here's another: What exactly is a "mojo story teller?" And...while I'm at it, what exactly is a "splatter punk?"

JRL: Actually, my wonderful webmaster, Lou Bank, came up with Mojo storyteller based on my use of the word as part of my title *Mucho Mojo*. It just means magical storyteller. But I didn't name myself that. I like it though. Splatterpunk was a horrible idea because it limited writers to fit a certain type of fiction. I may have written some stories that fit that definition, but I didn't want to define my career by it. It's clever, but frankly, I hate it. My friend David Schow came up with it. I think he and a few others wanted to make it a literary movement, and as soon as you can put a pin in it, put a name to it, it's over with anyway. I know a lot of writers who killed their careers with that label, and I was afraid it would get me even though I never embraced it; it puts too big a monkey on your back and again, for me, it's not accurate when it is used to define my career. It's a word that ended up in the dictionary, though, and David Schow is giving the credit, accurately.

ID: No shit? I figured you'd have said Skipp and Spector. What triggered your interest in the martial arts? Hey...maybe you and Chuck Norris could do a film together...

JRL: My father was forty or so when I was born and had been a wrestler and boxer from time to time at fairs during the Depression. He had picked up some judo and jujitsu, so he was my first instructor of self-defense and sparked my interest for life.

ID: If you could meet your favorite writer(s), who would it be? And...what would you do to entertain them? Dinner and drinks? Pizza and a DVD? Or...a verbal reading of The Night They Missed the Horror Show?

JRL: I've met some of my favorites. Robert Bloch. Richard Matheson. Ray Bradbury. William F. Nolan. Andrew Vachss, who is a dear friend and brother. I'd like to have met Flannery O'Conner. We'd have to have had fried chicken and gravy and taters.

ID: Sounds tasty. By the way, how's your book Leather Maiden *doing? Unfortunately, I haven't had a chance to read it yet.*

JRL: I won't know how *Leather Maiden* is doing until royalty time, but I think it's doing pretty good.

ID: Well, Joe, I know you are a busy man, so I will let you go for now. Any last words before you leave us?

JRL: Last words...hmm...Nope!

ID: Cool. Take it easy, Joe.

Bibliography

Novels

Hap Collins and Leonard Pine mysteries
Savage Season (1990)
Mucho Mojo (Cemetery Dance Publications, 1994)
Two-Bear Mambo (1995)
Bad Chili (1997)
Rumble Tumble (1998)
Veil's Visit (includes the eponymous story, written with Andrew Vachss; 1999; limited edition)
Captains Outrageous (2001)
Vanilla Ride (2009; previously referred to as *Blue to the Bone*)
The *Drive-In* series
The Drive-In: A "B" Movie with Blood and Popcorn, Made in Texas (1988)
The Drive-In 2: Not Just One of Them Sequels (1989)
The Drive-In: A Double-Feature (1997, omnibus; compiles the first two)
The Drive-In: The Bus Tour (2005; limited edition)
The *Ned the Seal* trilogy

These are all limited editions published by Subterranean Press:
Zeppelins West (2001)
Flaming London (2006)
The Sky Done Ripped (release date unknown)

Other novels

Act of Love (1980)
Texas Night Riders (1983; originally published under the pseudonym Ray Slater)
Dead in the West (1986; written in 1980)
Magic Wagon (1986)
The Nightrunners (1987; written in 1982 as *Night of the Goblins*)
Cold in July (1989)
Tarzan: the Lost Adventure (1995; with Edgar Rice Burroughs)
The Boar (1998; initially a limited edition, later republished)
Freezer Burn (1999)
Waltz of Shadows (1999; written in 1991; limited edition, *Lost Lansdale*, Vol. 1)
Something Lumber This Way Comes (1999; Children's book; limited edition, *Lost Lansdale*, Vol. 2)
The Big Blow (2000; limited edition)
Blood Dance (2000; written in the early '80's; limited edition, *Lost Lansdale*, Vol. 3)
The Bottoms (2000)
A Fine Dark Line (2002)
Sunset and Sawdust (2004)
Lost Echoes (2007)
Leather Maiden (2008)

Pseudonymous Novels

Molly's Sexual Follies (as Brad Simmons; Pseudonymous porn novel written with Brad W. Foster)
Mark Stone: MIA Hunter series

These are a few novels Lansdale wrote under the pseudonym "Jack Buchanan." These novels were probably co-writeritten with Stephen Mertz. Some people erroneously report that Lansdale is responsible for the entire series, which is definitely not true.

Hanoi Deathgrip (Stone: MIA Hunter #3)
Mountain Massacre (Stone: MIA Hunter #4)
Saigon Slaughter (Stone: MIA Hunter #7)

Short Stories: Collections

By Bizarre Hands (1989)
Stories by Mama Lansdale's Youngest Boy (1991; aka *Author's Choice Monthly #18*)
Bestsellers Guaranteed (1993)
Electric Gumbo: A Lansdale Reader (1994; Quality Paperback Book Club exclusive)
Writer of the Purple Rage (1994)
A Fistfull of Stories (and Articles) (1996)
The Good, The Bad, and the Indifferent (1997; limited edition)
Private Eye Action, As You Like It (1998; with Lewis Shiner; limited edition)
Triple Feature (1999; limited edition)
The Long Ones: Nuthin' But Novellas (2000)
High Cotton (2000)
For a Few Stories More (2002; limited edition, *Lost Lansdale, Vol. 4*; the "ultra-limited" edition of this book included a previously unpublished Young Adult vampire novel called *Shadow Time* which has not appeared anywhere else)
A Little Green Book of Monster Stories (2003; limited edition)
Bumper Crop (2004)
Mad Dog Summer and Other Stories (2004; initially a limited edition, reissued in paperback)
The King: and other stories (2005; limited edition)
The Shadows, Kith and Kin (2007)
Chapbooks
On the Far Side of the Cadillac Desert With Dead Folks (1991; limited edition)
The Steel Valentine (1991; Pulphouse Short Story Hardback #7)
Steppin' Out, Summer '68 (1992; limited edition)
Tight Little Stitches In A Dead Man's Back (1992; limited edition)
My Dead Dog Bobby (1995; limited edition)
Bubba Ho-Tep (2003; novella; published standalone as a movie tie-in)
Duck Footed (2005; novella; limited edition)

Uncollected Short Stories

"Castle of Shadows" (written with Ardath Mayhar) from *Weirdbook #21* (1985)
"Boo Yourself!" from *Whispers VI*, ed. Stuart David Schiff (1987), republished in *100 Tiny Tales of Terror*, ed. Martin H. Greenberg
"Dead in the West: Screenplay" from *Screamplays* (1997)
"Disaster Club" from *Cemetery Dance #32* (1999)

Comic Book-Related Writings

Batman: Captured by the Engines (1991; novel)
Batman: Terror on the High Skies (1992; junior novel; illustrated by Edward Hannigan & Dick Giordano)
"Belly Laugh, or The Joker's Trick or Treat", short story in *The Further Adventures of The Joker*, ed. Martin H. Greenberg (1989), reprinted in *Adventures of the Batman*, ed. Greenberg (1995)
"Subway Jack", short story in *The Further Adventures of Batman*, ed. Greenberg (1989); features Lansdale's character The God of the Razor; reprinted in *Tales of the Batman*, ed. Greenberg (1994)

Graphic Novels And Comic Books

Lone Ranger & Tonto (1993; 4 issues; Art by Tim Truman and Rick Magyar, also TPB, Topps Comics)
Jonah Hex: Two Gun Mojo (1993; 5 issues; Art by Tim Truman, also TPB, DC Comics)
Jonah Hex: Riders of the Worm and Such (1995; 5 issues; Art by Tim Truman, DC)
Blood and Shadows (1996; 4 issues; Art by Mark A. Nelson; DC/Vertigo)
The Spirit: The New Adventures #8 (1998; art by John Lucas, Kitchen Sink Comics)
Red Range (1999; graphic novel; Art by Sam Glanzman. Mojo Press)
Jonah Hex: Shadows West (1999; 3 issues; Art by Tim Truman. DC/Vertigo)
Conan and the Songs of the Dead (2006; art by Tim Truman; 5 issues; also TPB, Dark Horse Comics)
Marvel Adventures: Fantastic Four #32 (January 2008; art by Ronan Cliquet; Marvel Comics)
Pigeons from Hell (2008 adaptation of the Robert E. Howard short story; Art by Nathan Fox; 4 issue mini-series ongoing from Dark Horse Comics)[1] [2]

Short Stories

"Drive-By" (1993, adapted from a story by Andrew Vachss- Art by Gary Gianni); originally published in *Andrew Vachss: Hard Looks #5*; reprinted in *Andrew Vachss: Hard Looks* TPB; subsequently reprinted in a limited edition eponymous trade paperback containing Vachss' original story, Lansdale's comic script, and the as-published illustrated story
"Grease Trap" in *Creature Features* (1994; art by Ted Naifeh, Mojo Press)
"Shootout at Ice Flats" in *Supergirl Annual #1* (1996; co-writer: Neal Barrett Jr.; art by Robert Branishi and Stan Woch, DC)
"The Elopement" in *Weird War Tales #2* (of 4; July 1997; art by Sam Glanzman, DC)

"The Initiation" in *Gangland #4* (of 4; Sept 1998; co-writer: Rick Klaw; art by Tony Salmons; DC/Vertigo)
"Betrothed" in *Flinch #5* (Oct 1999; art by Rick Burchett, DC/Vertigo)
"The Split" in *Strange Adventures #3* (of 4; Jan 2000 — Art by Richard Corben. DC/Vertigo)
"Red Romance" in *Flinch #11* (May 2000; DC/Vertigo)
"Brer Hoodoo" in *Flinch #13* (July 2000; art by Tim Truman, DC/Vertigo)
"Devil's Sombrero" in *Weird Western Tales #2* (of 4; May 2001, DC/Vertigo)
"Steam Rider: The Steam-Powered Heart" in *Amazing Fantasy #20* (June 2006, Marvel Comics)
"Mice and Money" in *Marvel Romance Redux #5* (subtitle "Love is a Four Letter Word"; June 2006, Marvel Comics); reprinted in *Mighty Marvel Romance* trade paperback
"Gunhawk: Midnight Gun" in *Strange Westerns starring the Black Rider* (Aug 2006; art by Rafa Garres, Marvel; reprinted in *Mighty Marvel Westerns* hardcover)
"The War At Home" parts 1-3 in *Zombie Tales #1-3* (July-September, 2008, Boom Studios; full story collected in *Zombie Tales* trade, published December 2008)
"A Ripping Good Time" in *Tales from the Crypt #6* (July 2008; co-writer: John L. Lansdale; art by James Romberger and Marguerite Van Cook; Papercutz)
"Moonlight Sonata" in *Tales from the Crypt #7* (Aug 2008; art by Chris Noeth; Papercutz; both stories collected in *Tales from the Crypt Graphic Novel #4*)
"Virtual Hoodoo" in *Tales from the Crypt #8* (Oct 2008; co-writer: John L. Lansdale; art by James Romberger and Marguerite Van Cook; Papercutz)

Adaptations of Previously Published Stories, by Lansdale unless noted

Dead in the West (1993; 2 issues; adapted by Neal Barrett Jr.; Art by Jack Jackson; covers by Tim Truman; Dark Horse)
By Bizarre Hands (1994; 3 issues; adaptations by Neal Barrett Jr. and Jerry Prosser; art by Phil Hester and Dean Rohrer; Dark Horse)
Atomic Chili: The Illustrated Joe Lansdale (1996 — TPB; Mojo Press)
"Dog, Cat, and Baby", in *Murder by Crowquill #1* (1999 — TPB; with Keith Lansdale, art by Tim Truman; Amazing Montage Press)
"Bob The Dinosaur Goes To Disneyland" (adapted by Rick Klaw; art by Doug Potter; first publication at RevolutionSF; 2001 in color; first book publication in *Geek Confidential: Echoes From the 21st Century* by Rick Klaw, Monkeybrain, Inc.; 2003 in black and white)
Lansdale & Truman's Dead Folks (2003; from the story "On the Far Side of the Cadillac Desert With Dead Folks"; 3 issues; also TPB; Art by Tim Truman; Avatar Press)
The Drive-In (2003; 4 issues; also TPB; adapted by Chris Golden; art by Andres Guinaldo; Avatar)
By Bizarre Hands (2004; 6 issues, adaptations by Neal Barrett, Jr., Keith Lansdale, and Rick Klaw; Art by Dheeraj Verma, Armando Rossi, and Andres Guinaldo; Avatar)
The Drive-In 2 (2006; 4 issues, adapted by Neal Barrett, Jr.; Art by Andres Guinaldo; Avatar)
"Incident On and Off a Mountain Road" in *Masters of Horror #1-2* (2006; Adapted by Chris Ryall)

Anthologies Edited

The Best of the West (1989)
New Frontier (1989)
Razored Saddles (1989, with Pat Lobrutto)
Dark at Heart (1991, with Karen Lansdale)
Weird Business: a horror comics anthology (1995, with Richard Klaw)
West That Was (1994; co-ed: Thomas Knowles)
Wild West Show (1994; co-ed: Thomas Knowles)
The Horror Hall of Fame: The Stoker Winners (2004)
Retro-Pulp Tales (2006; limited edition)
Lords of the Razor (2006; limited edition)
Cross Plains Universe: Texans Celebrate Robert E. Howard (with Scott A. Cupp, 2006)

Chet Williamson

Chet Williamson (born June 19, 1948) is the author of nearly twenty books and over a hundred short stories published in The New Yorker, Playboy, Esquire, *and many other magazines and anthologies. He was born in Lancaster, Pennsylvania. He attended Indiana University of Pennsylvania, receiving a B.S. in 1970, and went on to be a teacher at public schools in Cleveland, Ohio. He then became a professional actor before becoming a freelance writer in 1986. His earlier novels include* Second Chance, *an ecological thriller/romance,* Ash Wednesday, Reign *and* Dreamthorp. *His story "Gandhi at the Bat" was recently made into a short film by Stephanie Argy and Alec Boehm.* Figures in Rain, *a collection of Williamson's short stories, won the* International Horror Guild Award. *He has been short-listed twice for the World Fantasy Award, six times for the Horror Writers Association's Bram Stoker Award, and once for the Mystery Writers of America's Edgar Award. His books have been translated and published in many languages and countries, including France, Germany, Russia, Italy and Japan. Williamson's most recent work has been in the field of theatre, and a ghost story/psychological thriller, "Revenant," was recently produced at Theater of the Seventh Sister in Lancaster PA. From 2001 to 2007, he was the lead singer and guitarist for the Irish duo Fire in the Glen, in which he was partnered with fiddler and bodhranist Tom Knapp. A lifelong member of Actors' Equity Association, he recently resumed his acting career, and has performed in plays and musicals at Lancaster's Fulton Opera House and Theater of the Seventh Sister.*

ID: *Believe it or not, the first time I read one of your stories was in* 100 Hair-Raising Little Horror Stories. *I believe the title of the story was "Night Deposits." That's been some time ago, but I remember it clearly as one of the most outstanding pieces in the collection. What is it about the horror genre that makes it stand out so prominently, no matter how much it may change from decade to decade? What's the attraction, in your personal opinion?*

CW: I think that the horror genre will be around forever, but not necessarily as a *genre*. As has been said over and over, fear is one of the basic emotions of mankind, and literature that deals with it is as permanent as literature that deals with any of the other primal and basic emotions: love, hate, hunger, need. And on a less visceral level, there are always going to be those among us who are drawn to the dark side, both as readers and as writers.

ID: Stephen King once said that "We create our own horrors in order to deal with the real ones." Do you agree? Do you believe horror can be an escape as well as a creative outlet?

CW: I think that can be true. I prefer horror not to be an escape, but a confrontation with the realities of life. The best horror illuminates the darkness within us, tells us something new about ourselves and our abilities to deal with the harsh realities of life.

ID: I tend to agree with that. I think...What first prompted your interest in the macabre?

CW: When I was a little kid, my grandfather owned a grocery store with a large, eerie, winding cellar, and Bob Hill, the older stock boy, would tell me the stories of Edgar Allan Poe in that dark cellar. That was the template of my imaginative life, and I've really never come out of that cellar. I discovered Poe in the originals, the old Universal horror films on TV, *Famous Monsters of Filmland* (I was definitely a child of Forry Ackerman), and then H. P. Lovecraft and the great *Ballantine* paperback horror collections and anthologies of the early '60s. I still love that stuff. Just the other day I found in a used bookstore an anthology I'd never come across before: 1947's *Tales of the Undead*, edited and illustrated with evocative scratchboard illos by Elinore Blaisdell. A terrific mixture of classic stories and some *Weird Tales* reprints. It's nice to know that there are still some books out there that I've missed!

ID: I heard that! I see you're acquainted with Joe R. Lansdale. You know what I think would be really cool? You and Joe collaborating on a story together. What do you think?

CW: I concur. I've known Joe for decades and he's a good friend and a great writer. Neither one of us is really a collaborative writer, though he and I have thrown some film ideas around, and he's really fun to work with. Maybe one of those ideas will bear fruit one of these days.

ID: I hope so. Your book, Hell: A Cyberpunk Thriller, *sounds more than just a little interesting. Is a cyberpunk anything like a splatterpunk? Or should I ask John Skipp and Craig Spector about that one? LOL!*

CW: Hell was a novelization of a computer game done back in '95. It was a bizarre blend of horror and cyberpunk SF, and really had nothing to do with splatterpunk. I'd never done anything like that before and haven't done anything since, but I enjoyed writing it.

ID: Good enough. I see you have won an International Horror Guild Award for your book Figures in Rain. *Do you prefer writing short fiction as opposed to novels? I personally find it easier, myself.*

CW: Short stories are easier in some ways — obviously, they take far less time to write. But when you write a novel you can stretch out more and relax a bit. In a short story, every word has to count, and the demands are far greater in terms of being concise and economical with your words. When I finish a short work and am happy with it, I usually find it much more satisfying than completing a novel. The problem is to come up with short story ideas that are worthy of the telling. So many short stories today seem to be retreads of ideas that have been dealt with better in earlier works.

ID: How true. Sometimes just the book title alone really captures my eye — as well as my imagination — and the title of your book, The Story of Noichi the Blind, *is one of them. Is it horror? Fantasy? It's hard to tell by the title, but still sounds intriguing, nonetheless.*

CW: Well, you should read it and find out! *Noichi* is a novella, which is really my favorite length in which to work, especially with the horror genre. Rich Chizmar of CD Publications commissioned me to do a novella in his CD series, so I decided to go very dark. It's a "traditional" Japanese folktale presented as a possibly unknown Lafcadio Hearn work, complete with a framing introduction and a scholarly afterward. The title character is "blind" all right, but it's an emotional blindness that enables him to deny the reality of some of those real life horrors I spoke of earlier. It's a tender little tale of love, necrophilia/bestiality, Japanese demons, and animals that like their friend Noichi a little *too* much. It's both fantasy and horror, and very, very twisted.

ID: Sounds like my cup of tea. You strike me as the kind of guy who would enjoy a really well-crafted horror film. Any favorites come to mind? I actually enjoyed some of the '80s slashers, myself.

CW: "Well-crafted" are the key words here. Horror movies get a bad rap because there's so much crap out there. The recent trend in torture-porn, like the *Saw* and *Hostel* movies, I find repellent, though I thought the first *Saw* fairly clever, and I can get a kick out of the imaginative ways the filmmakers snuff the idiots in the *Final Destination* series, and I find many Japanese horror films excellent, making you think while you cringe (like *Audition*). But I think the days of classic horror films are over. Everything has to be in your face, when what I find most terrifying is *suggestion*. Horror films today tend to lack subtlety and nuance.

ID: That is stating it mildly. Do you see yourself still writing, say, ten years from now? Twenty? What's on the horizon for Chet?

CW: I'll never retire, that's for sure. I love what I do too much. In the past few years I've gotten into playwriting and, as a result, acting, which was my first love before I started writing. I joined a local playwriting group, started doing some readings, and then acting again. I got my Actors Equity membership reinstated, and am lucky enough to have a few really fine Equity-associated theatres in my area, so I've been busy on the stage. I've recently been writing a show about W. B. Yeats, in which I hope to eventually perform. I've also been involved in writing the scenario and dialogue for another project — an online computer mystery game I've been commissioned to do, and that's been great fun. I hope to do more of it. And of course I'm trying to keep up with my reading — just got Andrew Vachss' new novel, which I'm looking forward to starting. Right now I'm in the middle of reading M. T. Anderson's two-volume *The Astonishing Life of Octavian Nothing, Traitor to the Nation*. Though marketed as a young adult work, it's incredibly mature and brilliantly written — and quite horrific in spots.

ID: All sounds great. Any last words before you go?

CW: I'll leave you with my favorite old Zen saying: "One inch ahead is all darkness." It's a great saying for horror writers, and a good thing for everyone to remember. So do what you're planning to do *now*.

ID: I will go along with that.

Bibliography

Novels

Soulstorm (1986)
Ash Wednesday (1987)
McKain's Dilemma (1988)
Lowland Rider (1988)
Dreamthorp (1989)
Reign (1990)
Mordenheim (1994)
Second Chance (1994)
Hell: A Cyberpunk Thriller (1995)
The Crow: City of Angels (1996)
Murder in Cormyr (1996)
The Crow: Clash By Night (1998)
Pennsylvania Dutch Night Before Christmas (2000)
Uniting Work and Spirit: A Centennial History of Elizabethtown College (2001)
The Story of Noichi the Blind (2007)
Pennsylvania Dutch Alphabet (2007)
The Final Verse (chapbook/CD, 2007)

Collections

The House of Fear: A Study in Comparative Religions (1989)
Figures in Rain: Weird and Ghostly Tales (2002)

Series

Searchers
1. *City of Iron* (1998)
2. *Empire of Dust* (1998)
3. *Siege of Stone* (1999)

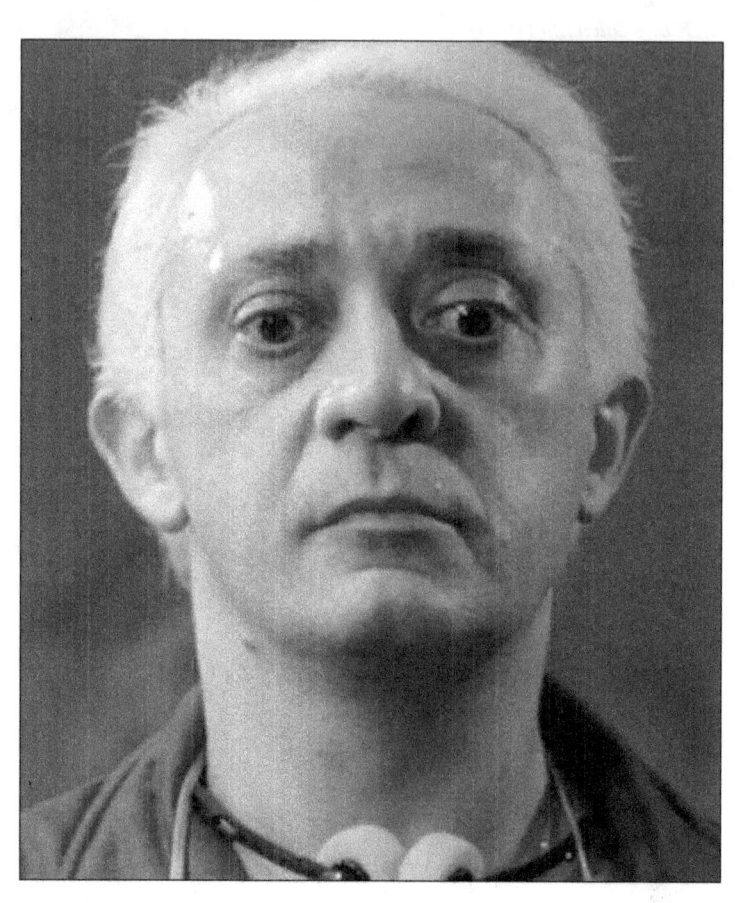

Don Calfa

Don Calfa is best remembered for his role as mortician Ernie Kaltenbrunner in the 1985 cult classic The Return of the Living Dead. *Don's career spans over 40 years in both film and TV. Born in Brooklyn, New York, and raised in Ozone Park, Queens, and later Westchester, Long Island, Don was originally interested in a career in the fine arts. He got the acting bug after seeing films such as* Rebel Without a Cause *and* Vertigo. *After dropping out of high school to study at Irwin Piscotor's The Dramatic Workshop (he finished his degree in night school), Don spent two years in summer stock which enabled him to join Actors Equity and eventually get his SAG card. Don has starred alongside some of cinema's greats including Warren Beatty in* Bugsy, *Michael Douglas in* The Star Chamber, *Jack Nicholson in* The Postman Always Rings Twice, *Robert DeNiro in* New York, New York, *Dudley Moore in Blake Edwards'* 10, *and many more. Among Don's most memorable roles were as Ralph Wilum in* Chopper Chicks in Zombietown, *Paulie in* Weekend at Bernie's, *Scarface in* Foul Play, *Mr. Pitts on the TV series* Beverly Hills, 90210, *and many more. His stage work includes extensive off-off-Broadway work, and he appeared on Broadway in* Lenny. *Don still works in the movie business and more recently starred in such independent movies as* Lewisburg *and* Jukebox California. *Don works the convention circuit in the USA, along side the rest of the cast of* The Return of the Living Dead. *Don has also attended conventions in Germany and the United Kingdom. In March 2007 Don, along with the rest of the ROTLD cast, recorded an ensemble commentary for the new Collectors Edition DVD of the* Return of the Living Dead *(released on September 11, 2007). Don appreciates his fans' comments and continued support.*

Don now resides in California, and has one child (Evan) from his second marriage. Don is a member of the Oscar Board and enjoys visiting the cinema and keeping up-to-date on today's biggest releases.

ID: How are you this fine December day?

DC: Great, just came back from Birmingham in the United Kingdom; I was at a signing convention and had a ball meeting UK fans. I love the UK and had a blast going to Warwick Castle, Blackpool and Birmingham itself.

ID: Let me start off by saying that I loved your performance in Return of the Living Dead. *Have you always been a big fan of the horror genre?*
DC: No, not really. I was never really into genre movies. I loved the old classics with Marlon Brando. Horror wasn't really my thing; however, over the years I have come to appreciate the genre for what it is and now enjoy the genre. Obviously I have been very lucky to be part of such films as *Return of the Living Dead* and *Chopper Chicks in Zombietown* which are both cult classics in their own rights. With *Return of the Living Dead* we changed the rules and made zombies scary again. So if anything, *Return of the Living Dead* re-charged the zombie genre for the 1980's audience.

To be honest, at first *Return* was just another job sent through my agent... it wasn't until reading the script that I realized how special the film was. I knew we had a hit on our hands as the script was so fantastic; the pace was amazing. When I saw the colors of the sets and clothes, I thought this could be a winner. It felt good; it didn't seem like just another job.

ID: And a winner it was, indeed. Your character in that film, Ernie Kaltenbrunner, seemed almost too real. Were you by some chance breathing life into a character that was based on someone you knew in real-life?
DC: A lot of people assume there was a lot of improvisation, but they're wrong! All what you see on screen was in Dan O'Bannon's fantastic script. Before we shot a frame of film, we had three weeks of rehearsals, which was terrific. Dan went for the fast, overlapping Howard Hawks dialogue, and by giving us time to practice it, nobody stepped on each other's lines.

My character's full name was Ernie Kaltenbrunner. I have a friend who is a real Nazi historian; he loves all World War II books and programs. When he heard my character was called Ernie Kaltenbrunner, he said, "Get out of here! Don, Kaltenbrunner was a high-ranking Nazi who was executed at Nuremberg." Dan O'Bannon allowed me to develop Ernie's Nazi past; on the bulletin board I put up a picture of Eva Braun from a 8mm film, I put the whole board together; it even has pictures of caricatures of Hitler and Goebbels.

ID: Very interesting. Speaking of films, Chopper Chicks in Zombie Town *seemed like it would have been a lot of fun to make. How was the atmosphere on the set?*

DC: The atmosphere was very good. I had just literally come from the shoot of *Weekend at Bernie's*. We finished *Bernie's* on one day and the next day I was on the set of *Chopper*. The original title was *Chrome Hearts* but Troma being Troma changed the title to *Chopper Chicks in Zombietown*. It was a nice little movie. Billy Bob Thornton was a total unknown at the time; he did well. Ed Gale who played the midget was great; he later went on to be *Howard the Duck*.

You may notice that my eyes are blue in the movie. I chose to wear blue contacts as blue eyes are more prominent and I think it suited the character of Ralph Willum well. I am very fond of the movie and it has a huge fan base.

ID: I'm sure it does. How about Weekend at Bernie's? *That must have been a wild ride, too.*

DC: Bernie's was great! Again, it is what it is and has become a cult favorite; my forte is comedy and I always enjoy those roles — the character of Paulie the Iceman was great. I love the line, "yeah, yeah, so where's your house." Terry Kiser was great as Bernie and we became great friends. I am in regular contact with him and have just finished a new comedy with him in Texas called *Losing Faith*.

Bernie's was a "wild ride" and is a fan favorite. I often get asked to sign photos, posters and DVD covers from *Bernie's*.

ID: In your forty-plus years of acting, you have starred in films with such noted actors as Robert DeNiro and Jack Nicholson. Have you ever felt that the character actor, at times, is not recognized for how talented they really are? You are such a versatile actor, yet I feel you are very underrated.

DC: I am very happy with the choices that I made; some of these small roles are the most memorable and sometimes the co-star will get a line that will carry the whole movie. The life of a character actor is a great one and it allows you to be versatile playing a variety of characters. It also allows you to be involved in films such as *Return of the Living Dead* that can become cult classics. So I feel very privileged to have worked among some of the great actors and directors of my generation.

ID: I was thrilled to see that you and a friend are wanting to publish your graphic novel, Revenge of the Living Dead. *I hope it does well. What prompted the idea for that project?*

DC: Revenge came about not long after *Return of the Living Dead* was released, everyone had such a great time on *Return of the Living Dead* and the film was a hit, we were all promised a chance to appear in the sequel so I decided to write a treatment for *Revenge of the Living Dead*, the story was a continuation to *Return of the Living Dead* rather than a sequel, it picks up directly after the events of the first film. The idea was that you could watch both films together as a 3 hour gore-fest. I sent the treatment to Dan O'Bannon and Producer Tom Fox, Dan loved it as we kept to the same vein as *Return of the Living Dead*, I didn't hear from Tom, and then news came about of *Return of the Living Dead* part 2, but these things happen in the business. The only thing was is that a scene from *Revenge* involving a severed hand attacking the survivors in a car later appeared in the script for *Return of the Living Dead* part 2...but, who knows!

ID: Let's keep our fingers crossed. Here is one for fun: What type of role do you enjoy playing most? Serious or comedic? Please don't take offense, but I think you'd make a good bad guy. Maybe a slasher or a tough guy.

DC: I enjoy comedy more; I think that's what I'm good at, films like *Greasers Palace, Weekend at Bernie's*. I like that challenge more; it's very hard life as a comedic actor, very challenging. I love the old British Ealing comedies, such as the *Ladykillers, The Man in the White Suit*. These films are classics and are an inspiration. Alec Guiness was amazing in them as was Peter Sellers in the *Ladykillers*. Obviously I'm known for playing villains, low lifes; but, hey, if that's what the fans want to see, then that's fine with me.

ID: What is on the horizon for Don? Would you still like to be in front of the camera say...ten years from now? I always believed that if you find a niche you are happy with, stay there.

DC: I'm semi-retired now, I still have a huge passion for films and the business and if someone wants me to be in their film then I'd be honored. I would love to work with directors like Rob Zombie.

ID: Yeah...I'd work with Rob myself.

DC: My new film *Losing Faith* alongside Terry Kiser is due out next year and could be very successful. Also on the horizon is a little independent movie called *Lewisburg*, also starring my friend Richard Lynch.

Then there's the *Revenge of the Living Dead* graphic novel...at the moment we are trying to locate the copyright owners of the series. I love life and am enjoying it — "all good things."

ID: Any last words before you leave us?

DC: Yeah — check out the official Don Calfa website at *www.doncalfa.com* and the official *Myspace* at *www.myspace.com/doncalfarotld*. Enjoy!

ID: I'm sure I will. Bye for now!

Selected Filmography

The Return of the Living Dead (1985) as Ernie Kaltenbrunner
Weekend at Bernie's (1989) as Paulie
Night Creep (2003) as Mr Blunt/Night Creep
Chopper Chicks in Zombietown (1991) as Ralph Willum
Twin Peaks (1 episode, 1990) as Vice Principal Greege
Treasure of the Moon Goddess (1987) as Harold Grand
Bugsy (1991) as Louie Dragna
10 (1979) as Neighbor
New York, New York (1977) as Gilbert
Corpses are Forever (2003) as Jack Stark
Progency (1998) as Jimmy Stevens
Stay Tuned (1992) as Wetzel
Barney Miller (7 episodes, 1977-1981)
Columbo (1990) as Rudy
Murder She Wrote (2 episodes, 1988-1993)
1941 (1979) as Telephone Operator
Greasers Palace (1972) as Morris
Pound (1970) as Italian Terrier
Me Myself and I (1992) as Irving
Dr Dolittle (1998) as Patient at Hammersmith
The Presidio (1988) as Howard Buckely

The Star Chamber (1983) as Lawrence Monk

Fred Olen Ray

ID: I must admit, I've never interviewed a director/producer/screenwriter who is also a wrestler before. I think I just made history here. What prompted your interest in pro wrestling, pray tell?

FOR: Wrestling came as an off-shoot of my boxing. I damaged a rotator cuff and had to stop when a friend, who was a wrestler, suggested that I try that since I wasn't really ready to get out of the ring. I kind of took to it and went from there — and a pile of new injuries!

ID: I also have to admit this is the first time I have interviewed someone who has directed a film about Hollywood Chainsaw Hookers. *Please, share your inspiration for this film with me. Or...should I be afraid to ask?*

FOR: It really was a matter of trying to find a title that would be the star of the show. Something that would make people sit up and pay attention. It was a low-budget affair, but has certainly garnered its fair share of notoriety.

ID: Is it true you made a film starring Buster Crabbe? Now, that would have been interesting...

FOR: I met Buster when I was a cameraman at the Golden Age Olympics which he was the Grand Marshall of. When I made *ALIEN DEAD* I rang him up and offered him the part and he said "yes"! The rest is pretty grim...

ID: Did you ever feel offended by your films ending up in grindhouses and drive-ins? I think it would have bothered some directors, especially considering the fact they worked so hard with miniscule budgets just to get the films finished.

FOR: Playing in a Drive-In was one of my proudest moments. Finally I had become part of my own history. I loved seeing the films on a Drive-In screen, even more than on 42nd Street, but that was magical as well.

ID: I see you grew up reading Famous Monsters magazine. *Did you ever get a chance to meet Forry Ackerman? He was one of a kind. He almost seemed immortal, actually.*

FOR: I had Forry in a handful of films...he even played Dracula, or a wax museum version of him, that comes to life in *Attack of the 60 Ft Centerfold*. I think I made maybe six or seven films with Forry, so I guess I knew him as well as a lot of people. He was iconic to the max.

ID: What's it like working on films at your age as opposed to 24? Or 34? Is it a lot easier for you now that you have been doing it so long?

FOR: My knowledge base is pretty broad by now and I'm not as worried as I might have been back on *Armed Response*, but it's still an incredibly arduous job that most people (who think they can do it) are not nearly cut out for.

ID: I heard you had some "mishaps" on the set before, concerning special effects. Regardless of this, which type of effects do you prefer? I always liked the old "hands-on" style myself. Now it's all CGI.

FOR: I personally like to see what I'm getting, so I rely on foreground miniature and live action stuff a lot, but we all have to take CGI seriously. I just don't like CG for the sake of CG. Give me an old fashioned pipe ramp any day!

ID: What is on the horizon for Fred?

FOR: Coming soon...*Silent Venom*, a snakes-on-a-submarine movie with Luke Perry and Tom Berenger, and *Dire Wolf*, a return to my bloodiest roots, with Maxwell Caulfield and Gil Gerard.

ID: Any last words before you leave us?
FOR: Keep on rocking.

Filmography

Director

Dire Wolf (2009)
The Lair (15 episodes, 2007-2008)
Voodoo Dollz (2008; TV; as Nicholas Medina)
Recoil (2008)
Bikini Royale (2008; TV; as Nicholas Medina)
Polar Opposites (2008)
Solar Flare (2008)
Tarzeena: Jiggle in the Jungle (2008; TV; as Nicholas Medina)
An Accidental Christmas (2007; TV)
The Girl from B.I.K.I.N.I. (2007; V; as Nicholas Medina)
Girl with the Sex-Ray Eyes (2007; TV; as Nicholas Medina)
Super Ninja Bikini Babes (2007; TV; as Nicholas Medina)
Bewitched Housewives (2007; TV; as Nicholas Medina)
Nuclear Hurricane (2007; TV)
Bikini Girls from the Lost Planet (2006; V; as Nicholas Medina)
Ghost in a Teeny Bikini (2006; V; as Nicholas Medina)
Bikini Pirates (2006; V; as Nicholas Medina)
Bikini Round-Up (2005; V; as Nicholas Medina)
Glass Trap (2005; as Ed Raymond)
Bikini Chain Gang (2005; V; as Nicholas Medina)
Bikini a Go Go (2004; V; as Nicholas Medina)
Tomb of the Werewolf (2004; V)
Genie in a String Bikini (2004; V; as Nicholas Medina)
Haunting Desires (2004; TV; as Nicholas Medina)
Teenage Cavegirl (2004; V; as Nicholas Medina)
The Bikini Escort Company (2004; V; as Nicholas Medina)
Bikini Airways (2003; V; as Nicholas Medina)
Final Examination (2003; V; as Ed Raymond)
Southern Discomfort: Wrestling on the Indie Circuit (2002)
Thirteen Erotic Ghosts (2002; as Nicholas Medina)
Venomous (2001; V; as Ed Raymond)
Emmanuelle 2000 (2001)
Air Rage (2001; V; as Ed Raymond)
Mach 2 (2001)
ACW Wrestling's Wildest Matches! (2001; V; as Sherman Scott)
Emmanuelle 2001: Emmanuelle's Sensual Pleasures (2001; V; as Nicholas Medina)
Kept (2001)
Stranded (2001)
Submerged (2000)
Sideshow (2000)
Active Stealth (2000; V)
Critical Mass (2000; as Ed Raymond)
Inviati Speciali (2000)
Invisible Mom II (1999; V)

Fugitive Mind (1999; V)
The Prophet (1999)
The Kid with X-ray Eyes (1999; V; as Sherman Scott)
Counter Measures (1999; V)
Scandal: On the Other Side (1999; as Nick Medina)
Mom, Can I Keep Her? (1998; V)
Invisible Dad (1998; V)
Illicit Dreams 2 (1998; as Roger Collins)
Billy Frankenstein (1998)
Dear Santa (1998; as Peter Stewart)
Mom's Outta Sight (1998; as Peter Stewart)
Inferno (1997)
Rapid Assault (1997; V; as Sherman Scott)
The Shooter (1997/I; as Ed Raymond)
Masseuse 2 (1997; V; as Peter Daniels)
Little Miss Magic (1997)
Hybrid (1997)
Night Shade (1997; as Nicholas Medina)
Bikini Hoe-Down (1997; V; as Roger Collins)
Maximum Revenge (1997)
Friend of the Family II (1996; as Nicholas Medina)
Fugitive Rage (1996; V)
Over the Wire (1996; as Nicholas Medina)
Invisible Mom (1996; V)
Masseuse (1996; as Peter Daniels)
Droid Gunner (1995)
Bikini Drive-In (1995)
Attack of the 60 Foot Centerfolds (1995)
Star Hunter (1995; V; as Sam Newfield)
Inner Sanctum II (1994)
Joe Bob's Drive-In Theater (1 episode, 1994)
Attack of the Queen Bees Month: Part 1 (1994; TV episode)
Possessed by the Night (1994; V)
Mind Twister (1994)
Dinosaur Island (1994)
Dinosaur Girls (1993)
Witch Academy (1993)
Evil Toons (1992)
Haunting Fear (1991)
Inner Sanctum (1991)
Wizards of the Demon Sword (1991)
Spirits (1991)
Scream Queen Hot Tub Party (1991; V; as Bill Carson)
Bad Girls from Mars (1990)
Mob Boss (1990; V)
Alienator (1990)
Demon Cop (1990)
Beverly Hills Vamp (1989)
The Phantom Empire (1989)

Terminal Force (1989)
Deep Space (1988)
Hollywood Chainsaw Hookers (1988)
Warlords (1988)
Evil Spawn (1987)
Commando Squad (1987)
Prison Ship (1987)
Cyclone (1987)
Armed Response (1986)
The Tomb (1986)
Biohazard (1985)
Scalps (1983)
Alien Dead (1980)
The Brain Leeches (1977)
Honey Britches (1971)

Producer

Reptisaurus (2008; TV; executive producer)
Dante's Cove (supervising producer; 10 episodes, 2006-2007)
Tiki (2006; V; executive producer)
Genie in a String Bikini (2004; V; executive producer; as Bill Carson)
The Bikini Escort Company (2004; V; associate producer; as Bill Carson)
Thirteen Erotic Ghosts (2002; executive producer; as Roger Collins)
ACW Wrestling's Wildest Matches! (2001; V; producer; as Sherman Scott)
Invisible Mom II (1999; V; producer)
Fugitive Mind (1999; V; producer)
Mom, Can I Keep Her? (1998; V; producer)
Illicit Dreams 2 (1998; producer)
Masseuse 2 (1997; V; producer; as Peter Daniels)
Little Miss Magic (1997; producer)
Hybrid (1997; producer)
Night Shade (1997; producer)
Bikini Hoe-Down (1997; V; producer; as Roger Collins)
Fugitive Rage (1996; V; producer)
Invisible Mom (1996; V; producer)
Droid Gunner (1995; producer)
Bikini Drive-In (1995; producer)
Jack-O (1995; executive producer)
Sorceress (1995; producer)
Biohazard: The Alien Force (1995; V; executive producer)
Attack of the 60 Foot Centerfolds (1995; producer)
Star Hunter (1995; V; producer; as Sam Newfield)
Dinosaur Island (1994; producer)
Dark Universe (1993; executive producer)
Angel Eyes (1993; executive producer)
Witch Academy (1993; producer)
Fatal Justice (1993; V; executive producer)
One Million Heels B.C. (1993; producer; as Bill Carson)

Evil Toons (1992; co-producer)
Teenage Exorcist (1991; associate producer)
Haunting Fear (1991; producer)
Inner Sanctum (1991; co-producer)
Wizards of the Demon Sword (1991; co-producer)
Scream Queen Hot Tub Party (1991; V; producer; as Bill Carson)
Bad Girls from Mars (1990; co-producer)
Mob Boss (1990; V; producer)
Demon Cop (1990; producer: new footage)
Beverly Hills Vamp (1989; producer)
The Phantom Empire (1989; producer)
Terminal Force (1989; co-producer)
Sexbomb (1989; executive producer)
Deep Space (1988; co-producer)
Bulletproof (1988; associate producer)
Hollywood Chainsaw Hookers (1988; producer)
Warlords (1988; co-producer)
Evil Spawn (1987; producer)
Commando Squad (1987; co-producer)
Prison Ship (1987; producer)
Moon in Scorpio (1987; co-producer)
Armed Response (1986; co-producer)
The Tomb (1986; producer)
Biohazard (1985; producer)
Alien Dead (1980; producer)
Honey Britches (1971; producer; new footage)

Writer

The Lair (15 episodes, 2007-2008)
Voodoo Dollz (2008; TV; written by; as Nicholas Medina)
The Girl from B.I.K.I.N.I. (2007; V; written by; as Nicholas Medina)
Girl with the Sex-Ray Eyes (2007; TV; written by; as Sherman Scott)
Bewitched Housewives (2007; TV; written by; as Sherman Scott)
Ghost in a Teeny Bikini (2006; V; written by; as Nicholas Medina)
Bikini Pirates (2006; V; written by; as Nicholas Medina)
Bikini Round-Up (2005; V; screenplay; as Nicholas Medina)
Bikini a Go Go (2004; V; screenplay; as Sherman Scott)
Tomb of the Werewolf (2004; V; writer; as Sherman Scott)
Genie in a String Bikini (2004; V; writer; as Sherman Scott)
Haunting Desires (2004; TV; screenplay; as Sherman Scott)
Teenage Cavegirl (2004; V; writer; as Sherman Scott)
The Bikini Escort Company (2004; V; screenplay; as Sherman Scott)
Bikini Airways (2003; V; screenplay; as Roger Collins)
Southern Discomfort: Wrestling on the Indie Circuit (2002; writer)
Thirteen Erotic Ghosts (2002; written by; as Sherman Scott)
Jack-O (1995; story)
Inner Sanctum II (1994; writer; as Sherman Scott)
Possessed by the Night (1994; V; story)

Stepmonster (1993; story)
Evil Toons (1992; writer; as Sherman Scott)
Teenage Exorcist (1991; story)
Haunting Fear (1991; writer; as Sherman Scott)
Soldier's Fortune (1991; story)
Scream Queen Hot Tub Party (1991; V; writer; as Bill Carson)
Bad Girls from Mars (1990; writer; as Sherman Scott)
The Phantom Empire (1989; writer)
Deep Space (1988; writer)
Bulletproof (1988; story)
Hollywood Chainsaw Hookers (1988; screenplay; as Dr. S. Carver)
Prison Ship (1987; story)
Cyclone (1987; story)
Armed Response (1986; story)
Biohazard (1985; writer)
Scalps (1983; screenplay; story)
Alien Dead (1980; screenplay)

Actor

Zombiegeddon (2003; V; voice; Fred)
Thirteen Erotic Ghosts (2002; uncredited; Professor Ted Isor)
The Voyeur (Dr. Howard Wexler; 1 episode)
The Prophet (1999; as Sherman Scott; Hunter's Men)
Ghost Taxi (1999)
Ride with the Devil (1999; Sleazy Filmmaker)
Alien Escape (1997; Boris)
Inferno (1997; as Ed Raymond; Interpol Chief)
Just Write (1997; Couple at Mandalay)
Bikini Hoe-Down (1997; V; as Sam Newfield; Chicken Thief #2)
Maximum Revenge (1997; as Bill Carson; Lieutenant Burke)
Fugitive Rage (1996; V; Mob Attorney)
Invisible Mom (1996; V; Cabbie)
Theater Dark Video Magazine (1996; TV; Host)
Babe WatCH: Forbidden Parody (1996; Radio Announcer)
Droid Gunner (1995; Fighter Pilot #1)
Bikini Drive-In (1995; as Randy Rocket; Randy Rocket)
Sorceress (1995; Bill Carson)
Hard Bounty (1995; Ringo)
The Wasp Woman (1995; TV; Tex)
Star Hunter (1995; V; Tracker)
Rebellious (1995; Ratty)
Vampire Vixens from Venus (1995; Man in Lot)
Inner Sanctum II (1994; Officer Scott)
Possessed by the Night (1994; V; Waiter)
Mind Twister (1994; Photographer)
Double Deception (1993; TV; Director)
Angel Eyes (1993; as Sam Newfield; Eddie)
Munchie (1992; Piano Player)

Scream Queen Hot Tub Party (1991; V; uncredited; Psycho slasher guy)
Naked Obsession (1991; Announcer)
Bad Girls from Mars (1990; as Sherman Scott; Robber #2)
Alienator (1990; uncredited; Tech #3)
Deep Space (1988; Workman #2)
Commando Squad (1987; uncredited)
Prison Ship (1987; voice; Mouse Robot)
Cyclone (1987)
Armed Response (1986; Soldier #2)
Biohazard (1985; Medic #2)
Alien Dead (1980; Pool Player)
The Brain Leeches (1977)

Second Unit Director or Assistant Director

Gale Force (2002; V; second unit director; as Ed Raymond)
Jack-O (1995; second unit director; as Sherman Scott)
Sorceress (1995; second unit director)
Dark Universe (1993; second unit director; as Sherman Scott)

Additional Crew Credits

Ice Spiders (2007; TV; production consultant)
Sadomaster (2005; V; CGI blood provider)
Invisible Dad (1998; V; blue screen effects designer)
Attack of the 60 Foot Centerfolds (1995; digital effects designer)
The Channeler (1990; executive consultant)
My Best Friend's Birthday (1987; camera provider)
Dogs of Hell (1982; special effects)
Alien Dead (1980; special effects)
Shock Waves (1977; still photographer)

Muse Watson

ID: Greetings and salutations, Muse. I trust you are doing well?
MW: I guess that is relative. I feel as busted up as an old rodeo clown, but then you probably didn't want a real answer to that one. I'll be nice — I'm finer than a frog's hair!

ID: Let me start off by saying that I have followed your career — from afar, if you will — for quite some time now, and after seeing you portray the character of Mike Franks in NCIS, it confirmed my belief that you should be one of the most sought-after actors working today. Tell me, what is it about Mike's character that you find so interesting? You seem as though you are really enjoying that role.
MW: Mike is a complex guy. Here is a guy who lost contact with his family by being a workaholic, who devotes his entire being to keeping the world safe from bad guys. When he warns the powers that be of a terrible attack on humanity, his warning gets caught up in the bureaucracy and many folks die in the Kobal Towers attack. Devastated, he leaves NCIS, but being a professional, he leaves it in the competent hands of his protégé, Jethro Gibbs (Mark Harmon). Mike is a "by the book" kind of guy, but the book has changed and every now and then he takes a brief moment to fire his Glock and make a small correction in the process of justice.

I knew at the casting session that I wanted to give him a gruff voice and a competent stance, but I learned a great deal about where he had been and his relationship to agents in *NCIS* by reading a book Mark Harmon gave me entitled *Special Agent, Vietnam* by Douglass H. Hubbard Jr. Mark wrote in the cover: "Muse, I wanted you to have this if you feel like reading. What I found important is that this guy is completely NIS, a different time and as a result, a different attitude, all of which come from specific character. Franks and Gibbs would have understood. Look forward to seeing you, amigo. SF/MH."

Please understand that Mike served at a time when law enforcement did not have their hands tied by political correctness and although he believes in the principles "correctness" tries to speak to, he is unwilling to let the new rules keep him from his mission. Being retired, he is able to "solve" cases with his usual cunning, but is not above eliminating players who are manipulating justice. He is a dying breed of men who devoted their lives to protecting our democracy before we castrated them with beliefs that we could talk to our enemies and they would no longer want to kill us.

Personally, Mike is a loner. I can't wait to show the changes in his persona because he is now living with his grand-daughter and Muslim daughter-in-law. I hope I am given the opportunity. These profound changes would be subtle at *NCIS*, but huge at home. Mike is the closest thing to a cowboy an electronic, three piece suit world has.

ID: What are the other actors you work with on that show like in person? They strike me like a group of people who would be a lot of fun to work with.

MW: The tone of any show comes from the star, and Mark Harmon expects people to be civil with each other. His influence makes the set pleasant and a great place to work. Let me tell you a story. When Jethro became disenchanted with his life at NCIS and came to live with me in Mexico, the wardrobe department suggested I wear shorts on the beach. I told them, "I am a grown man, I don't wear shorts." The designer said, "What do you see him wearing?" and I responded with, "I see him in long flowing linen pants like Hemingway's *The Old Man and the Sea*." They custom-made several pair which I wore in the episode: when I commented to Mark how much I loved them, a pair showed up in my trailer for me to take home. When I asked Mark if he had given the order for me to have a pair he said, "I just told them how much you loved them — I believe that should be enough said to people who want to do what's right." See what I mean about Mark? A great man — and a great leader.

Sean is a great guy. A guy some people might overlook, but that would be their loss. A guy I knew years ago playing volleyball at a popular condo complex where Love Hewitt and I both lived for a while. I was so glad to see he had died and gone to *NCIS*. LOL. He deserves his success and I love being around him.

Cote is beautiful inside and out. I would rather watch her walk away from me than eat cake. But when she is facing you talking, she is as articulate and intelligent as any agent could be. She is a fine woman and I hope her personal life is filled with the respect she deserves.

Pauley is a classically beautiful woman who is such fun to be around. Her "fun" is always inspired by a desire to love as much and as many as she can. I love watching the transformation into her character. It's not like a real drastic change as much as it is like a bud blooming into a huge flower.

David McCallum was a childhood hero of mine. The first day I was on the set he walked over to me and said, "It is going to be great to have another *Man* on the set." I knew exactly what he meant and we have been great friends from that day. His performance is a wonder to watch.

Michael is fun. He has one thought about his character: and that is to do whatever his mind tells him he should not do. LOL. I never worry about what he thinks because it is superfluous to him.

ID: Forgive me, I should have asked this first: What first prompted your interest in becoming an actor?
MW: Honestly?

ID: Yes, honestly.
MW: My life was so sad, I was looking for a way to live as someone else and be happy. As I experienced some success I found out that it was OK to be drawn to acting by anything, but that I was going to have to work hard at it and become an emotionally balanced person if I was going to be able to let go of my own hang ups and portray other people. I think it would be a mistake to consider working actors as people who are incomplete. They may start out that way, but after many different characters, it is imperative that they find themselves and become comfortable in their own skin.

I was at Berea College and taking a beginning speech course because it satisfied the curriculum. The course was being taught by Paul Power who was the theater director. He announced that he was interested in seeing some new faces at the auditions for *Taming of the Shrew*. Being shy, but knowing this was my shot, I went home and grabbed a fifth of Jack Daniels and my *Complete Works of Shakespeare*. As I drank and read, I thought, "I can do this guy." Paul later noted he almost did not cast me because I sounded to him like Clark Gable. A friend, John Chisholm, told him Gable might have made a good Petruchio — and I got the role in the play. I was on my way.

ID: I'd like to get away from the subject of acting for a moment, to ask you about your early background with the Baptist Church. I, myself, attended a Baptist Church when I was young. Did you actually sing in the church choir? Me too! Forgive me for saying this, but, your persona doesn't exactly exude a "I used to sing in my church choir" type of personality. No offense intended, of course.

MW: LOL. I know. But in reality I was a skinny little boy who was somewhat funny looking and played the clarinet in the school band and sang in the church choir. But don't let your head go in the wrong direction with that. We were on our way to being men. I was disciplined at Church for hitting a boy with a dirt clod and the song we sang as we marched in the Louisiana Tech band went something like, "s...t, f....k, hell, p....y, gobble, nibble, chew, Tech band boys 'a bunch of mean mother f......s." I could be whipped by a lot of boys, but few tried, because I was known for not giving up. Once you attacked me, you had better have brought a lunch and a lantern because if you didn't disable me, I would get up and up and come at you again and again.

The choir was innovative for the time with an orchestra and tours around the country, and the band was so creative in half time shows that it gave us a following in the crowd and on the football team.

My love of music gave me pleasure in choir and band, and the training I got was instrumental in my performances as Cervantes in *Man of La Mancha* and Sky Masterson in *Guys and Dolls*.

ID: Let me ask you about your role in I Know What You Did Last Summer. *Have you always been a fan of horror films, or were you just recommended for the role? I must say, you did a great job of being "creepy."*

MW: I have to say, I was not a fan of horror and never understood the attraction. But the fans of horror are so devoted they won me over. I took on the role as any other and studied him until I became the character. I was recommended for the role by a producer who had worked with me on *Something to Talk About* with Julia Roberts. They needed a bad guy who would be willing to hang around the set to motivate the young actors if they needed it. They didn't, but my reputation for being a guy who would do anything for the picture got me the role. As for being creepy, I studied the role — I asked Ben to take over my body and do what he wanted. He did, much to my wife's dismay. He is not welcomed in our home. LOL.

ID: I can see why. I understand you are also a music lover. Your role in Prison Break *entails you being a kitty lover. Is the latter true about yourself? You can tell me if you are really a pussycat underneath that tough guy persona: I won't tell!*

MW: LOL. Music is my life. I love every form of music. Rap is not music.

As for kitties? My pal and long time companion, Sancho (a large German Shepard who passed away this Christmas), ate cats. I always wanted to let a cat live in our barn to keep the rats away, but Sancho would not allow it. I actually enjoy visiting with my friends' cats, although I am not sure their aloofness would fit it with my demand for interaction between those I am close to. If my daughter wants one I will get her one — and I will try to convince Sancho's sister not to eat it.

As for *my* persona? I am a man who has looked the Devil right square in the eye and told him to go f — k himself. I haven't felt fear since. By the same token, when a man is described as a Gentleman, there are two parts to the description. He is a "man," and he is "gentle" in that context. And a grown man is a gentleman. I hope to be known as a grown gentleman.

ID: What's this about you teaching acting classes at Georgia State Penitentiary? That sounds interesting...as well as a little frightening.

MW: The director of the Chattanooga Little Theater had been going every year for 10 years when he moved to Memphis. He asked me to take his place at the prison. I agreed to go one year. I did not want to establish the kind of relationships that he had with the inmates. It did not seem right to me. There were as many strange stories as there were inmates. I decided that our commencement play would be from the Texas Trilogy and was called *Lonestar*. I decided to double cast since the leads were brothers. One cast was black and the other was white. I told the inmates that if one of the members of their cast was moved to solitary that we would go with the other cast at the competition of Georgia Penitentiaries for best play. I thought this would motivate them to behave. When it was time to go to the competition we only had the two brothers who were white and the best friend who was black. It worked well, and I understand that it has become a trend in presenting the play. We won best play and best lead actor. It was a great experience.

ID: In my personal opinion, you would make a "good bad guy" in a Western. You could be a gunslinger, and...hmm...let's say Sam Shepard could be the Sheriff. Who do you think would win the quick-draw competition?

MW: I was told that once I got to Hollywood I would be playing one cowboy after another. Being raised on a horse, I was satisfied with that future. It has not turned out that way. As for Sam, we got to know each other on *Steel Magnolias*. I stunt doubled him in a vehicular stunt at the end. We ate together and partied hard. He would ask my advice like when he was shooting the scene where he was supposed to be working on his truck, he asked me what he could be doing — and I gave him a screw driver and taught him how to adjust the brakes. As for the quick draw — he's a dead man. I really like Sam and loved being around him. One day he asked me to go team roping with him but I told him the reason he was "off work" that day was because I was playing him. I would have loved to team up with him on horses. But, put face to face — he wouldn't get it out of the holster.

ID: Just out of curiosity, what would you say is your favorite film? I know that may cover a lot of ground.

MW: The Unbearable Lightness of Being and Princess Bride...and because it covers a lot of ground, I'll stop there.

ID: Fair enough. What about literature? Favorite book? Magazine? By the way, did you ever read Forry Ackerman's magazine Famous Monsters of Filmland? *It was one of my favorites growing up.*

MW: When I was at Berea College I saw an ad for a set of literature "classics." I ordered them. It was about four dollars a month, which was a lot of money to a Berea student then. Every month I would receive a new hard cover book. Montaigne, Thoreau, D. H. Lawrence were just a few in a set of about 30. Being dyslexic, it was tedious work. Once I was entertaining a young lady in my digs. She was washing the dishes from dinner as I read to her from Sophocles and she said, "Shouldn't you be studying for your test tomorrow?" To which I replied, "I never let my classes interfere with my education." And my grades showed it.

At any rate, I am not much for fiction. I have never seen the publication you mentioned. We subscribe to *Smithsonian, Southern Living* and *Sunset*. I love looking at pictures of well designed homes and gardening.

ID: Nothing wrong with some beauty in the world. What was it like growing up in Louisiana in the '50s and '60s? Did anything in particular from your childhood help form your career choices in later years?

MW: This question could be a book of its own. It was an exciting time. Raised by an African American woman who would not answer unless I called her "Black Moma," my father died when I was six years old, my Grandfather Muse was a truly great man and gave me a high standard for being a grown MAN. I was arrested for bombing the Wallace headquarters in the Humphrey campaign for President. I got kicked out of college. I really enjoyed a lot of ladies' company. No one raised in the sixties missed the message about pursuing their dreams. Some of us chose to take the chance and some of us didn't, but all of us understood it.

ID: Makes my "formative" years sound boring. LOL. What would you say is on the horizon for you right now? More NCIS, *I hope!*

MW: I feel it in my bones. I will be a "regular" on a TV series (*NCIS*, I hope), but my break out performance will be of an endearing old man in a feature (if you really feel I need to be on *NCIS* more, please write CBS and tell them).

ID: Don't worry, I will. Any last words of wisdom before you leave us?
MW: Return your shopping carts!
Try having one conversation with anyone where you don't interrupt each other.
Do what ever you must to get Chris Dodd and Barney Frank to retire and take Nancy Pelosi with them.
Support President Obama after his celebrity is gone.
Go tell your kids you love them right now!
Practice moderation before it is necessary.
Go to some Church a lot.
Think about growing up.
Be the old man you wish you had in your life.
Praise your mother.
Use your turn signal.
Make your first look at any woman as if you just saw Aphrodite.
Store your broom bristles up. If you don't have a broom, go get one and use it.
Always keep a hundred dollar bill in your boot.
Be on time. No, really.
It is hard to be grateful when you are an asshole.
To stay on track, Google your dream and print a picture of it.
Follow your heart.

— Muse Watson

ID: Amen, brother. Amen.

Where to write to see Muse on *NCIS* regularly:
Charles Floyd Johnson
c/o Valencia Studios
28343 Ave. Crocker #1
Valencia, CA 91355

To ask Muse a question:
http://movies.groups.yahoo.com/group/musewatsonclub
Muse's web site:
http://www.musewatson.com/
Muse Watson film clip:
http://www.youtube.com/profile?user=musewatson

Filmography

Film

House of Grimm, Old Man
End of the Spear, Adolfo
Frankenfish, Elmer
Dead Birds, Father
Iowa, Sheriff Walker
A Day Without a Mexican, Louis McClaire
The Christmas Child, Jimmy James Carstair
The Season of the Hunted, Frank
The Last Summer, Dad
American Outlaws, Burly Detective
Hollywood Vampire, Dr. Fulton
Wild Turkey, Floyd
Songcatcher (Winner, 2000 Sundance Film Festival), Parley Gentry
All the Rage, Todd
Art of the Bullet, Captain Walters
Austin Powers II, Klansman
Morgan's Ferry, Sheriff Billy Ray Barnwell
I Still Know, Ben Willis
From Dusk Till Dawn II, C.W. Niles
Break Up, Baker Cop #1
Shadrach, Captain
I Know What You Did Last Summer, Ben Willis
Acts of Betrayal, Trenton Fraser
Heartwood, James Keller
Rosewood, Henry Andrews
Lolita, store clerk
If I Die Before I Wake, Daryl
Assassins, Ketchum

Something to Talk About, Hank Corrigan
The Journey of August King, Herman Zimmer
Sommersby, The Drifter
Chattahoochie, Lucas
Handmaid's Tale, Guardian
Black Rainbow, State Trooper

Television

Close to Home, Bob Peters, CBS
NCIS, Mike Franks, CBS
Prison Break, Charles Westmoreland, Fox
Jane Doe, Captain Barnes, Hallmark
The Last Cowboy, Otis, Hallmark
Saturday Night Live, Guest Star, NBC
Walker, Texas Ranger, Forbes, CBS
JAG, Admiral Fessenden, CBS
Lazarus Man, Dawkins, TNT
American Gothic, Wash Sutpen, CBS
Gramps, father, NBC
Tecumseh, Whitley, TNT
Tad, Tom Pendel, Family
Justice in a Small Town, Robert Stubbs, NBC
Leave of Absence, Guy, ABC
Matlock, security expert, NBC
Birds II, Jessie, Showtime
Young Indiana Jones, Rudy, CBS
Separate But Equal, vehicular stunt, ABC
Blind Vengeance, Varsac, USA
Matlock, patrol officer, NBC
I-40 Paradise, Doctor, TNN

Theater

Taming of the Shrew, Petruchio, Berea College Theater
Cat on a Hot Tin Roof, Brick, Summer Arena Theater
Charley's Aunt, Jack, Summer Arena Theater
Passionella, Producer, Summer Arena Theater
Wilderness Road, Otho Turner, Wilderness Road Outdoor Drama
Wizard of Oz, Capt. of Uglies, Henrietta Child Children's Theater
Child's Play, Father Mozian, Berea College Players
A Streetcar Named Desire, Stanley, Berea College Players
Wilderness Road, Jed Willis, Wilderness Road Outdoor Drama
Humbug & Holly, Young Willie, Tidewater Dinner Theater
Romeo & Juliet, Mercutio, Oak Ridge Playhouse
Charley's Aunt, Jack, Oak Ridge Playhouse
Man of LaMancha, Cervantes, Oak Ridge Playhouse
Song of the Whippoorwill, Jack, Oak Ridge Playhouse
Much Ado About Nothing, Benedict, Oak Ridge Playhouse

Guys & Dolls, Sky Masterson, Oak Ridge Playhouse
Everything in the Garden, Paul, U T Theatre in the Round
Man of LaMancha, Cervantes, Chattanooga Little Theater
Hamlet, Hamlet, Chattanooga Little Theater
Fiddler on the Roof, Tevye, Chattanooga Little Theater
A Midsummer Night's Dream, Oberon, Chattanooga Little Theater
Perils of Cedarville, Prod./Director, Ragtime on the River
Shadow Box, Joe, Performing Arts Center
Lonestar, Director, Georgia State Penitentiary
Lonestar, Director, Performing Arts Center
Ain't Misbehavin', Director, Bessie Smith Foundation
Burn This, Pale, Centre Stage-South Carolina
Home, Hershel, Benefit Homeless Shelter

Jason Paul Collum

Jason Paul Collum (born July 15, 1973 in Brookfield, Wisconsin) is an American filmmaker. He formerly worked at Femme Fatales *and* Cinefantastique *magazines. Collum is the author of* Assault of the Killer Bs: Interviews with 20 Cult Film Actresses *(McFarland, 2004). He wrote and directed the horror starlets documentary* Something to Scream About *(2002). Collum now works with Tempe Entertainment and is director/writer of the* October Moon *franchise.*

ID: *While glancing through your resume, I see you have written some scripts for film sequels, one of which was for* Last House on the Left. *Interesting choice. What became of that project?*

JPC: *The Last on the Left, Part 2: A Weasel Walks Among Us* was a spec script I'd written in the hopes of getting a film career started back in 1992. It sat with Kushner-Locke (who owned the sequel rights) for six months. They really seemed to like the script and at some point gave it to Jonathan Craven (son of Wes), but ultimately passed because they feared an NC-17 for its extreme sexual violence, which in 1992 would have basically killed the film in its theatrical release. I sent it on to other studios, but they all basically responded the same way. It did ultimately get me my first writing/directing job with MDM Productions out of Virginia, who wanted me to change the title to *The First House on the Right*. I was such a devout horror fan at the time I knew that would be sacrilege, so I said "no," then made *Mark of the Devil 666: The Moralist* instead for their company.

In 1999 I re-wrote the *Last House 2* script and tried Kushner-Locke again, but it was still too sexually intense and violent, and they turned it down again, only this time it was refused pretty quickly. At that point I let it die, though I always think someday I'll just change all the characters names and title and make it myself, though "torture porn" seems to be on its way out, so I may have missed the ball...again.

ID: Your first film project was the Danny Bonaduce film, America's Deadliest Home Video. *Very interesting choice. What is Danny really like? I mean, he does have somewhat of a reputation, you know.*

JPC: I wish I had some vulgar story to tell, but the truth is I never met him. The film was actually complete before I came on to begin publicity. I do know that Danny had been on his way to jail (this may have been for beating up the tranny), and it was this film that got him out. The producers paid his bail so they could get him in the movie. So there's some juicy gossip...

ID: Juicy enough...Ok, on to your book Assault of the Killer Bs. *What was it like interviewing all those B-girls? I love interviewing the ladies of horror myself. They are much more intelligent than they are normally given credit for.*

JPC: It was one of the best experiences of my life. Honestly. I'd idolized each of them, and to be able to sit with them one-on-one for an hour or so and chat was simply euphoric. They're all incredibly smart and I learned so many interesting things about their careers, their families, and backgrounds. Very generous. Not a snot in the bunch.

There was only one actress, who shall remain unnamed other than to say she was in one of the *Friday the 13th* films, who was just a train wreck. I took her to lunch and could barely make out what she was saying. She was very frail and ate her sandwich like she hadn't eaten in a week. Then she went to the bathroom and came back with cocaine all over her nose and cheeks. I'd brought a copy of the film for her to sign, but was so depressed I never pulled it out of my bag. After the "interview" she asked me to drive her to her "friend's" house...which I discovered was actually a crack house once I got there. No one has been able to hunt her down for interviews since, but oddly she's the most requested contact I receive from other authors and filmmakers. That was my only truly negative experience with the book.

ID: I also see you have written for Femme Fatales *and* Fangoria. *I've been reading* Fangoria *since the early 80s. Are you just naturally a big fan of the horror genre?*

JPC: I was a HUGE fan of the genre as a teenager and into college. It countered all my teen angst. I always saw myself as the hero or heroine of each film. Battered and bruised and put through hell, but a survivor in the end. I'd literally go to the video store every single day and pour over the horror section. I re-watched just about everything a minimum of five times, some as many as 50 times. I mean, I've seen *Slumber Party Massacre II* about 75 times, so that must tell you something about devotion.

When I picked up my first copy of *Fangoria* in 1989 with the cover story on the killer Santa Claus from TVs *Tales from the Crypt*, I knew I'd found my Bible. I devoured every page so much that the ink wore off where my thumbs rested. It had a fold out in the front of Mrs. Voorhees' head in the fridge, and an article on *The Stepfather II* which I couldn't stop re-reading. I've collected every issue since, though these days I'm more apt to go to the review sections and the elegy by Tony Timpone and skip a lot of the actual articles. Bizarre, I know.

As I've grown older I've found I don't "need" horror the way I used to. Plus I'm simply too busy now. I'm lucky to see any single movie within a four-week period. When I do, it's usually pre-2000. Nowadays it seems anything new that comes out is a remake of something old, even if it isn't an official remake. Take *Wrong Turn*. Well done movie, but it's a combination of the original *The Hills Have Eyes*, *The Last House on the Left* and *Friday the 13th* (among others). So my love for the genre seems to be stuck from films released in the 1950s through the 1990s. I'm sure that's why I'd rather read an article about Brinke Stevens and Linnea Quigley than any of the newer girls.

ID: Which do you enjoy more? Script writing or books? I tried my hand at writing some short film screenplays once, and failed miserably.

JPC: I actually prefer scripts. I wrote a lot of short horror stories in high school and college, but rather than trying to get them published I always turned them into screenplays. I'm not sure why. I'm much more visual, so although I'm going to make myself seem stupid, I really do enjoy looking at things with pictures. I'd much rather "read" *People* magazine than pick up a Stephen King book.

Scriptwriting is a faster process for me. It's cleaner, and ultimately something which would be turned into a moving picture rather than black and white on a page. Again, bizarre, I know. That's just how my brain works and how my interest in a project is held.

Also, a screenplay is altered as it rolls in front of a camera. If dialogue looks good on the page but doesn't work once actors speak it out loud, it can be made better. With a book, once it's written down and passes through an editor, it is what it is.

ID: As far as your taste in cinema goes, what genre do you enjoy the most? Wait...was that a dumb question?

JPC: Not at all. Like I said, I'm not the die-hard horror fan I used to be. From ages 12 through my mid-20s, I watched horror exclusively. Then I started to expand my horizons and discovered all these other wonderful genres. Horror will always be my number one love, but even within that genre I find my tastes have changed between the subgenres. I used to crave slasher movies, but now much prefer a deep dose of psychological terror. *Rosemary's Baby*, *The Omen* and *The Exorcist* now freak me out, but they didn't when I was a teenager. In turn, the *Nightmare on Elm Street* and *Friday the 13th* films don't hold my interest like they once did. Now, my "Top 10" list is more diverse:

1. *Carrie* (1976)
2. *Elvira, Mistress of the Dark* (1988)
3. *Moulin Rouge!* (2001)
4. *Friday the 13th, Part 2* (1981)
5. *Edward Scissorhands* (1990)
6. *The Color Purple* (1985)
7. *Crash* (2005)
8. *Finding Nemo* (2004)
9. *The Electric Grandmother* (1983)
10. *Watership Down* (1979)

Additionally, the horror I used to write has changed into more "thriller" style stuff. I don't know that I could write that *Last House 2* script these days. A very angry 19 year old wrote that script from a very dark and lonely place in his heart, mind and soul. I'm so much different now internally... emotionally. I'm more jaded, but I'm also more in control of my own life. Even *October Moon* and *November Son*, though written only two years apart, seem to have been done by two completely different people. *October Moon* is a much more emotion-filled, passionate piece, whereas *November Son* is much colder, and I'm less attached to it.

I tend to write based on where my head is at in my own life. I was madly in love and trying to hold on to a relationship that really didn't exist during *October Moon*. With *November Son*, I had detached myself from most of my friends and family. I was deeply depressed, and my response was to shut off and loathe everyone. Now, two years later, I can look at that film and see what was going on at that time in my head, and say "That was an angry, confused bitch who wrote that script."

At the same time, I'm also more aware of "the market." What's selling? I know that the gritty, vulgar scenarios of *Last House 2* aren't in me as much these days, but also that with all the negativity towards "torture porn" now, it's something which likely won't sell anyway. But hey, talk to me in another two years and I might give you completely different answers.

ID: What is on the horizon for Jason Paul Collum? Some more interview books, I hope.

JPC: Possibly. I'm actually working on two children's books and a martini book. How's that for stepping away from the horror fold?! I'm also circulating scripts for my next film project. I've toyed with doing a "sequel" book to *Assault of the Killer B's*. I have a healthy number of interviews which can be culled into a nifty volume: chats with Ginger Lynn Allen, David DeCoteau, Tanya Dempsey, Pricilla Barnes, Sam Irvin, Kathleen Kinmont, and many others. I need to 1). Figure out how to roll them in to a theme, and 2). Find the time to do it. So many ideas, so little time.

ID: Any last words before you leave us?
JPC: Yes. Go buy my movies. I need to pay my mortgage.

ID: You too, huh?
JPC: Also, if filmmaking is your dream, go make an f-ing movie!!! Don't wait for someone else to make it happen. Pick up a camcorder, gather your friends, and make the freakin' thing. That's what I did. Technology is better and cheaper today, so if a kid in junior high is making mini movies and showing 'em on You Tube, then certainly you can too! Now go visit the site I never update: www.jasonpaulcollum.com.

ID: Been there, done that!

Education

University of Wisconsin — Parkside; Major: English; Writing Concentration. Minor: Communications. Graduated August 1996.

Writing Experience: Screenplays

Optioned & transcribed dramedy *Shy of Normal;* B+Boy Productions, 2007
Created psychological thriller *November Son;* B+Boy Productions, 2007
Wrote psychological thriller *October Moon;* B+Boy Productions, 2005
Documented *Something To Scream About;* Tempe Entertainment, 2003
Wrote *5 Dark Souls, Part 3: Retribution;* B+Boy Productions, 2003
Commissioned to write *Sleepless Nights;* Rapid Heart Pictures, 2000
Created psychological thriller *Julia Wept;* B+Boy Productions, 2000
Wrote horror script *Somewhere, He Waits;* Majestic World Entertainment, 1999
Documented *Brinke Stevens Private Collection IV;* Think Brinke Inc., 1999
Developed mystery sequel *5 Dark Souls, Part 2*; MDM Productions, 1998
Wrote commercial *Program Activities & Opportunities at Sienna Center;* Racine Dominicans, 1996
Created action-thriller screenplay *5 Dark Souls;* MDM Productions, 1996
Wrote mystery script *Mark of the Devil 666;* MDM Productions, 1995
Developed screenplay *Deranged 2;* MDM Productions, 1994

Writing Experience: Journalism

Authored the book *Assault of the Killer B'S: Interviews With 20 Cult Film Actresses.* McFarland & Co. Publishers, 2004
Wrote chapter "Into the Post-Modern Era" for the book *Attack of the B Queens.* Luminary Press, October 2003
Wrote "Slashback: Where Did the Friday the 13th Girls Go?" and "The Hills Still Have Eyes" retrospectives, *Alternative Cinema* #21, Summer 2003
Researched and documented 50+ retrospectives for *Femme Fatales* Magazine._SEE COMPLETE LIST BELOW
Wrote "Elvira's Haunted Hills Busts Out," *Fangoria* Magazine #212, June 2002
Profiled "Witchouse 2," *Fangoria* Magazine #197, October 2000
Critiqued eight movies and film business, *Fangoria* Magazine, 1991 — present
Commentated "Horrified by Harris," *Video Store* Magazine, December 17, 1995
Wrote "A Mess in the Making," *Independent Video Magazine* #6, 1994
Published short story in the Christian book *Dreams* Alives (1991) and the text book *Creating A Christian Lifestyle* (1996)

Film Experience

Director, *Something to Scream About* (documentary); Tempe Entertainment, 2003
Director, *5 Dark Souls, Part 3: Retribution* (horror);B+Boy Productions, 2003
1st A.D. / Actor, *Bad Movie Police* series (comedy); Tempe Entertainment, 2003
1st A.D. / Actor, *Deadly Stingers* (horror); 20th Century Fox, 2003
Actor, *Hell Asylum* (horror); Full Moon, 2002

Director of Photography, *Behind the Scenes Hell Asylum* (documentary); Full Moon 2002
Production Coordinator/2nd A.D., *The Frightening* (horror) Amsell, 2001
Production Coordinator/2nd A.D., *The Brotherhood 2* (horror); Regent, 2001
Director, *Julia Wept* (psychological horror); B Boy Productions, 2000
Production Coordinator/2nd A.D., *Final Stab* (horror); Rapid Heart, 2000
Production Coordinator/2nd A.D., *The Brotherhood* (horror); Regent, 2000
2nd A.D., Sega "Prank Caller" (commercial); Copper Media, 1999
2nd A.D., *Ancient Evil: Scream of the Mummy* (horror); Rapid Heart, 1999
1st A.D., *Worlds* (drama); Giddy-up Productions, 1999
Director, *5 Dark Souls, Part 2* (horror); MDM Productions, 1998
Coordinator/Script Supervisor, OFF! Coils (commercial); Cowles Films, 1997
Director, Lake Cook Health Care Center (commercial); LCHCC, INC., 1997
Assistant Location Manager, *Harp* (action); Harp Productions, Inc., 1996
Director, *5 Dark Souls* (thriller); MDM Productions, 1996
Script Supervisor, Skintastic (commercial); Cy DeCosse, Inc., 1996
Director, *Mark of the Devil 666* (mystery); MDM Productions, 1995
Director, *Sacrifices* (documentary); Student Pictures, 1994

Additional Credentials

Publicity Director, Tempe Entertainment, 2003
Editor-in-Chief, *Cinefantastique* Magazine, 2002
Assistant Editor, *Femme Fatales* Magazine, 2001-2002
Head of Advertising and Marketing, *Cinefantastique* and *Femme Fatales* Magazines, 2001-2002
Representative for *Femme Fatales* Magazine: Los Angeles Bureau, 2000-2001
Developed text book and taught "Film Genre: American Horror 1968-1994" at University of Wisconsin — Parkside; Spring 2000, Fall 2002
Media Relations Manager, Rapid Heart Pictures, 1999-2002
Writer/Director/Production Assistant at TCI Television, 1996-1997
Designed customer brochure for Moore Video Company, 1996
Distribution Director for *America's Deadliest Home Video*; Randum Films & Entertainment, 1994-1995

Published Journalism

"The Beauty in Darkness...." *Femme Fatales*. Volume 11, Number 8. July 2002. Pgs 24-30. Q&A interview with splattertographer Ward Boult.
"Brinke Stevens: 20 Years Later...." (Cover story) *Femme Fatales*. Volume 11, Numbers 5/6. May 2002. Pgs 72-81. Career retrospective includes interview with Brinke Stevens.
"The Brotherhood." *Femme Fatales*. Volume 10, Number 4. September/October 2001. Pgs 48-49. Film coverage includes interview with Director/Producer David DeCoteau, Line ProducerWendy Kutzner and actresses Elizabeth Bruderman and Rebekah Ryan.
"Brotherhood: Elizabeth Bruderman." *Femme Fatales*. Volume 10, Number 4. September/October 2001. Pgs 53-54. Interview with newcomer/actress Elizabeth Bruderman.

"Brotherhood: Rebekah Ryan." *Femme Fatales.* Volume 10, Number 4. September/October 2001. Pgs 50-52. Interview and career piece with actress/model Rebekah Ryan.

"The Brotherhood II: Young Warlocks." *Femme Fatales.* Volume 10, Number 4. September/October 2001. Pgs 55-56. Film coverage includes interview with Producer/Director David DeCoteau and actress Jennifer Capo.

"Brotherhood II: Jennifer Capo." *Femme Fatales.* Volume 10, Number 4. September/October 2001. Pgs 57-58. Interview with new actress Jennifer Capo.

"Brotherhood II: Stacey Scowley." *Femme Fatales.* Volume 10, Number 4. September/October 2001. Pgs 59-60. Interview with new actress Stacey Scowley.

"Cheerleader Ninjas." *Femme Fatales.* Volume 11, Numbers 10/11. September/October 2002. Pgs 58-63. Film coverage and review includes interviews with Screenwriter/Director Kevin Campbell and Cinematographer Brendan C. Flynt.

"Danny Draven." *Femme Fatales.* Volume 11, Number 1. January 2002. Pgs 21-24. Interview introducing new director includes interview with Danny Draven.

"David DeCoteau: Rapid Heart's Low-Budget Auteur." *Femme Fatales.* Volume 9, Number 7. November 2000. Pgs 16-31. Career retrospective includes interviews with David DeCoteau, Linnea Quigley, Michelle Bauer, Brinke Stevens.

"Debra DeLiso." *Femme Fatales.* Volume 11, Number 8. July 2002. Pgs 46-51. Career retrospective includes interview with Debra DeLiso and Brinke Stevens.

"Debra Mayer." *Femme Fatales.* Volume 11, Number 8. July 2002. Pgs 40-43. Interview introducing new actress Debra Mayer.

"Elvira's Haunted Hills Busts Out." *Fangoria.* Number 212. May 2001. Pgs 75-78. Film coverage of Elvira's Haunted Hills includes interviews with Elvira portrayer/creator Cassandra Peterson, producer Mark Pierson and director Sam Irvin.

"Felissa Rose." *Femme Fatales.* Volume 11, Numbers 5/6. May 2002. Pgs 38-41. *Sleepaway Camp* film retrospective and interview with star Felissa Rose and Jeff Hayes.

"Filmmaker Sam Irvin: Child of the Drive-In." *Femme Fatales.* Volume 10, Number 5. November 2001. Pgs 22-31, 62. Career retrospective includes interviews with Sam Irvin, Stella Stevens, Musetta Vander, Cassandra Petersen, Julie Brown, Brinke Stevens and Mary Woronov.

"Final Stab." *Femme Fatales.* Volume 10, Number 5. November 2001. Pgs 18-21. Film coverage includes interviews with director David DeCoteau and actors Melissa Renee Martin, Erinn Carter and Laila Reece Landon.

"Firestarter II: Rekindled." *Femme Fatales.* Volume 11, Numbers 5/6. May 2002. Pgs 48-51. Film coverage includes interviews with director Robert Iscove, producer Jeff Morton, screenwriter Philip Eisner, and actress Marguerite Moreau.

"The Hills Still Have Eyes 26 Years Later." *Alternative Cinema.* Number 21. Summer 2003. Pgs.70-73. Retrospective/critique of why the film has retained its power.

"The Independent: Ginger Lynn — Part 1." *Femme Fatales.* Volume 11, Numbers 10/11. September/October 2002. Pgs 48-49. Film coverage and interview with Ginger Lynn Allen.

"J.R. Bookwalter: King of Guerilla Filmmaking." (Cover story) *Femme Fatales.* Volume 11, Number 1. January 2002. Pgs 8-20. Career retrospective includes interviews with J.R. Bookwalter, Ariauna Albright, David DeCoteau.

"Julie Brown." *Femme Fatales.* Volume 10, Number 5. November 2001. Pgs 42-47. Career retrospective includes interview with Julie Brown.

"Judith O'Dea." *Femme Fatales*. Volume 11, Numbers 5/6. May 2002. Pgs 10-15. Career and *Night of the Living Dead* retrospective includes interview with star Judith O'Dea.

"Karen Mistal." *Femme Fatales*. Volume 11, Number 7. June 2002. Pgs 26-31. Career and *Return of the Killer* Tomatoes retrospective includes interview with Karen Mistal.

"Kelly Jo Minter." *Femme Fatales*. Volume 11, Numbers 5/6. May 2002. Pgs 110-113. Career retrospective includes interview with Kelly Jo Minter.

"Killjoy 2." *Femme Fatales*. Volume 11, Number 4. April 2002. Pgs 10-19. Film coverage includes interviews with director Tammi Sutton and actors Nicole Pulliam, Olimpia Fernandez, Rhonda Claerbuat.

"Lar Park-Lincoln." *Femme Fatales*. Volume 11, Numbers 5/6. May 2002. Pgs 52-55. Career and *Friday The 13th, Part VII* retrospective includes interview with Lar Park-Lincoln.

"Lisa Wilcox...Her Nightmare Became a Dream Come True." (Cover story) *Femme Fatales*. Volume 11, Numbers 5/6. May 2002. Pgs 96-103. Career and *A Nightmare on Elm Street 4* retrospective includes interview with Lisa Wilcox.

"Lisa Zane." *Femme Fatales*. Volume 11, Numbers 5/6. May 2002. Pgs 118-120. Career retrospective included interview with Lisa Zane.

"Mannequin Mayhem in the Heartland." *Femme Fatales*. Volume 11, Numbers 10/11. September/October 2002. Pgs 72-77. Film coverage of *Jigsaw* includes interviews with writers/directors Harry James Picardi and Don Adams and actors Aimee Bravo, Maren Lindow, James Palmer, and Arthur Simone.

"A Mess in the Making." *Independent Video* Magazine. Issue 6. Winter 1994. Candid diary of a beginning filmmaker's mistakes.

"Michelle Nordin: Ancient Evil — Scream of the Mummy." (Cover story) *Femme Fatales*. Volume 9, Number 7. November 2000. Pgs 8-11, 13-15. Film coverage and career interview with lead Michelle Nordin.

"Pamela Susan Shoop." *Femme Fatales*. Volume 10, Number 3. July/August 2001. Pgs 56-60. Career retrospective interview with Pamela Susan Shoop.

"Panic Room." *Femme Fatales*. Volume 11, Numbers 5/6. May 2002. Pgs 8-9. Film coverage and special FX interview with Pixel Liberation Front artist Ron Frankel.

"Q&A with Lezlie Deane." *Femme Fatales*. Volume 11, Numbers 5/6. May 2002. Pgs 114-117. Film and music career retrospective included interview with Lezlie Deane.

"Rapid Heart Pictures." *Femme Fatales*. Volume 9, Number 7. November 2000. Pgs 11-12. New Production Company interviews with David DeCoteau and Michelle Nordin.

"Slashback: Where Did the Girls of *Friday the 13th* Go?" *Alternative Cinema*. Number 21. Summer 2003. Pgs. 64-69. The search for the women of one of horror's most beloved franchises.

"The Slumber Party Massacre Saga." (Cover story) *Femme Fatales*. Volume 9, Number 3. August 11, 2000. Pgs 8-10, 13-16, 19, 21, 23, 26-27. Film franchise retrospective includes interviews with Brinke Stevens, Heidi Kozak, Juliette Cummins, Marta Kober, Brandi Burkett.

"Slumber Party Massacre: Brinke Stevens." *Femme Fatales*. Volume 9, Number 3. August 11, 2000. Pgs 11-13. Retrospective includes interview with Brinke Stevens.

"Slumber Party Massacre: Robin Rochelle Stille." *Femme Fatales.* Volume 9, Number 3. August 11, 2000. Pg 14. Career retrospective of late actress includes interviews with Brinke Stevens, David DeCoteau and poet Rhonda Baughman.

"Slumber Party Massacre 2: Heidi Kozak." *Femme Fatales.* Volume 9, Number 3. August 11, 2000. Pgs 17-18. Career retrospective includes interviews with Heidi Kozak and Kevin Blair Spirtas.

"Slumber Party Massacre 2: Juliette Cummins." *Femme Fatales.* Volume 9, Number 3. August 11, 2000. Pgs 19-20. Career retrospective includes interview with Juliette Cummins.

"Slumber Party Massacre 3: Brandi Burkett." *Femme Fatales.* Volume 9, Number 3. August 11, 2000. Pgs 24-25. Career retrospective with Brandi Burkett.

"Slumber Party Massacre 3: Marta Kober." *Femme Fatales.* Volume 9, Number 3. August 11, 2000. Pgs 21-22. Career retrospective includes interview with Marta Kober.

"Stacey Nelkin." *Femme Fatales.* Volume 11, Numbers 5/6. May 2002. Pgs 85-87. Career and *Halloween III: Season of the Witch* film retrospective includes interview with Stacey Nelkin.

"Taking a Bite Out of Crime...." *Femme Fatales.* Volume 11, Number 8. July 2002. Pg 57. Interview with actress Elizabeth Bruderman on roles in *America's Most Wanted, The Brotherhood* and *The Frightening.*

"Tammi Sutton...In a Class By Herself." (Cover story) *Femme Fatales.* Volume 11, Number 4. April 2002. Pgs 20-25. Career interview with new director Tammi Sutton.

"Tanya Dempsey: Horror's Fresh Femme." (Cover story) *Femme Fatales.* Volume 11, Number 8. July 2002. Pgs 32-39. Interview introducing new actress includes Q&A interviews with Tanya Dempsey and Danny Draven.

"*There's Nothing Out There*...The 10th Anniversary." *Femme Fatales.* Volume 10, Number 3. July/August 2001. Pgs 42-47. Film Retrospective interview with writer/director Rolfe Kanefsky.

"Thinking Outside Hollywood." *Femme Fatales.* Volume 11, Numbers 5/6. May 2002. Pg 84. Interview with indie film star Tina Ona Paukstelis. (Written under pseudonym "Bud Windale.")

"...What Are You Doing, Tuesday Knight?" *Femme Fatales.* Volume 11, Numbers 5/6. May 2002. Pgs 104-109. Career and *A Nightmare on Elm Street* 4 retrospective includes interview with actress Tuesday Knight.

"*Witchouse 2: Blood Coven* — Another Lilith Scare." *Fangoria.* Number 197. October 2000. Pg 10. Film coverage includes interviews with director J.R. Bookwalter and actress Ariauna Albright.

Fangoria Mini-Reviews:

C.L.A.M.P.ing Down: Religion vs. Horror (April 2000, #191)

Blair Witch Project vs. *America's Deadliest Home Video* (November 1999, #188)

Scream: The Battle Between Mirimax/Sony/MPAA (September 1997)

Halloween: The Curse of Michael Myers (March 1996)

Movie Studio's Poor Business Ethics (July 1993)

Prom Night IV: Deliver Us From Evil (October 1992)

Silent Night, Deadly Night 5: The Toy Maker (April 1992)

The Howling VI: The Freaks (October 1991)

John Kenneth Muir

John Kenneth Muir became a full-time, professional writer/journalist in the year 1996 at the age of 27, just before his first book, *Exploring Space: 1999* (McFarland, 1997), was published. Since 1997, John has — on average — seen at least two books a year released from various publishers including Applause Theatre and Cinema Books and Powys Media. John now has over sixteen successful books in print.

ID: Greetings and salutations, John. How are you? Long time, no hear.
JKM: Very busy, thank you, and doing quite well. I hope the same is true for you. It's an honor to be here today.

ID: I must say: it is a real thrill to have you drop by. I have wanted to interview you since I read your book, Horror Films of the 1980s. *Wow...that's a BIG book! How long did it take you to write it?*
JKM: It took me over a year to write that one. I think it was fifteen months. But, it was a very fun fifteen months.

ID: I love the way you put the book together. Just how many horror films have you seen?
JKM: I love the horror film as an art form, and I have watched as much of it as possible while still maintaining a profession and a family life. For *Horror Films of the 70s*, I watched over 225 films. For the 80s book, it was around 325. I'd venture to say I have seen over a thousand horror films. And that total is bound to go up soon, because I just signed a contract to write *Horror Films of the 90s*. I just put around 187 films in my Netflix queue...

ID: Speaking of horror films in general, I feel compelled to ask you this for sure: What is your overall opinion of horror cinema these days? Things have changed a lot from decade to decade, and sometimes not for the better.
JKM: Taking the "big" historical view, I'd say every period in horror history has had its ups and downs. But fifteen years from now, we'll look

back and see, I am certain, that there are some very strong titles among the weak titles, and I think that's true of every decade.

ID: I see you also penned a book about my favorite director, John Carpenter. Have you ever met him in person?
JKM: No, I've never had the pleasure, but maybe someday...

ID: What prompted you to become a writer/journalist? My inspiration came from reading old EC Comics like Tales from the Crypt *and watching old horror films on late night TV.*
JKM: Well, I became infatuated with film and TV at an early age. An episode of *Space: 1999* had an indelible impact on me when I was around six years old, in 1975. The episode was called "Dragon's Domain," and it was about this monster lurking around on an abandoned space ship. It had a glowing eye and dozens of tentacles, and it would hypnotize its victims, sucking them into its gaping maw. Then, the monster would digest them, and spit up their steaming bones. The imagery in that show was absolutely unforgettable to me, and even though it was on a science fiction show, it cemented my love of horror.

ID: You should have known I'd ask this; have you ever written any horror fiction? If so, I'd love to take a peek at it. I'd even post it in my on line magazine!
JKM: All right, buddy, you asked for it. As soon as I can, I'm sending some of my horror fiction your way, so beware!

ID: How about a favorite horror film? Or book? I know that may cover a lot of ground.
JKM: It would be difficult for me to name my favorite horror film, because I love so many of them. I have different favorites on different days. I think the original *Texas Chainsaw Massacre* is work of art, a real masterpiece. I also love Carpenter's original *Halloween*, as well as the original *The Hills Have Eyes, Night of the Living Dead, The Exorcist, Don't Look Now,* and *Picnic At Hanging Rock*. That too many?

ID: Good enough! Hey...what's this about you being interviewed on Dateline NBC*?*
JKM: Well, I had the good fortune to be interviewed on the *E! True Hollywood Story* as well. The *Dateline* thing was interesting, though. It was around the time of my Wes Craven book, *The Art of Horror*, and *Dateline* called me and did a phone interview with me about the *Scream* series, and

the Columbine shootings and the popular response to horror films. We talked a long time and the producer decided to fly me out to do the show. Then, that weekend, there was an ice storm — the worst I have seen in this area in eight years — so I didn't get to do the show. So, yeah, I did an interview, but I didn't get to be on TV.

ID: Darn...oh well, they were thinking about you at least. Now, this may sound like a REALLY dumb question, but here goes: What is your favorite type of film? I mean, some folks enjoy writing horror, but otherwise never read it, or watch it on the screen.

JKM: My favorite type of film is indeed the horror film. But I should amend that to say "the intelligent, well-crafted" horror film. I mean, I can't stomach the sight or sound of a *Troma* film. I don't like having my intelligence insulted. I believe horror is a serious business, and I appreciate filmmakers who treat the genre with respect.

ID: I must agree. Finally, last, but not least, what are your present and future projects? More books on my favorite subject, I hope?

JKM: Well, I will be turning in *The Horror Films of the 90s* by the end of 2009, and I am currently in post-production for the third season of my internet show called *The House Between*. Also, I blog on a daily basis, so let me direct your readers here: *http://reflectionsonfilmandtelevision.blogspot*. There, I review films and TV shows, and also look at nostalgia items like electronic toys from my youth.

ID: Well, John, I have to sign off for now, even though I'd like to ask you about ten thousand more questions, but please, drop by again sometime, ok?

JKM: To quote someone famous..."I'll be back..."
Thanks, David.

ID: No...thank you!

Christopher Golden

Christopher Golden is the award-winning, bestselling author of such novels as The Myth Hunters, Wildwood Road, The Boys Are Back in Town, The Ferryman, Strangewood, Of Saints and Shadows, *and (with Tim Lebbon)* Mind the Gap. *Golden co-writerote the lavishly illustrated novel* Baltimore, or, The Steadfast Tin Soldier and the Vampire *with Mike Mignola, which they are currently scripting as a feature film for New Regency. He has also written books for teens and young adults, including the thriller series* Body of Evidence, *honored by the New York Public Library and chosen as one of YALSA's Best Books for Young Readers. Upcoming teen novels include* Poison Ink *for Delacorte,* Soulless *for MTV Books, and* The Secret Journeys of Jack London, *a collaboration with Tim Lebbon. With Thomas E. Sniegoski, he is the co-author of the dark fantasy series* The Menagerie *as well as the young readers' fantasy series* OutCast *and the comic book miniseries* Talent, *both of which were recently acquired by Universal Pictures. Golden and Sniegoski also wrote the upcoming comic book miniseries* The Sisterhood, *currently in development as a feature film. Working with actress/writer/director Amber Benson, he co-created and co-writerote* Ghosts of Albion, *an original animated supernatural drama for BBC online, from which they created the book series of the same name. (www.ghostsofalbion.net)*

As an editor, Golden's work has included the Hellboy *novel series, a trio of* Hellboy *short story anthologies, and co-editing duties on* British Invasion, *from Cemetery Dance. His non-fiction work includes collaborative efforts such as* The Stephen King Universe, Buffy the Vampire Slayer: The Watcher's Guide, *and the upcoming* Neil Gaiman Companion. *His other writing has included video games, numerous comic books, and short stories.*

Golden was born and raised in Massachusetts, where he still lives with his family. His original novels have been published in fourteen languages in countries around the world.

ID: *Keeping busy as usual?*

CG: Always. Although I'm going to try to take it as easy as I can over the holidays. I work at home, but somehow still don't manage to spend as much time with my family as I'd like.

ID: I recently purchased a copy of Joe Hill's Twentieth Century Ghosts, *and I really enjoyed your introduction. In it, you state that "...modern horror is not often subtle." I tend to agree. Why do you think so many writers seem to go for the jugular?*

CG: I can think of two reasons that jump immediately to mind. One is film. Once upon a time, cinema was most often a reactive medium when it came to horror fiction. Horror fiction — both supernatural and otherwise — had a greater ratio of elegance to deviance. But my generation grew up on slasher movies, and the influence of those films cannot be overstated. They influenced good writers and bad writers alike. The second reason is another major influence — Splatterpunk. Skipp and Spector, David Schow, and a handful of others wrote wonderful, visceral fiction, but like the boundary-pushing horror in films, the Splat-Pack influenced both good writers and bad writers.

By the way, the quiet, eerie, subtle stuff also influences good and bad writers...I'm not saying otherwise. But I will suggest that that special breed of writer — those who remind me of the most tragic of *American Idol* auditioners — do seem to gravitate more toward the bloodier, more outrageous horror, and that the subtleties that the talented practitioners of such fiction manage to achieve are lost on them.

ID: Speaking of Joe Hill, I think it's great that he opted not to cash in on his father's name. What is he like in person?

CG: Wow. Amazingly, you're the first person to ask the "what's he really like?" question. But to be honest, I don't know how to answer it. I find celebrity to be a very curious thing. A lot like sushi, actually. People seem to love it, but I don't see the fascination. Joe's a good guy. I'd definitely call him a friend. He doesn't go around making balloon animals or enter a room doing a little soft shoe. What readers need to know about any writer they can learn by reading him.

ID: That's good advice. What was it that first prompted your interest in the macabre? Just a genuine love for the genre?

CG: From birth, yeah. My favorite movies, TV shows, comics, and books were always horror, or at least weird. I remember watching *Frankenstein* at the age of seven, and crying when he threw the little girl in the lake, not in fear but because of how tragic that scene is. I don't know where the interest comes from, but it was always there.

ID: I see you have collaborated with Tim Lebbon on a book. Tell me a little about it.
CG: Tim and I have actually just finished our third collaboration. The first two, *Mind The Gap* and *The Map Of Moments*, are part of a series of thematically related standalone novels we're doing for Bantam called *The Hidden Cities*. Each book is set in a different city with a different cast of characters and an unrelated story, but they all deal with the hidden histories, forgotten parts, and secret magic of a city. *Mind The Gap* is set in London, and I'm really pleased with it, but *The Map Of Moments* — which is set in post-Katrina New Orleans — is something Tim and I both believe is some of our best work ever. The third book we wrote together, *The Secret Journeys of Jack London: The Calls of The Wild* is the first in a new YA series.

ID: My, my, you are a busy fellow. What's this about being co-creator/writer on the BBC series Ghosts of Albion*?*
CG: Back in the days when I was writing lots of *Buffy the Vampire Slayer* related novels, comics, video games, non-fiction books, etc., Amber Benson and I collaborated on several comics together. BBC got in touch and wanted us to create an original online animated series for them, and *Ghosts of Albion* was born. We did two hour-long serials, and have since written two novels, a novella, and a short story in that world. The role-playing game has recently been released. Amber and I had a blast working on all of it, most especially the time we spent together in London in the studio with the cast. She directed the first hour, and the actors loved her.

ID: Has becoming a family man affected the way you approach horror fiction? I see you have published teen and young adult books as well.
CG: I've been writing for teens nearly as long as I've been writing professionally. But I'm sure the answer to the question is yes. Everything affects you. Growing older, getting married, having children...it all comes into play. But the one book of mine where I think it is especially evident is *Strangewood*, which came out nearly ten years ago. I wrote it when my sons were very, very small, and being a father is really what the story is all about. It's still among my favorites of all my novels.

ID: How about horror cinema? What is your opinion of all this money being spent on more remakes, like Friday the 13th *and* The Evil Dead*?*

CG: Perhaps if some of them were actually good, my opinion would be different. I fear that most of what passes for horror coming out of Hollywood studios these days is being made by people who have no understanding of or real interest in horror. Maybe the next wave will be different. I certainly hope so. The remake of *The Fog*, one of my favorites, was literally one of the worst movies I have ever seen in my life. The whole thing was a mess, impossible to follow, loaded with mistakes...what a waste.

ID: What's on the horizon for you right now?

CG: I've just finished co-writeriting a TV pilot based on a YA book series of mine for the CW. I'm currently working on a new draft of the screenplay for *Baltimore* for New Regency, and I've just wrapped up work on my longest novel ever, a big fat thriller called *The Ocean Dark*.

Selected Bibliography

Novels

Strangewood (Signet, 1999)
Straight On 'Til Morning (Signet, 2001)
The Ferryman (Signet, 2002)
The Boys Are Back in Town (Bantam, 2004)
Wildwood Road (Bantam, 2005)

THE VEIL
The Myth Hunters (Bantam, 2006)
The Borderkind (Bantam, 2006)
The Lost Ones (Bantam, 2008)

THE SHADOW SAGA
Of Saints and Shadows (Berkley, 1994)
Angel Souls and Devil Hearts (Berkley, 1995)
Of Masques and Martyrs (Ace, 1998)
The Gathering Dark (Berkley, 2003)

THE MENAGERIE
The Nimble Man [w/Tom Sniegoski] (Ace, 2004)
The Tears of Furies [w/Tom Sniegoski] (Ace, 2005)
Stones Unturned [w/Tom Sniegoski] (Ace, 2006)
Crashing Paradise [w/Tom Sniegoski] (Ace, 2007)

GHOSTS OF ALBION
Accursed [w/Amber Benson] (Del Rey, 2005)
Witchery [w/Amber Benson] (Del Rey, 2006)

HELLBOY
Hellboy: The Lost Army (Dark Horse, 1997)
Hellboy: The Bones of Giants (Dark Horse, 2001)
Hellboy: The Dragon Pool (Pocket Books, 2007)

BODY OF EVIDENCE
Body Bags (Pocket, 1999)
Thief of Hearts (Pocket, 1999)
Soul Survivor (Pocket, 1999)
Meets the Eye (Pocket, 2000)
Head Games (Pocket, 2000)
Skin Deep [w/Rick Hautala] (Pocket, 2000)
Burning Bones [w/Rick Hautala] (Pocket, 2001)
Brain Trust [w/Rick Hautala] (Pocket, 2001)
Last Breath [w/Rick Hautala] (Pocket, 2004)
Throat Culture [w/Rick Hautala] (Pocket, 2005)

OUTCAST
OutCast: The Un-Magician [w/Tom Sniegoski] (Pocket, 2004)
OutCast: Dragon Secrets [w/Tom Sniegoski] (Pocket, 2004)
OutCast: Ghostfire [w/Tom Sniegoski] (Pocket, 2005)
OutCast: Wurm War [w/Tom Sniegoski] (Pocket, 2005)

PROWLERS
Prowlers (Pocket, 2001)
Laws of Nature (Pocket, 2001)
Predator and Prey (Pocket, 2001)
Wild Things (Pocket, 2002)

BUFFY THE VAMPIRE SLAYER
Halloween Rain [w/Nancy Holder] (Pocket, 1997)
Blooded [w/Nancy Holder] (Pocket 1998)
Child of the Hunt [w/Nancy Holder] (Pocket 1998)
The Gatekeeper, Book One — Out of the Madhouse [w/Nancy Holder] (Pocket 1999)
The Gatekeeper, Book Two — Ghost Roads [w/Nancy Holder] (Pocket 1999)
The Gatekeeper, Book Three — Sons of Entropy [w/Nancy Holder] (Pocket 1999)
Immortal [w/ Nancy Holder] (hardcover, Pocket, 1999)
Sins of the Father (Pocket, 1999)
Spike & Dru: Pretty Maids All in a Row (hardcover, Pocket, 2000)
The Lost Slayer — Parts 1 through 4 (Pocket 2001)
Oz: Into the Wild (Pocket, 2002)
The Wisdom of War (Pocket, 2002)
Monster Island [w/Tom Sniegoski] (hardcover, Pocket, 2003)

Additional Novels for Teens

Beach Blanket Psycho (Bantam YA, 1995)
Bikini (Bantam YA, 1995)
Force Majeure [w/Tom Sniegoski] (Pocket, 2002)
Poison Ink (Delacorte, 2008)
Soulless (MTV Books, 2008)

Other Media Tie-ins

X-Men: Mutant Empire-Siege
X-Men: Mutant Empire-Sanctuary
X-Men: Mutant Empire-Salvation
X-Men: Codename Wolverine
Daredevil: Predator's Smile
Battlestar Galactica: Armageddon
Battlestar Galactica: Warhawk
Gen13: Netherwar [w/Jeff Mariotte]
Justice League: Exterminators

Non-Fiction

Cut!: Horror Writers on Horror Film (Berkley, editor, 1992)
The Watcher's Guide: The Official Buffy the Vampire Slayer Companion [w/Nancy Holder] (Pocket 1998)
The Sunnydale High Yearbook [w/Nancy Holder] (Pocket, 1999)
Buffy the Vampire Slayer: The Monster Book [w/Stephen R. Bissette and Tom Sniegoski] (Pocket, 2000)
The Stephen King Universe [w/Stanley Wiater and Hank Wager] (Renaissance, 2001)

As Editor

Hellboy: Odd Jobs (Dark Horse, 1999)
Hellboy: Odder Jobs (Dark Horse, 2004)

Video Game Scripts

Buffy the Vampire Slayer [w/Tom Sniegoski] (Fox Interactive/Electronic Arts, 2002)
Buffy the Vampire Slayer: Chaos Bleeds [w/Tom Sniegoski] (Fox Interactive, 2003)

Jim O'Rear

Jim O'Rear has been involved in the entertainment industry for over twenty five years, beginning his career on tour as The Youngest Professional Magician with David Copperfield, Harry Blackstone Jr., and The Great Tomsoni and opening for acts like Cheap Trick and John Anderson.

With his "magical" background and having been trained in New York at The American Academy of Dramatic Arts, it was only natural that Jim move into the realm of film, television, and theatre, where he has worked steadily as an actor, stuntman, and special make-up effects artist on such projects as Day of the Dead, Star Trek IV, The Vampire Wars, Lethal Weapon 3, Creature Feature, Hayride Slaughter, Cop & ½, Psycho Beach Party, Evita, Little Shop of Horrors, No Retreat No Surrender 3, Mortal Kombat: Conquest, *and many more with actors including Martin Sheen, Burt Reynolds, Mel Gibson, Amanda Plummer, Maximilian Schell, Robert Englund, Jon Voight, Chris Sarandon, and others.*

ID: I really appreciate you taking the time to do this, Jim, and I'm sure Uncle Forry would have been happy about it, too. Been keeping busy as usual?

JO: Of course! Gotta stay busy...it keeps me from getting into trouble!

ID: A man with your background was surely a fan of the '60s and '70s pop culture. Were you a fan of Famous Monsters Magazine*?*

JO: I LOVED *Famous Monsters*...everything about it: the Basil Gogos cover art, the silly humor, the great film photos, and, of course, all the crazy ads in the back. I still remember going to the newsstand to pick up each new issue as it was released. Forry's love for the genre really shinned through in that publication.

As a side note: I was the creator, publisher, and editor of a horror magazine, myself, for five years (quite some time ago), and was honored when Forry became a subscriber to my publication. It's strange how things come full-circle in life, sometimes.

ID: Yes, very strange — but nice — indeed. You know, I recently heard a rumor that you were once "immortalized" as a comic book character. What was that all about?

JO: I was...very briefly...in Marvel Comics. It was MANY years ago, though. It's funny you should ask because it all ties back to the magazine I created and was just discussing with you. The magazine also focused on comic books and my crew and I would often appear at conventions to interview guests for the magazine as well as for the companion television show that mirrored the publication. During that time I became friends with several comic book artists and writers. Well, one of them decided to make me a character in the current issue they were writing and drawing...it was me and Thor. So, I can officially say that I was a Marvel comic book character alongside Thor in one issue.

ID: I think it is great to see a man of your obvious talents having been cast in films with (so-called) big names like Jon Voight and Mel Gibson. It lets Hollywood producers get a bird's eye view of what kind of talent lies within the indie film industry. What was it like working with Jon Voight, for example?

JO: Jon Voight is great. Very focused and into his craft when he is on set. Most everyone I've worked with have been a joy to be around, especially Martin Sheen, Henry Winkler, Robert Englund, Andrew Divoff, Chris Sarandon, and Ron Howard. They were some of my favorites. Very genuine people who love what they do.

ID: I see you have been busy selling your screenplays, too. Horror films, I suppose?

JO: Yep...horror films. They say "write what you know," and I happen to know horror. I'm about to branch out, though. I've been hired to write a romantic comedy later this year. I look at this opportunity as exciting, challenging, and terrifying all at the same time because I haven't written anything like that before. Keep your fingers crossed that it doesn't suck! Ha ha ha!

ID: Already crossed them. Speaking of horror films, tell me about your film with Kane "Jason" Hodder, Old Habits Die Hard. *Kane looks as though he could be pretty "menacing" on the set. (laughs).*

JO: Old Habits is a crazy, fun, dark horror comedy about a family of morticians who kill people in order to increase revenue for their funeral business. The family structure is very much like *The Devil's Rejects*. Kane and I play brothers, Tricia Cast (Emmy winner from *The Young and the*

Restless) plays our mom, Roger Hewlett (from *Road House, X-Files,* and *Dexter*) plays our cousin, and Stacy Dixon (from *Shudder*) plays our sister.

Kane was fantastic to work with and he is REALLY good in this role. He seems menacing, but don't let that fool ya. He's a big, talented teddy bear. We had a good chemistry on set, naturally falling into the roles of dysfunctional brothers easily: so much so that we ad-libbed a lot of our lines because we were so comfortable with the characters and each other's abilities.

I think horror fans will really like this one.

ID: In my experience, I've found that the actors and actresses who can really creep you out on film are usually some of the nicest, most normal folks otherwise. How about you?

JO: That is very true. I play a lot of creepy characters, myself, and find that you get to release a lot of your creepiness and ugly urges through the character, making you a much more balanced person off-set. That's how it works for me, anyway. But, yes, most of the actors I know that creep people out are some of the nicest and most gentle people you'll ever meet.

ID: Now that you are a contributor to horror magazines — getting into writing in general — do you think you might even conjure up a good piece of horror fiction for us someday?

JO: Actually, my first horror novel was just released. It's currently only available online, as we are testing the waters to see how it is received, but we hope to make it available in stores soon. It's called *Mortuary of Madness* and is very reminiscent of the style of the early *EC* horror comic books. It's a twisted and darkly-humorous story about a mortician who is slowly losing his marbles and slipping over the edge of madness. Amazon is the best place to currently purchase a copy.

ID: What's on the agenda for you right now?

JO: I've got tons of films shooting over the next year, including *Jingle Hell, Beverly Lane, Survival: GMF, Love Don't Let Me Down, Santa Versus The Zombies, Dark Moon,* and *Lesferatu,* just to name a few. I'm also working with *The Hollywood Ghost Hunters* (made up of horror professionals such as myself, Kane Hodder, Chris Carnel, Adam Green, RA Mihailoff, and Rick McCallum) on paranormal investigations...we recently completed the TV pilot for that. You can check out more info on the *Hollywood Ghost Hunters* at www.HollywoodGhostHunters.com. I have another paranormal book being published soon titled *Hollywood's Paranormal Movies.* And, of course, lots of personal appearances at conventions, including Paranormal Scare Fest, Cirque Du Terror, Full Moon Tattoo & Horror Festival, A-Kon, and many more.

ID: Any last words before you leave us?

JO: I just want to thank you for including me in your publication. It's been a pleasure. If anyone wants to check out more details about my upcoming films and appearances they can do so at my website *(www.JimORear.com)*.

Sara Karloff

ID: Good morning, Sara. How was your holiday season?

SK: Hello Dave. Please forgive my very tardy reply to your New Year's Day interview. I am running so very much behind and I'm still reeling from the loss of my beloved husband, Sparky, this summer. Many of the fans knew him. As a matter of fact, Forry knew him also.

ID: My heart-felt wishes go out to you and yours. It's an honor to have you here with us, and to be my first interview of the New Year! First of all, let me ask you what is was like "growing up Karloff"? I've always understood your father was a very nice man, kind, gentle, unlike his on-screen image of all sorts of monsters.

SK: You are absolutely correct when you say my father was a kind and gentle man. He was the complete opposite from the roles he portrayed. He was a soft spoken British gentleman with a lovely sense of humor who loved to garden, was a voracious reader, adored animals, and was passionate about the English game of Cricket. He was very self-effacing and modest and didn't talk about himself or his career unless asked about his work in an interview.

ID: He sounds like a man I would have liked to have met in person. I'm sure Forry Ackerman would have been thrilled to see you here, too. Did you ever get a chance to meet him in person?

SK: Indeed I knew Forry. My two sons, now grown men, knew Forry when they were young boys. They were even featured in an article in *Famous Monsters in Filmland* when we went to visit Forry for the first time at the Acker Mansion. It was a real treat for all of us.

Through the years I don't think there was anyone who did as much as Forry did to introduce new generations to the classic horror genre and to the actors behind the roles. He did so much to perpetuate the legacies of these men. My family owes him a great debt of gratitude.

ID: Believe me, A LOT of people out there owe Forry a great deal of gratitude. Tell me, what was it like growing up in the '30s and '40s in L.A.? I've only seen old black and white photos and heard stories, but it was enough to give me the impression it would have been a somewhat magical time within the film industry.

SK: Although I left Southern California when I was seven years old, the area was absolutely magical both to live in and to visit. Hollywood, of course, had its own mystic, but the weather, the architecture, the palm trees, the wide streets, the fancy cars, the beaches all made Southern California a heavenly place.

ID: You are very pretty, and carry an air of class about you as well. Had the thought of getting into acting ever crossed your mind?

SK: I thank you for the compliment, but acting was not on my list of desires.

When my father was appearing on stage in *Peter Pan* in Chicago, he arranged for me to visit him for a week and for me to see the play from backstage, from the wings, from the front row, from just about anywhere. When my visit was just about over, he said, "I can tell you will never be an actress. You just don't have the 'fire in your belly.' You paid more attention to Nana the dog on stage than you did to me." He was right, of course: I never did want to be an actress. And of course, he cast a pretty big shadow!

ID: He did indeed. Did you spend time with your father on the set of his films?

SK: I did have the chance to visit my father while she was on stage, making films and doing TV. Each time it was incredible. I also was able to take my two sons to a couple of TV sets on which my father was working.

My favorite set was *A Comedy of Terrors*. Those old men were having such a good time spoofing their boogey men images and pulling practical jokes on one another driving the Director crazy.

ID: I bet! Did you ever get the chance to meet any of your father's co-stars, like Bela Lugosi or Lon Chaney?

SK: Although I never had the pleasure of meeting Bela Sr. or Lon Chaney Sr. or Jr., Bela Jr. and Ron Chaney are good friends of mine.

I did know Vincent Price, and he reminded one time when I was an adult that he used to carry me around on his shoulders when I was a child. I met Basil Rathbone and Peter Lorre on the set of *A Comedy of Terrors*.

ID: Just out of curiosity — not to be intrusive SK: why did your father change his legal name?

SK: My father said that he felt the name Pratt would not be a particularly fortunate name up on a marquee, perhaps due to the term pratfalls. He never did take the name Boris Karloff legally however. It was an AKA. He signed all legal documents William Henry Pratt AKA Boris Karloff. However, on my Birth Certificate, my legal name is Sara Jane Karloff Pratt which actually makes me the only legal Karloff. That and $3.00 will maybe buy you a Starbucks!

ID: Tell me about Karloff Enterprises. It sounds very interesting.

SK: In 1993 at the *Famous Monsters of Filmland* Convention I met Bela Jr. and Ron Chaney and Dwight Frye Jr. all for the first time. It was at that time I learned about the enormous fan base for my father and also I learned about the laws which protect the persona rights of deceased celebrities. It was not long after that that I decided I should form a company the purpose of which would be to protect and perpetuate my father's legacy. Protect it from the misuse mainly by the studios and perpetuate it through the availability of appropriate products for the fans.

In the last 16 or so years I have worked with the US Post Office, Madame Tussaud's, The Screen Actors Guild, but most importantly, with my father's fans. That's been the most fun of all.

ID: It all sounds wonderful. What's on the horizon for you right now?

SK: Right now, Dark Horse Comics is about to release Volume 2 of its four-volume set of my father's 1960s 97-issue comic book series *Boris Karloff's Takes of Mystery*. Dark Horse, through their Archival Division, has done the most amazing restoration job of these beautiful comics and now they are once again available for a new generation of fans. They can be purchased from comic book stores, specialty book stores, Amazon.com and from my website's gift store www.karloff.com, where both Volume 1 and 2 will be available for $49.95 plus shipping.

ID: Wonderful! Any last words before you leave us?

SK: I want to thank my father's fans for their continued support of his legacy. I always enjoy hearing from them and meeting them at the conventions I attend. They always treat my father's memory with the utmost respect for which my family is most grateful.

ID: You are very welcome, and thank you — and your Father — as well.

Iron Dave
Interviewed by Roberta Lannes

Roberta Lannes sold her first story, "Lorraine," to Stone River Review *in 1966. Her high school creative writing teacher, Marjorie Bruce, encouraged Roberta to write towards publishing as well as to find her personal voice.*

Ms. Bruce mailed Roberta's story to fiction magazines, along with other stories by her classmates, and that brought about the sale of the story. Roberta believes that without Ms. Bruce's encouragement and belief in her ability, she might never have gone on to publish. The power of a good teacher is equal to that of a good parent, so it inspired Roberta not only to write, but to go on to teach as well.

From 1983 to 1990, Roberta attended extension writing courses at UCLA, where she received experience and gained insight into her strengths as a writer. An assignment in her class on Horror Writing with teacher Dennis Etchison (a master short story writer in the genre) caught the attention of Etchison, who bought the story "Goodbye, Dark Love" for his award-winning anthology Cutting Edge. *With his encouragement and backing, she was able to meet and establish relationships with authors, publishers and editors in the field, two of whom remain her friends and most supportive editors, American Ellen Datlow, and Brit Stephen Jones.*

With Cutting Edge *published in eleven languages, Roberta's work began to build a fan base in Italy, France, Japan, The Netherlands (where filmmaker Ian Kerkhof created* Ten Monologues from the Lives of the Serial Killers *using her work), and especially the United Kingdom. Her strong sci fi, dark fantasy, and horror fiction is disturbing, yet it is considered to be powerful and effective storytelling by reviewers and fans alike.*

She was approached by Silver Salamander Press in 1995 to publish a collection of her short stories. John Pelan, a fan and publisher/writer, edited the collection which can be found in specialty bookstores, and even though it is now out of print, it can also still be found on Amazon.com and other internet vendors.

Her stories approach the darkest of thoughts, passions and behaviors with vivid descriptions and convincing detail from a remarkable imagination. People who meet her after reading her work are surprised to find a personable, happy and normal person — nothing like expected, judged from her deliciously dark writing. She asks her readers to relinquish their safe worlds and immerse themselves in the worlds of disturbed thinkers and brutal monsters. Extensive research into some of the darkest macabre and deviant minds has given Roberta fodder for the most chilling of tales.

When asked how such a 'nice person' could write such dark and disturbing fiction, Roberta has said, "I'm fascinated by things that are not in my reality and I believe others are fascinated, too. I don't want to live in the dark realms, in futuristic sci fi worlds, but I enjoy visiting from the safety of my armchair, and I hope many readers do, as well. I write from my research, meetings with some of the most discomforting, creepy people, and those who treat them. In understanding these people, their needs and perceptions, and how they got there, I can be their voices in the same way an actor might portray them. It doesn't change that I'm a good person. In fact, it fuels my desire to fill my life with sane, sweet, and loving friends. At the end of the day, I want to come home to my wonderful husband and have good times with my friends. I guess that makes me an enigma."

Though she continues to publish in the sci fi, dark fantasy and horror genres, she writes mystery, poetry and articles as well.

RL: Hello, David. It's my pleasure to know you, call you friend, and now learn more about you. I've got a load of questions, so I hope you're ready!

ID: The feeling is mutual, and I'm as ready as I'll ever be, babe. Shoot.

RL: Can you remember the moment in your youth when you realized you loved horror? What, in hindsight, was the evolution of your fascination?

ID: Well, I first realized my fascination with the horror genre when I was about eight years old. My third grade teacher, Betty White, was holding a "scary story contest" for Halloween that year, and the first prize was a HUGE bag of Halloween candy. So naturally, I wrote up a story for the contest. It was called "Bats," and was about two vampire bats who were my secret friends, and would take up for me when one of my classmates would pick on me. I was a bookworm, you see, and at my grade school, the bookworms were marked for death by the local bully. The story was, in all honesty, a "creative outlet" for my childhood fears.

Anyway, in the story, the bully was picking on me on Halloween night — stole my candy — and I summoned my two bats to gobble him up. It was the winner of the contest, and my mother was mortified when she read it. But, I won the candy, and one of the little girls in my class had a crush on me, so all was well!

In later years, it was the old Hammer films, and old comic books like *Tales from the Crypt* that got me interested in the horror genre again, and I still enjoy it to this day.

RL: Ahhh, the power of sugar and female s...So you were a bookworm when you were young. What were your favorite books and authors growing up? What turned you off? And how did the good and bad stuff influence your tastes?

ID: I was not only a bookworm, but an avid reader of fiction as well. My main study subjects in school had been spelling, English, and creative writing, so it was just natural to be drawn to reading and writing fiction. I read Poe and Lovecraft in grade school, and went on to read the masters like Stephen King and Clive Barker later on. To me, these men were true visionaries in the horror genre, and although I knew my own writing would never hold a candle to theirs, I still wanted to use their influence to keep my inspiration going, hang in there when times were tough. I must have received around 100 rejection slips before making my first sale, a story called "Dead Birds" about a little boy who lived in a small farmhouse with his grandmother, and after she died, he'd kill birds and shove the bird guts down her throat to keep her "fresh."

It was a mortifying tale, and had to be "toned down," before the magazine would even publish it. The magazine is defunct, now. *What a bitch.*

Least liked writers? Hmm...well, I can't honestly say that there any writers I actually *dislike*, but there were certain "styles" of fiction I didn't care much for: really GRAPHIC Splatterpunk, the subgenre of sci-fi/horror, and, most of all, zombie fiction. To me, there isn't much scary about drooling, staggering, mindless, smelly, flesh-eating sub-human waste walking around gobbling up people's guts. It isn't scary — it's stupid. I'll have to admit I have seen some zombie movies I found amusing, but that's as far as it goes. It seems to me that a lot of writers have lost their grasp on what TRUE horror really is, as well as divided it up into so many sub-genres, the reader doesn't know where true horror begins or ends. It's a shame, really. Horror has grown stale, clichéd.

RL: So define TRUE horror for us. I once heard a horror author describe his genre as having "one true purpose — disturbing the reader."

ID: Now first of all, don't take the term "true horror" the wrong way. I am not suggesting that a lot of the popular horror writers have not put out some really good fiction, because it wouldn't be true. What I meant by "true horror" was the fact that I believe that writers like Poe, Lovecraft, and Stoker were the true "pioneers" of horror fiction, and I guess in the past, I based my personal opinions on that. No offense intended toward anyone. And sure, if a writer accomplishes what he or she sets out to do with their work, then more power to them. That's what all writers of horror set out to do, I think: to achieve the desired effect they set out to achieve with their fans.

RL: What about film? Have you always loved horror movies or did you find yourself
attracted to other noir sorts of movies?
ID: Hmm...well, I am a big fan of the '80s slashers. Now, mind you, a lot of those films were pretty much the same-old-same-old, too, but, it was something NEW, and it spawned a lot of the horror film icons that are still popular today. Case in point: the character of "Pinhead" from the *Hellraiser* films by Clive Barker — to me, he is the epitome of the true horror film icon, the personification of horror. As far as noir films, it depends on what you mean by "noir." Nowadays, there are a lot of noir films around, and that term has been divided into sub-genres, too. Horror-noir, scifi noir, and so on. Personally, I like the "crime noir," or "dark noir" types of films, like the Coen Brothers' 1984 film, *Blood Simple*, or Sam Raimi's *A Simple Plan*. Noir films actually began a long time ago, in old Hollywood films that showcased popular characters like Mike Hammer and Mickey Spillane. Films like *The Maltese Falcon*. It seems there are no longer any "true noir" films around, either. Another dirty shame.

RL: When you were all grown up (if you consider yourself at all grown up — wink,
wink), which authors, filmmakers, directors, actors became inspirational? How?
ID: Well, I consider myself about as grown up as I am ever going to get, I guess. At 50, it's hard to act young and toss caution to the wind, unless you want to have a stroke. My main worries at being "grown up" are high blood pressure, hemorrhoids, and the rising cost of cigarettes. Don't get me started, please.

RL: That's a whole other interview!

ID: Back to the subject at hand — I'll start with fiction, first. Inspirational? I'd say King and Barker are still on my top ten list, along with my buddies Joe R. Lansdale, Chet Williamson, and YOU, of course. Your story "Goodbye, Dark Love," from the first *Splatterpunks* book has always remained one of my favorites, and it even inspired me to write a story of my own about "a woman scorned," entitled "The First Cut Is the Deepest." I have only *dreamed* of being in the same class as you, as far as writing ability, but we are now friends, so that is something much more valuable than any story or book. (wink-wink).

RL: Back at you!
ID: Here's my list then...

Filmmakers/directors:
John Carpenter — director of *Halloween*
Ridley Scott — director of *Alien, Hannibal*
The Coen Brothers — directors of *Blood Simple, No Country for Old Men*
Just to name a few.
Actors/actresses? Okey dokey. The ladies:
Pauley Perrette — star of *NCIS* — she is absolutely ADORABLE.
Emily Proctor — star of CSI Miami — tough, yet fair and sweet. And a beautiful smile.
The guys:
David Caruso — *CSI Miami* — tough, hard-nosed, bad-ass, yet good hearted, and loves children.
Mark Harmon — star of *NCIS* — same as David Caruso in character traits.
Just to name a couple.
And how did these people inspire me? It's simple: they have all had to overcome personal tragedy and tough obstacles in their life, yet have managed to keep a sense of grace, integrity, and style, and are very underrated, in my opinion. People that work within the horror genre aren't the only ones with talent, you know. Enough said.

RL: Have you met any of these people? How?
ID: None of them, unfortunately, except for Pinhead himself, Doug Bradley. In person, he is very polite, intelligent, and caring person. Very sociable, too. He stood with me outside the auditorium where he was speaking for about an hour, just talking and smoking cigarettes. He was really nice.

RL: Pinhead. Very cool. How did NVH come into existence? Did you see a need that wanted filling or was it something you felt a burning desire to create?

ID: Well, it went live on the 'net back in December 2007 on the premise we were going to showcase new writers, ones who hadn't had any luck submitting to more "upscale" horror mags. I felt it would be a good venue for the unknown writers of horror to show just how much recognition they really deserved for their writing. Believe me: I have pulled books off the local library shelves that wouldn't even hold a candle to some of these unknowns. I thought that was a shame, so I decided to do something about it.

It was a success until about two or three months ago, when the combination of the crushing economy and general lack of interest by my readers led me to close it down. I have now opened NVF Films, a small indie film company that promotes indie filmmakers, and I have three films in the works right now that I am acting as producer on. Things are looking up a tad bit now, and maybe 2010 will be better. Keep your fingers crossed.

RL: Note — fingers crossed! Only good things should come to you. If your friends were asked "What's David Byron like? What drives him?" what do you think they would say?

ID: Hmm...well, it might just be more than a tad bit scary to hear what some of them have to say. Any time you have done a lot of "social networking," like I have, you can make enemies whether you've done anything to warrant ill feelings or not. Overall, though, I have made some really good friends, and one of them recently referred to me as "the hardest working 'unknown' man in horror," which was flattering, but came at a time when I had decided to explore other genres in fiction and film. Go figure, huh? (Laughs).

RL: It's great to get the compliments when you're riding the wave, instead of on the beach. I know what you mean. Would you say you've had to face adversities in your life that have taken you off your course? How have these events or experiences affected your work?

ID: I've had plenty, but NONE of them have accomplished detouring me for very long. The deaths of friends or family, personal health issues, financial problems, nothing out of the normal context, no. But I was raised to believe in myself, and stick to my guns, and that's what I've always done. Sometimes it isn't easy, but it is necessary to survive life's curveballs. I'm a tough old fart!

RL: When you look to the future, say five years from now, ten, twenty, what would you like your life to look like? What would be your most important accomplishments?

ID: Hmm...got plenty of coffee and cigarettes handy? (Laughs) Well, if I am still alive then, I'd like to picture myself having become a success at what I've worked so hard to achieve, and if not, then so be it. At least I can say I gave it my best shot, made a lot of good friends, and produced a lot of enjoyable books and films.

My most important accomplishment? Remaining who I am now. It has served me well so far.

RL: Being true to yourself is tough, so that is a huge accomplishment! Do you have any regrets (that you want the public to know)?

ID: A lot of them really, but none worth mentioning here. I tend to keep my private regrets private, unless you want them plastered all over the internet.

RL: (Warm smile) Then tell me what makes you laugh? Makes you choke up? Pisses you off?

ID: My sense of humor is very broad, so it would really depend on what I was reading or watching. I like older comedies, films like *Some Like It Hot* with Jack Lemmon and Tony Curtis, and newer ones like *The Game Plan* with The Rock. It just depends.

Reading comedy? Believe it or not, some of the stories in the *Splatterpunks* book series cracked me up. I don't know why, but they did. There was a story in the first one (the one you were in) called "Reunion Moon," about a 350-pound ex-football player named "Bubba," who had been constipated for a week, and had to enlist the help of a witch doctor to help him poop. It was a riot.

Chokes me up? Hmm...sad movies...my cat's litter box...people who don't bathe regularly. (Roberta laughs here)

What pisses me off? Don't get me started; we will be here all day. But here's one example: folks who think they poop rose petals and pee champagne, never perspire, and always look immaculate. They can't be as perfect as they claim to be, and I intend to launch an investigation into this phenomenon soon.

RL: HA! And here I thought all my attempts to appear perfect had fooled you! Lastly, what future projects should we be looking to see coming up?

ID: Funny you should ask! There are a bunch! Here is a list.

Books:

Darc Karnivale / a collection of short horror fiction / due for release December 18, 2009

Deadly Dolls / a collection of short horror fiction writen by an all-female lineup / available now

Hot & Horrifying: The 1st ladies Of horror / due out in Spring of 2010 (interviews with women in horror films)

The Indie Filmmakers Handbook / due out in Summer 2010 (interviews with filmmakers)

Horror Prodigies & Legends / due out in January 2010/(a collection of interviews with established and up-and-coming writers of horror fiction)

Films:

Horror Prodigies & Legends / a documentary film featuring horror writers

The Good Bad Guys / a film documentary featuring "bad guys" in crime and action films

Hot & Horrifying / a film documentary featuring women in horror films
Whew! That's about it for now.

RL: Well, no one could call you a slacker. Wow! You're a one man corporation. I'm impressed. May all your projects bring you all you're looking for, my friend. Thanks for this — it was fun!

ID: Thanks for having me, and you take care and be well! HUGS!

Roberta Lannes.

John Everson

John Everson is the Bram Stoker Award-winning author of the novels Covenant *(Leisure Books, 2008) and* Sacrifice *(Leisure Books, 2009). Both novels were originally issued as limited edition hard covers by Delirium Books. A Polish translation of* Covenant *was also issued by Poland's Red Horse Books as* Demoniczne Przymierze *in late summer 2007.*

Over the past 15 years, John's short fiction has appeared in more than 50 magazines, including Space & Time, Dark Discoveries *and* Grue, *as well as in a couple dozen anthologies, most recently in* A Dark and Deadly Valley, Cold Flesh, Damned, *and* KolchAK: The Night Stalker Casebook. *His short stories have also been translated and published in Polish and French. A wide selection of his short fiction has been collected in three short story collections:* Needles & Sins *(Necro Books, 2007),* Vigilantes of Love *(Twilight Tales, 2003) and* Cage of Bones & Other Deadly Obsessions *(Delirium Books, 2000).*

"Letting Go," one of the short stories from Needles & Sins, *was nominated for a 2007 Bram Stoker Award and three other short stories from the collection have been included in the Honorable Mention List of the annual* Year's Best Fantasy & Horror Anthology *co-edited by Ellen Datlow.*

John is also the editor of the anthologies Sins of the Sirens *(Dark Arts Books, 2008) and* In Delirium II *(Delirium Books, 2007) and co-editor of the* Spooks! *ghost story anthology (Twilight Tales, 2004). In 2006, he co-founded Dark Arts Books (www.darkartsbooks.com) to produce trade paperback collections spotlighting the cutting edge work of some of the best authors working in short dark fantasy fiction today (they have since produced four anthologies). He is also a digital artist and musician — some of his dark techno songs serve as the soundtrack to the horror fiction CD-ROM anthologies* Bloodtype *and* Carnival/Circus, *and in 2003 he scored Martin Mundt's comedic serial killer stage play* The Jackie Sex-knife Show *in Chicago.*

John shares a deep purple den in Naperville, Illinois with a cockatoo and cockatiel, a disparate collection of fake skulls, twisted skeletal fairies, Alan Clark illustrations and a large stuffed Eeyore. There's also a mounted Chinese fowling spider named Stoker courtesy of fellow horror author Charlee Jacob, an ever-growing shelf of custom mix CDs and an acoustic guitar that he can't really play but that his son likes to hear him beat on anyway. Sometimes his wife is surprised to find him shuffling through more public areas of the house, but it's usually only to brew another cup of coffee. In order to avoid the onerous task of writing, he records pop-rock songs in a hidden home studio, experiments with the insatiable culinary joys of the jalapeno, designs book covers for a variety of small presses, loses hours in expanding an array of gardens and chases frequent excursions into the bizarre visual headspace of '70s euro-horror DVDs with a shot of Makers Mark and a tall glass of Newcastle.

His newest book is The 13th *from Leisure Books.*

For information on his fiction, art and music, visit John Everson: Dark Arts at www.johneverson.com *or MySpace at* www.myspace.com/johneverson.

ID: Good morning, John. How was your New Year holiday?
JE: Too short! I had all these plans to get various projects finished and suddenly...there I was, back at work!

ID: Been there, done that. How's your book The 13th *doing? I've read very favorable reviews so far.*
JE: It will be quite a few months before I get any numbers on how the book is doing sales-wise, but it has garnered quite a few positive reviews from those who like over-the-top horror. A reader on Amazon recently posted this, which definitely made my day:

> "I had so much fun reading this! Women disappearing, occult happenings, twisted minds...what more could you want? It takes an old idea to a whole new level. Everson masterfully keeps the action going, with creepy guys bringing women to a psycho doctor and his beautiful cohort for God-knows-what, and it doesn't get boring for even an instant. Everson really twists the sick cord tight, including horrific scenes I've never read in any other horror novel. Lots of 'Oh, my God!' moments. The doctor's ultimate purpose is where all the action culminates to a thrilling end, but no disappointment, even in the end."

And *Shroud* Magazine's review of the book called it, "Everson's strongest assembly of entertaining characters yet," before adding, "in a tale of blood sacrifice and demonic lust, Everson hits buried, quieter fears: that of hidden darkness in those thought closest. Hitting consistently on subtle terrors such as this is what will continue to carry Everson's career forward."

ID: Sounds great! Hailing from a suburban town in Illinois, did you dream of becoming a successful novelist as a child?
JE: Whether it was via novels or short stories, I did always want to write fiction that would move people in the same way I was moved by stories as a kid. I read constantly growing up, and loved to disappear into the worlds that authors created for me. I always wanted to somehow "give that back."

ID: And give it back you did, indeed. You strike me as the type to have enjoyed the pop culture of the '60s and '70s. Were you a fan of Forry Ackerman's Famous Monsters *magazine?*
JE: I loved *Famous Monsters* as well as the culture it covered. Horror was really kind of frowned upon in my house growing up, so the sneak peeks of the classic movie monsters that I saw in *Famous Monsters* and other zines like *Starlog* and *Fangoria* when I was a kid were like a glimpse at a wonderful hidden world.

ID: I've always wanted to ask you this, so now is as good a time as any: what exactly was the inspiration for your story "Pumpkin Head"? It had me mortified, but in a good way, of course (laughs).
JE: "Pumpkin Head" was one of those "where did THAT come from" inspirations. I was at work one day and something had made me think of how crazy it is that some guys actually try to masturbate using a hole in a tree trunk (maybe someone had made a joke about it or something, I don't recall.) That got me thinking about what might be a less...abrasive... vegetative "aid" and suddenly I had the first scene of "Pumpkin Head" in mind — a juvenile boy's masturbatory dare. Events devolve from there, as they will in a horror story!

I wrote most of that piece over the course of my lunch hour that day, and it has since gone on to be printed in *Grue* Magazine, *Delirium* Magazine, translated into French and collected in two of my short story collections.

ID: I can see why. You've been publishing short fiction for more than fifteen years now. Did you ever get any rejection slips for a story you thought was a sure-fire sale?
JE: Hundreds! When I was really actively submitting short fiction in the '90s and even well into the 2000's, I used to track my "average" rejection rate per story sent out. I think it generally took me six or seven rejections

on average before a story found a home — which, of course, meant some pieces that I really loved actually got shot down 10 or 12 times while others found their mark in one or two tries. But I'd say most of my stories that have appeared in magazines were rejected by an editor somewhere at least once. That's just the nature of the business — stories are very subjective, and up against lots of competition for every publication slot. So you have to find the right editor at the right time. Persistence counts as much as luck and a way with words!

ID: Tell me about your Bram Stoker award! How did that feel? Dumb question, huh?
JE: It was amazing, and totally unexpected. I went out to Burbank, CA, to attend the ceremony in the summer of 2005 not because I thought I would win, but because I thought, "hell, I may never be nominated for one of these again, and it would be a great opportunity to meet people." So when they announced the "First Novel" category was a tie, my stomach flip-flopped because suddenly I went from having a 1 in 4 chance of winning to a 50/50 chance! All I can say now is that if I'd ever believed that I was going to win and get up at the podium and be videotaped giving an impromptu speech, I would have worn a suit jacket!

ID: Here's one just for fun: if you could be any of your favorite monsters, which one would it be?
JE: I'd be a vampire. They live forever; they don't decompose; they seem to all be rich with big creepy mansions, and they get lots of girls!

ID: Hell — that makes ME want to be a vampire! Allow me to dig into your "psyche" a little more: what's your favorite horror film? How about book?
JE: Alien is probably my favorite horror film, because it combines the best things about my two favorite genres, horror and science fiction. It's a nightmarishly claustrophobic film, includes great characters and suspense and of course, in space, no one can hear you scream!

Book-wise, growing up, I was a big fan of the original *Dracula*, which I read two or three times. In modern horror, my favorites are Stephen King's *Pet Sematary* and *The Stand,* Clive Barker's *The Damnation Game* and *Great and Secret Show,* and Edward Lee's *Incubi* and *Slither.*

ID: If you could have said one last thing to Forry Ackerman before his death, what would it have been?
JE: Thanks for keeping the monsters alive for us.

ID: What's on the horizon for you right now?
JE: My fourth novel *Siren* is coming out this summer, which I'm really excited about. I'm really proud of this book, which delves into the dark places of desire and obsession...and water. And I've just signed on with Leisure Books to write my fifth novel, *The Pumpkin Man,* which is what I'll be working on over the next several months.

ID: Any last words before you go?
JE: Uncle Forry, we miss you! R.I.P.

The Amazing Kreskin

For over four decades, The Amazing Kreskin has dramatized the unusual power of the human mind with a rare combination of wit and showmanship. His very name has become an integral part of pop culture invoked in comedy clubs, comic strips, print stories and TV shows from sitcoms to national magazines. Kreskin, who has performed for the likes of royalty and Presidential families, has also made well over 500 television appearances in addition to those as host of his own highly rated series and specials. Ever-earning his status as "the world's foremost mentalist," Kreskin offers $50,000 to anyone who can prove he employs paid assistants or confederates during any of his performances. On stage and television, Kreskin seeks to reveal the thoughts of audience members, plant suggestions in fully aware subjects and dazzle with feats of extraordinary mental projections. As one of the highlights of his stage show, he regularly asks to have his check hidden anywhere in the premises. If he fails to find it, he will forfeit his fee.

Kreskin dismisses any association with the occult and labels like psychic and medium. "I am not a mind reader, because that implies I can totally penetrate the process of the human brain," he explains. "On many occasions I can perceive a single thought or a series of simple thoughts if the subjects are tuned to me and willing to open their imaginations to receive or project. I am totally helpless if they refuse."

Kreskin maintains that this silent communication is within the capability of many people, once trained and self-sensitized. "Basically, I apply the power of positive thinking which may be mankind's ultimate tool."

Kreskin's name and face have gained a household recognition from over 500 appearances on national television including 118 episodes of the Mike Douglas Show, *98 installments of* The Merv Griffin Show *and a record 88* Tonight Show *stints. Legend has it that Johnny Carson, who saw Kreskin trip and fall during his first appearance on* The Steve Allen Show, *modeled his own clumsy-yet adept Carnac the Magnificent after the mentalist. In addition, Kreskin's recent guest spots include* The Late Show with David Letterman, *MTV, Live with Regis and Kathie Lee, The Howard Stern Show, Larry*

King Live *and* CNN Morning News. *Kreskin astonished viewers of* Lifestyles of the Rich and Famous *by finding Robin Leach hidden somewhere in New York City. In 1997, Kreskin amazed not only the Academy of Motion Pictures Arts and Sciences, but also the entire world, when he successfully predicted the top 9 categories of the Academy Awards the day before on* CNN Morning News.

In 1977, the legendary magazine, Famous Monsters of Filmland, *devoted two lengthy cover stories to Kreskin's analysis of the use of hypnotism in movies. Recently, Stephen King re-wrote his classic novel for television,* The Shining, *where he renamed the boy as "Little Kreskin."*

Kreskin especially enjoys working Halloween. In 1997, Kreskin conducted a séance on The Howard Stern Show. *The appearance (lasting over two hours) included flying tables and over 30 completely bewildered fans who participated in-studio. Howard Stern summed it up best when he said, "This is the most amazing thing I've ever seen!"*

The mentalist has dazzled millions of international viewers each week for years with his television series The Amazing World of Kreskin *and starring in* Kreskin's Quest, *a series of internationally syndicated specials. In 1997, Kreskin brought Sprint's latest campaign to millions of consumers as the spokesperson for the "Amazing Dime Find." This promotion took place throughout the United States and garnered media appearances the world beginning with an appearance on NBC's* Today Show. *Kreskin has appeared in several commercials this past year for Wendy's Restaurants. He also headlined the premier promotion of the Burnet Swiss Watch Company.*

Kreskin, who has always enjoyed the challenge of a casino (those of which he is allowed to enter), made two incredible appearances in Atlantic City in the summer of 1997. First, he appeared in front of Trump Plaza on the hottest day of the summer and caused crowds to shiver, shake and run for blankets. Kreskin proved that your "Mind Could Beat the Heat" and The Philadelphia Inquirer *was on hand to document that participants' hands were cold and shaking. Later in the fall, Kreskin broke his own personal record by winning 21 straight hands of blackjack at Resorts Casino. The casino spokesperson said, "It's one thing for casinos to deal with card counters, but handling Kreskin is something else. There's not much we can do about ESP, if you got it, you got it." Kreskin's unparalleled contribution to the study of parapsychology has made him the subject of articles in numerous scientific journals and magazines, along with earning him an honorary Doctorate of Letters from Seton Hall University, where he majored in psychology. Among thousands of volumes in his personal library on the subject of parapsychology (reportedly the largest private collection in the world) are eight books by Kreskin himself.*

Kreskin's books include The Amazing World of Kreskin *(Random House), Kreskin's Mind Power Book (McGraw-Hill), Fun Ways to Mind Expansion (Doubleday), Secrets of the Amazing Kreskin (Prometheus), How to Be a Fake Kreskin (St. Martin's Press) and Kreskin's Secrets, a privately published mail-order tome which has sold nearly 500,000 copies. Kreskin credits the childhood influences of Mandrake the Magician comic books, radio/television pioneer Arthur Godfrey and magnetic televangelist Bishop Sheen for the direction of his career.*

Born in Montclair, New Jersey, Kreskin was fully fascinated with magic by age five, after which he began to perform for the neighborhood children. To this day, Kreskin often warms up an audience with a deft display of sleight-of-hand as a preparation for the thought reading to come. He enjoys defying the eye and admits, "The ESP factor needs a solid mental foundation to be successful. Once the audience members become mystified, they are more susceptible to suggestion."

The roots of Kreskin's abilities can be traced to a simple childhood game. While trying to find a hidden object based on the verbal hints of "hot" and "cold," he discovered he could locate the object without the verbal communication if the person who hid it concentrated on its location. From this and other exercises, Kreskin gradually developed a telepathic-like sensitivity. At age eleven, he developed an uncanny determination beyond his years when he received permission to study the entire psychology section of his local library. Soon Kreskin began to perform professionally, billed as "The World's Youngest Hypnotist." From his early experiments, Kreskin developed a theory into his special talent: "In most cases the phenomenon of thought transference can be explained as a kind of hyper-aesthesia — an almost unconscious raising of the threshold of one's senses to a degree far exceeding one's everyday feelings."

With a hectic schedule of ever 300 appearances a year worldwide, Kreskin is constantly challenging the impossible with amazing results. The Sally Jessy Raphael Thanksgiving Day Show once featured Kreskin discussing "How to Pick Lottery Numbers." His performance offered amazing discussions over Thanksgiving dinner throughout the world. Music has also served as an effective medium for the mentalist who made his professional debut as a pianist at Carnegie Hall with Skitch Henderson and the New York City Pops, subsequently soloing as a guest artist with the symphonies throughout the U.S. and Canada. During one performance with the Hamilton Philharmonic in Ontario, thirty people slumped over in their chairs onstage as Kreskin played Brahms' Lullaby. *At a seance in Nashville, Kreskin played* Love Me Tender *on the piano as he summoned the spirit of Elvis Presley — through Kreskin's* extraordinary powers of suggestion, bystanders suddenly began to drop to their knees! Kreskin has also used his unique gifts to make a positive social contribution.

His highly developed skills have led to the discovery of crucial evidence in several major criminal investigations. He has also devoted a great deal of time in and out of the nation's courtrooms questioning the validity of testimony given by hypnotized witnesses and the reliability of hypnosis in general. Kreskin even appeared on the television series Missing Reward to offer $100,000 to any hypnotist, psychologist or psychiatrist who could prove the very existence of a "hypnotic trance" under scientific conditions. To date, no one has collected on this challenge.

ID: Greetings and salutations, kind sir. It is a pleasure to have you with us. How was your Thanksgiving?

AK: Thank you for asking, Dave. My Thanksgiving was a very pleasing one with close members of my family. I hope yours went well.

ID: Thank you for your kind wishes as well. I see you were born in New Jersey. Was that a good venue for someone of your talents?

AK: Certainly New Jersey worked for me as a kid, although I happen to believe that my career would have evolved no matter where I was born, since I really envisioned my entering the field in which I am in by four or five years old. I was given a comic book by one of my visiting relatives in Bethlehem, PA, the Polish side of my family. My Sicilian side lived in NJ, and I was born in Montclair, NJ. While visiting, one of my earliest first memories was of a fellow, probably a teenager, giving me a comic book, and one of the cartoon stories in the comic was Mandrake the Magician. He really wasn't a magician in the traditional sense of stage illusions and sleight of hand. He had hypnotic and telepathic abilities and used them to solve crimes. I was immediately enchanted with this character, and since I was taught to read by the time I was 4½ — 5 years old, my mother often supporting and reading to me from comic books, I knew this would be my model.

ID: I've always been curious as to the exact meaning of the term "mentalist." Since the premiere of the TV series of the same name, the interest in the term has become wide-spread, to say the least. What would your definition of the term be?

AK: Regarding the meaning of the term "mentalist", it's interesting because Dr. Margaret Mead never wanted me to call myself a mentalist, she wanted me to call myself a "sensitive," but I used to say to her, this great anthropologist, most people would not know what that meant. A term that goes back to the 18-19th century, individuals in the old world who showed unique mental abilities were often called sensitives, rather than psychics or what have you. In my work, I do not claim supernatural powers, but I do claim to be able to tune in and perceive the thoughts of individuals and influence their thoughts and behavior. The term mentalist as an entertainment term captures it. It defines for me my ability to embrace the thoughts of those who are concentrating and also to dramatically influence their thoughts, usually mentally or by the power of suggestion.

The series *The Mentalist* is a refreshing take on crime solving stories, but of course in that series the character is shown to have been a fake psychic, mentalist, what have you, and now finding a new life and assisting crime investigation is really observing details around him, clay on people's feet, material under people's fingernails, objects lying around the room that could have referred to the murder. In truth, the series *The Mentalist* is a throw-back to the greatest fictional crime solver of all, who also had very little violence in the story, but who has charmed and captured people from all walks of life, including Presidents and statesmen, and that, of course, is Sherlock Holmes. So the new series *The Mentalist* is really a modern-times Sherlock Holmes story, which I think is extremely well done, but really does not refer to my work.

ID: I understand that your powers were evident even as a child. At what age did your unique capabilities of finding hidden objects begin?

AK: Early in my childhood in NJ, I practiced games with friends. When I was in third grade and was 9½ years old or so, I was in a class during which time we were to have outdoor play sessions. However, it was raining, and instead our teacher played a game which then was called Huckle Buckle Beanstalk. A person would leave the classroom, and while out of the room, we hid a beanbag, as I recall it was hidden in someone's desk, and Jane Hamilton, who was the first person to be picked, came in the room and walked around, and we talked around saying you're getting warmer, you're getting colder, depending on how close she came to finding the bean bag. The game is generally known as Hot and Cold. I was infused with intrigue about the game. I wished I had been picked to play it, but I was not once invited to leave the class while the beanbag was hidden. So while I was walking home from school, which was about a mile, I was imbued with playing this game. I met my brother at home, who was three years younger, and we walked over to my grandparents' house, who lived about 10 minutes away. It was an old two-story house built by my grandfather who was a construction worker. He built it with friends, and it still exists today. I invited my brother to go upstairs and hide the penny. My grandparents rented the downstairs in order to make ends meet. He called me, and I went up the wooden steps, walked into the old fashioned kitchen with a giant pot-belly stove. My grandmother was sitting at the kitchen table curious about what was going on. My grandparents did not speak English, but I was very close to them. I meandered into my uncle's bedroom — he was at work — climbed up an old, as I can recall, dark maroon chair, and since I was short, found myself reaching behind a curtain rod on which curtains were hanging, and I felt the penny. I found it, and it suddenly dawned on me that I never told my brother to speak to me. I never told him to talk to me. There was no verbal communication at all. My grandmother, being Italian, probably thought this was the evil eye.

My family became fascinated with this ability, and I started performing at private parties. In 4th and 6th grade, on Fridays for show and tell, my teacher for both years, Miss Galloway, would often have me perform for my fellow students, attempting to read their thoughts. I was already doing private performances for children's parties, but that was as a magician, doing sleight of hand magic and what have you. By the time I was in the 9th grade, I was beginning to use my abilities with the mind, and was already for two years performing as a hypnotist. Indeed, I did a two-hour concert in the 9th grade to raise funds for the school.

Incidentally, regarding the comic book *Mandrake* — a few years ago Lee Falk, who was the author, and is now no longer with us, was invited to a special gathering at Sardi's Restaurant in New York. It was hosted by a large group of university professors and writers, all of whom had researched and were highly knowledgeable in the areas of comics. They were saluting Lee Falk. He had created two major comics in his life, *Mandrake* and *The Phantom*, both which were tremendously successful even overseas, in Australia and in Italy in the Second World War. Mandrake was a tremendously popular comic but Mussolini would not allow the English verbiage, so he had someone in Italy do the writing for the dialogue of the comic, namely the great director Fellini. At that gathering at Sardi's, yours truly was invited to attend, since it had become known that the comic inspired my imagination, and inspired me with drive and ambition. It was one of the great moments of my life when Lee Falk was discussing the evolution of his comic, and then parenthetically said in all the years he'd written it, the person who came closest in actuality, in real life, to the character of Mandrake was...and he turned and nodded to yours truly. Certainly one of the most priceless moments of my life.

The telepathic-like ability increased more and more through the years, but it was the wonderful support of teachers in grade school, junior high, and high school encouraging me that certainly supported and gave confidence in my work. I'm fortunate, I've often said, that I embraced this area in my early life, because by doing so, no one had a chance to teach me that these things couldn't be done. So it started as magic tricks, and then became mind-reading tricks, evolved into an art form today that has carried me all over the world. Indeed, as of February of this year, the airline industry estimates I have flown over three million miles. Last year I did 198 appearances around the world. Just the past few weeks touring Canada, each performance lasted approximately two hours and 30 minutes.

ID: You have also been recognized as "the world's youngest hypnotist." What happened, exactly, that earned you this moniker?
AK: Needless to say, in the evolution of my career, I cannot minimize but instead must accentuate the tremendous early support of people like Steve Allen, who first gave me national attention. In the years I spent with *The Mike Douglas Show*, having done approximately 118 shows with Mike, and of course I could not ignore the appearances with Johnny Carson, some 88 appearances, which some say is a record for personal appearances. Indeed, it was Carson who saw my first national appearance on Steve Allen, for he had been looking in. When I walked out the lights in the 1960s were extremely bright. I turned and walked towards Steve Allen, who was rather tall, about 6'4" in height, and of course he was standing by his desk which was elevated, as all the desks have been since from Carson to Letterman. I was going over to shake hands with him and I tripped over the desk and fell flat on my face. Carson saw that incident and as a result created Carnac, who when he walked out fell over the desk. One of the last shows I did with Johnny, I thanked him for perpetuating my name and imaging even when I wasn't on the show, and he interrupted and said, "Oh, you mean the mighty Carnac!" Television continued to be important to me. Through the years I have done so far 109 shows with Regis, going all the way back to the days of Joey Bishop when Regis was an announcer for the show and Joey Bishop was so fascinated with my work that in the latter years of his show, he made me a regular, often having me on for one week at a time.

ID: I heard an interesting little story about you requesting that your appearance fee be hidden somewhere within the venue, with the understanding that if you could not find it, you would forfeit your fee. Did you ever lose a fee? (No offense intended, of course).

AK: In your inquiry about my fee being hidden, one of the features of my performances in almost all my shows is that my fee, my check for the evening, is turned over to a committee from the audience. Part of that committee escorts me from the theatre, or the nightclub, or the banquet hall, or the private home, as my audiences have varied extensively from 12 people at a private home to banquets of hundreds of people or a few thousand, to state fairs such as Oregon State, numbering some 20,000. But at all of these performances, my check is hidden while I am taken to an area where I cannot see or hear what is going on. When I return, there is no communication verbally with any of the committee, which usually numbers four or five people. The committee is simply admonished to concentrate and focus their attention on where it has been hidden. If I do not find my fee, I do not get paid. Some people ask if I have ever failed. I have nine times, which some would say is not many out of 6,000. It may not be many, but on my first trip to New Zealand at one event, a coliseum, I failed, and a press conference was held the next day. In fact, the money was turned over to a crippled children's hospital, and a wing has since been named after me. The night before I had lost a little over $51,000.

On the plus side, I have found my check in some of the most outrageous locations:

At a university gymnasium, some 2000-3000 students, I ended up pulling a gentleman in a suit to the stage, opened his jacket and found a revolver, and in spite of the insanity of what I'm about to say, turned the barrel of the gun towards me and looked down into the barrel. They had taken tweezers and stuffed the check in the barrel of the gun.

At the University of Illinois, amongst 8000 students and family, I found my way to a gentleman in the audience and had him stand. I asked him to open his mouth. There was no check. I asked if it had to do with the roof of his mouth, and he reached in, took out his upper plates, and handed me the check.

Recently at a private affair in Princeton, NJ, when I returned to the house and walked through the living room where there were some 40 or so people, I ended up in the kitchen, pulling out some of the china, where the check had been quietly placed behind a dish.

Certainly one of the singular incidents of my life was when I walked back into a banquet hall in New York City and some 1500 writers, TV, and radio people suspensefully silently watched. It was a dinner at the Waldorf in honor of Bob Hope, who was sitting on the dais with Walter Cronkite and a few others next to him. As I meandered through the audience, I ended up on the dais. After lifting a dish half a dozen times, which had turkey on it, I was in frustration. Why would I lift the dish when there was no check under the plate, until I realized that somebody was concentrating on a certain action. I took my tuxedo jacket off, and shoved my hand into the stuffing. They had cooked it into the stuffing of the turkey!

As of a few weeks ago during a tour in Canada, one night I ended up in the Orchestra Pit area on my knees, and I was absolutely frustrated to the point of being annoyed. There was no place to hide it. I was kneeling on a flat floor. There wasn't even a carpet that I could lift up. I will never forget that something possessed me to pull on tape, yards upon yards of black tape had covered the floor in place of carpeting, and although I thought this was an extraordinarily damaging thing to do, I thought I could cause the tape to give if I pulled a slight corner and pulled upward. When I did, the check was one foot into the area of taping, and I pulled out the check.

The career of yours truly has been like an adventure, even though I did not dream that Tom Hanks, until he came to me with the script, would release a movie in March of 2009 called *The Great Buck Howard*, and as all the press conferences, interviews, and television discussions have reported the movie climaxes with remarks beautifully made before the credits appear. The character star of the movie, Buck Howard, is based on the work of yours truly. In fact, John Malkovich, who plays me, studied videos of yours truly for days. The key theme of the movie is my check test, and all over the world people recognize it as part of my career, but even though in the movie it is suggested that electronic devices and stooges may be used by the character, at the end of the movie it is made clear that yours truly has never, ever, ever been shown to use electronic devices or employ secret paid assistants in any phase of his work.

With the release of the movie, yours truly released a book which he wrote in 2½ weeks in order to time it with the movie itself. The title of the book is *Kreskin Confidential*, and yours truly reiterates how for years he has offered $50,000 to anyone who can prove he employs paid secret assistants or confederates in any phase of his work. With the release of that movie, that has been dropped. I no longer offer that sum of money...

Instead, I will, to my last day on earth, offer to anyone who can prove that I employ paid secret assistants or confederates or any hidden electronic devices in order to accomplish my mental test the sum of *one million dollars*.

ID: You have helped law enforcement and security personnel as well. Did your services involve helping to solve cold-case crimes?

AK: Regarding my involvement with law enforcement cases, I've never done this to seek publicity, and I'm not suggesting that I'm solving the case, by no means. I'm not solving the case, but helping investigators to gain information, sometimes in the case of potential witnesses who are not aware that they were picking up information, perhaps on an unconscious level, that could be pertinent to the crime. In a case in Reno, Nevada, some years ago, a tragic one in which a girl leaving college was kidnapped and murdered, was without any clues for a sustained amount of time. Through the press, three individuals who were driving by when she was met at her car outside the university, volunteered to participate in some experiments with me, although they could not be certain they saw anything, but they had stopped at a long traffic light which seemed like it was around the time of the kidnapping. The bottom line is, seeing each of them separately with a court artist present, to cause two of them to develop in their mind a detailed image of what could be a suspect. Each of the two seemed to contribute and add to the other's image. That drawing was in the local newspapers for a number of days. Interestingly enough some time later, an individual was apprehended in Los Angeles, a suspect on another murder, and it turns out he fit the description and was the culprit of this crime.

In the past couple of years I've held seminars for law enforcement groups, training and teaching them how to use their own intuition as an aid in investigating crimes. No, I could not teach them to read thoughts. I would be misrepresenting myself and it would not work, as this has been a lifetime evolution. But I feel successful in borrowing what I've done privately through the years with business individuals, and that is training them to gain a second opinion, that is their unconscious mind, on details of a problem or a case that seems to have bogged them down.

ID: Do you have any amusing anecdotes from your career to share with us?
AK: When the *Buck Howard* movie was released, Cindy Adams, the famous New York columnist with the *New York Post,* devoted a column on which she expounded on my abilities and said if anyone thinks this is a gimmick, she became a conduit in a dramatic test years ago. It was when the TV series *Lifestyles of the Rich and Famous* was on the air. After Robin Leach and his people had come to my home, I offered them another segment to the show which they found absolutely intriguing and went through with it. Robin Leach said if it failed, they would leave the test out, but I said no, it would remain in. I've kept the integrity of what I do on stage and otherwise clear to the public, and if something fails, they should see it. It's not a magic act. The bottom line is, I was driven to Tavern on the Green in New York where a number of police cars had gathered, and I was escorted to a limousine, in which Cindy Adams sat. We were never to speak to each

other. I was only to speak to the driver, and tell him where to turn as he drove the car. The challenge was simply I had to find Robin Leach, who was hidden somewhere in the city of New York. It was a bizarre experience. The police later on told me I was driving them crazy. They didn't know where Robin Leach was, but they had to follow me, and there were times I was taking them down one-way streets the wrong way. I finally exited the car with Cindy Adams following me, entered a building, and found my way in an elevator to the top floor. It was a private swim club. I kept standing looking at this large Olympic size swimming pool. Cindy Adams later on told me she didn't know what to do. The camera people kept photographing me throughout the procedure, and couldn't say anything. Finally, after five minutes of staring at the pool, I saw a door at the other end of the pool room and went to that, opened it, and there was a bar, which was not opened yet, it was too early in the morning. People were cleaning glasses. I saw someone leaning across the bar, looking like he was intoxicated, face down on the bar. I went over and touched him on the shoulder, and said I think this is as far as I go. He lifted his head up and said to me, "Let's get out the champagne, you found me: it took you 32 minutes." Incidentally, Cindy Adams brought up the fact that I was standing looking at the swimming pool for about five minutes. He bolted out of his chair and said, "My God, when the crew radioed me and let me know that Kreskin was beginning his search, I thought it would be interesting for him to find me in the pool. I was swimming there for about 20 minutes, then finally I got waterlogged, dried off and got dressed, and here I can vividly remember staring at the pool as if I was supposed to see him in the pool."

Some years ago when the 50th anniversary of Orson Welles' CBS radio broadcast that terrorized part of the nation was coming about, the state of New Jersey approached me and asked if there was something I could contribute in order to celebrate this incident, and I jumped at the opportunity, because I had met Orson Welles and was a tremendous fan of his, and told him that someday I would do this. As we sat in a restaurant in London, he looked at me and said, "Kreskin, let's take my *War of the Worlds* radio show one step beyond." We gathered in the city in the location in New Jersey where in the radio version UFO's were supposed to have landed. That area was picked by one of the writers, getting gas one day driving into the city asked for a map. In those days all the gas stations gave out maps. He pulled out the map of New Jersey, closed his eyes, dropped his finger down, and the location he hit was the location used in the Orson Welles version. You must remember, it was broadcast like a radio news broadcast, and as a result caused thousands upon thousands to panic. When I appeared on a make-shift platform in the middle of nowhere with a grassy knoll around us, there were thousands of people, press, and what have you, and I invited a number of people to come up onstage, some 18 or so volunteers, all ages, teens all the way up to people in their 60's and 70's. I asked them if they'd ever seen a UFO. One or two raised their hands. A couple were uncertain, but most said no. I asked them if they believed in UFOs, and there was generally a weak belief, but no strong conviction except for one or two. I held a handkerchief in my hand, just as was done through the years when there was a firing squad. When the handkerchief was dropped, the guns were fired. The handkerchief was highly symbolic. As I talked to the committee on stage standing three, I dropped the handkerchief. Within a few minutes, a tremendous emotional wave went across the stage. Most of the people on stage started to "see" UFOs in the sky. They started to argue. Some saw them green, some saw them red. It was clear that the crowd standing around the stage, hundreds of people, knee-deep some of them, that these people were excited about seeing something very graphic. You could see fear on some of their faces. Others were screaming, "Look, look!" And then I pointed to the ground and said, "Doesn't it look like some of the UFOs are landing?" At that moment, subjects on stage had to crouch behind each other, because I suggested a door was opening on one of the UFOs, and some being was leaving. Within a few seconds, the attention of everyone turned to an elderly woman on stage, as she quietly walked off the stage and started to walk towards someone. Within seconds, I ran down, broke the spell in their minds that had created this hallucination, but it was clear that she was literally about to grab a gun from the holster of a policeman and fire point blank at this UFO figure that she "saw" coming towards her.

ID: Have you ever met any other famous "mentalists" in person?
AK: This answer is very simple...*No.*

ID: You've been dubbed the "Nostradamus" of the twentieth century. Do you feel that this moniker is befitting of your powers? Hold it in high regard?
AK: I can understand because the word "Nostradamus" has dealt with long-range prophecies, what have you, but I don't really consider myself a prophet. The bottom line is, while I can read thoughts, I do not look into a crystal ball. Some years ago CNN television came to me and said we've had psychics and astrologers on New Year's Day — why don't you make some predictions, and I pointed out to them that I really don't make predictions. But they reminded me of something. At that time I had flown probably some two million miles. They said to me, Kreskin, you travel endlessly around the

world dealing with how people are thinking. You must have some intuitive facts, and I began to reflect that a weatherman predicts the future by looking at present conditions that could project into the future, and I decided to tap into my unconscious intuitiveness, and that was the beginning of what has garnished me coverage all over the world. I predicted twice winners of the Academy Awards, and in one case it was only two hours before the awards were announced that I predicted the top 10 or 12. The following year I predicted the top eight. It was in 2001 on CNN that I had introduced a book called *Kreskin and Friends*, in which I went to 60 famous people and asked them to predict the future of their field, Regis in talk-show television, Seinfeld in comedy, Roger Ailes in television news, judges, etc. While this was being discussed on CNN New Year's morning, the anchorwoman said in the last two pages Kreskin has announced his predictions. That was January 1, 2001. She opened it and the first prediction dealt with war. I said while the public does not realize that we are at war, it is a war of terrorism, and could someday develop into biological warfare, and suddenly I interrupted and said I don't know why I'm saying this, but in September of this year there could be a disaster here in New York involving two airlines. Needless to say after 9/11, I was questioned by scores of authorities as to "what made me make such a statement". I had toured the Middle East for five years, Saudi Arabia, etc., and again as we've been warned through decades and decades is that the only thing we ever learn from history is that we never learn from history. I feel the handwriting is on the wall.

A few years ago in Canada in 2005 there was a liberal already in office who was running again for Prime Minister. One month before the election, I made my prediction, but not wanting to get into politics during the run, I insisted it be sealed, and it was placed in a safe on the evening news of the CTV Network where people saw it every night when the news was introduced and the news anchor referred to the safe as the Kreskin safe. I was flown in the night of the election to observe the results, and the next morning the safe was opened on *AM Canada*, a national show. I predicted that the liberal would win, but would not have a strong support of seats that he needed. I gave a specific number of seats that I thought he would carry, and I received headlines that I predicted the exact number. On that show live, after receiving the acclaim, and the enthusiasm, and credit, I interrupted and said if this government ever collapses, it will be within 14 months, and the individual will never be re-elected for office again. I forgot about this, and coming home from a trip one day I walked into my office and there were some 80 messages on the answering machine, all from reporters in Canada. The government had collapsed. Three parties went against the Prime Minister and his party, and I was only off by five days.

ID: What's on the horizon for you right now?

AK: I am already working on my 18th book, in fact my 18th and 19th book, one of which is dealing with techniques of self-help, and the other — well, I've been asked for years to write extensively my memoirs. The problem is it would be a book hundreds and hundreds of pages, so I'll have to do it piecemeal. As far as a biography, I would have to treat it the way P.T. Barnum did. First of all, if you write a biography and you put it on the market, doesn't that end everything? Obviously it doesn't end, because you are still working after that. So if I write a biography, I will follow in the footsteps of Barnum who added a chapter every year to keep things up to date.

At this point, I am in the development of an infomercial. I've done a number in the past. One of my favorite commercial successes was an Aflac commercial following Yogi Berra, and *Advertising Age* pointed out that the year my commercial appeared was the most recognized commercial for much of the year. It was interesting in the commercial hypnotizing a duck.

With my 75th birthday coming up in January, I've been asked if I ever plan to retire, with the hectic schedule I have. It's hard for anyone to conceive this, having now done in recent months three *Jimmy Fallon Show*s at NBC, the only guest to appear more than once on his show, and in this case three times, and my third show with Mike Huckabee on Fox News will be in January of 2010, and by the time this book is read, who knows how many more times. So the question is do I plan to retire, and my answer is very simple, as I've stated in performances all over the world. Yes, as of November, 2009, I have announced my plans, "I intend to retire ten days after I pass away!"

ID: That's the spirit! Any last words before you leave us?

AK: I would just want to reflect and simply state that my life, as has been told me over and over again by writers, television broadcasters, individuals in every area you can imagine, has been an adventure. It's hard to believe that one person can have this adventure in one lifetime. Through all this, one of the quiet personal satisfactions of my life — and who could have ever dreamt this — was to find my name used endlessly around the world in stories, books, television series, movies. There is one crime show on TV that uses my name every four or five stories, and all dealing with and usually captured in the phrase, "Who do you think I am, *Kreskin*?" It is an honor and a thrill to know that people will recognize the name, even used parenthetically, in a passing phrase.

Count Gregula

Back in 1998 A.D., after his centuries-long slumber, Count Gregula was "exhumed" on Halloween night at a party that was hosted by Rich Koz a.k.a. Svengoolie at The House of Monsters. It was a direct result of that very party which had brought about a certain creative force into the limelight for the subsequent years to come. Count Gregula had a goatee and pastier complexion that night...currently that look has now come to be fondly known as Dear Grandpa Gregula. However, The Count has gone through many different afterlives since then...

The Greg's Munster Fan Club website (http://community-2.webtv.net/GREATBIGG/GREGSMUNSTERFANCLUB/), which debuted in January of 2000 A.D,. was the very first incarnation of Count Gregula on the Internet. That site was dedicated to The Munsters and their fans. Then in 2003, the long awaited arrival of his own domain...CountGregula.com became reality. This new site included not just The Munsters, but also several other of The Count's interests such as Halloween, horror, ghost hunting, celebrities, conventions, Svengoolie, horror hosts and so much more! It was also the year that His Dearest Countess arose back from the fiery depths of Hell to be at his side forevermore.

In the year 2005 A.D., the new and improved Count-Gregula.com was created due to a need for a bigger webspace. As The Count has said himself, "There vill be even MORE photos and other goodies for your surfing displeasure!" Today, the Count and Countess live in the Transylvanian section of Illinois in the disguise of thirty-something mortals Linda and Greg, who spend way too much time watching sitcoms and eating fried chicken. They are currently making their Evil Plans (along with their Children of the Night: Igor, Figor, Shegor and Megor) to bring their special brand of Vampirey Fun to TV viewers in the Midwest as Horror Hosts!

ID: Greetings, Count. How are you this evening? Thirsty, I suppose.

CG: Ghoul Evening, Dave! I am alvays out for new blood, but these days it's Blood Lite. Have to vatch my figure you know! *(Vink)*

ID: Even though I rarely interview vampires, you seemed like a really nice bloodsucker, so I made an exception. What prompted your transition from full-time bloodsucker to part-time TV host?

CG: Vell, I vanted to show the world that us vampires don't just "bite and run." To be an entertainer vas alvays a nightmare of mine and vhen the opportunity arose to bring Da Crypt to TV, I jumped at the chance... fangs first!

ID: Did you ever get the chance to meet Sammy Terry? To me, he is the REAL Godfather of late night TV hosts. And let us not forget Forry Ackerman, of Famous Monsters!

CG: Yes, I have met the legendary Sammy Terry at the HorrorHound Convention in Indianapolis more than once. It vas an honor to meet one of the pioneers of Horror Hosting! Mr. Terry vas a pleasure to "meat" and he truly seemed to enjoy interacting vith his fans. My Countess and I even had our picture taken vith him (vhich you can see on my website — *www.Count-Gregula.com*) and not to brag...but you have never seen a better looking bunch of ghouls in your afterlife.

Unfortunately I never had the opportunity to "meat" Forry Ackerman in person, even though Countess and I traveled as far as Pittsburgh for Monster Bash 2007 to see and celebrate Forry's 90th B-Day Bash only to find out that he vas too ill to attend the event. (*sad face*) However, Forry's "Ultimate Fanboy" legend lives on and sets the example for the rest of us fiends of horror and sci-fi to follow for many more afterlives to come! May you rest in peace, Uncle Forry.

ID: I see you have met some interesting — as well as famous — people along the way: Brad Dourif, Fred Gwynne, Kyra Schon. What are they like in person? I met Doug Bradley (Pinhead) once, and in person, he is nothing at all like his on-screen persona.

CG: Fred Gwynne? I VISH I could have met Fred Gwynne, he vas one of my Horror Idols!!! But I did meet his *Munsters* co-star Al Lewis at a Munster Mansion Halloveen Party in Waxahachie, TX back in 2002. Mr. Lewis vas quite the party animal! He liked to have a good time and vasn't shy about it.

Vhen I met Brad Dourif at the Flashback Veekend Convention a few years ago, he told the story of vhen he vas filming *Child's Play* in Chicago and caught a cold while running through our streets in the opening scene. He vas pleasant, but he vouldn't do the Chucky laugh for us *(sad face)*.

Kyra Schon vas also a pleasure to meet. Ve got to meet her a couple of times, once at the Cinema Wasteland show in Cleveland and again in Pittsburgh at Monster Bash 2007. She vas very pleasant and looks really good vith a garden trowel IF you know vhat I mean *vink*!

And, on a side note, Countess and I met Doug Bradley as vell, first in 2007 at the Fango Convention in Rosemont, IL, then again in 2008 at the HorrorHound Convention in Indianapolis. My fondest memory in "meat"ing Mr. Bradley vas the second time vhen he served us cake vith his likeness on it as "Pinhead" at the HH Con after-party and I have two pics of that surreal experience to prove it!

ID: What — if any — is your opinion of horror cinema these days? I mean, there a lot of good films out there, but it seems to me that too many filmmakers these days have lost grasp on the key elements to a well-crafted horror film.

CG: Vell, I believe there are too many remakes of the good classic movies that ve all grew up vith. The originals are great and in no vay need to be re-imagined or redone. Also, the art of suspense seems to have faded. Horror films these days, especially out of Hollywood, seem to focus on the gore factor instead of the story. Now, don't get me wrong, I love a good gory flick (it vhets my appetite), but shock factor alone is not enough to entertain this vamp. I highly recommend checking out independent horror films for good old-fashioned entertainment.

ID: Speaking of horror films in general, what would you say is your favorite?

CG: John Carpenter's *Halloween* (1978) has alvays been a favorite of mine.

ID: Anything exciting on the horizon for you right now?

CG: Vell, Dave, Count Gregula's Crypt vill be rising from the grave again after a short hiatus! A friend of mine, Raul Benitez, has asked me to collaborate with him on a project vhich vill include a podcast of Countess and I hosting movies online. Ve are all excited to be bringing back our special Vampirey blend of entertainment to a computer near you.

Be sure to check out *www.strangefictionpodcast.com* for more details!

ID: Any last words before you go?

Ghoul night, sleep tight…don't let The Children of the Night bite! But if you do see them, please send Figor, Shegor and Megor back to the "BAT" room in Da Crypt!!!

Jim Wynorski

ID: How are you today?
JW: I couldn't be better: no one's ever asked me that question before in an interview. I appreciate you taking an interest.

ID: No problem, Jimbo. First of all, I couldn't resist asking you about one of your pseudonyms, "H.R. Blueberry." Who — or what — was the inspiration for that one?
JW: I don't know where these names come from...they just appear in my mind...usually right before I add the credits in Post Production. I think it's partially based on H.R. Pufnstuf and the French comic artist, Blue Berry.

ID: Fair enough. I have been a fan of yours since seeing the film Chopping Mall. *Although a lot of your films have been straight to video releases, I stand by my opinion that you were always a very underrated filmmaker. Do you feel that some of your films were much better than they were given credit for?*
JW: Kind of a back handed compliment there, but I get your drift. I always endeavor to do the best I can with whatever budget I'm allotted. And I've always felt that money is no substitute for creativity — although I'm positive big budget Hollywood wouldn't agree.

ID: No offense intended, and I agree. I've never seen Scream Queen Hot Tub Party, *but I hear it is a real hoot. What is it like working with Fred Olen Ray?*
JW: I've never seen *Scream Queen Hot Tub Party* either.

ID: No joke?
JW: Just kidding. Fred and I made that film in one day back in 1991. It was, as you say, quite a hoot. And Fred's a wonderful guy. We took turns directing *Dinosaur Island* together, and we've been good friends for over 25 years.

ID: In your personal opinion, what era in film did you enjoy the most? The '80s? '90s? It seems as though horror films change format from decade to decade as often as some folks change their socks. One decade it was the slasher craze, then in the '90s it was serial killers.

JW: There's something to be said for each new cycle of horror films. I can have just as much fun with the original *The Bride of Frankenstein* as I can with *Friday the 13th 3D* or the remake of *Hills Have Eyes*. If I was forced to pick one era above all others, I'd probably choose the '50s — the decade when science fiction films finally came to the cinema forefront. I grew up loving those pictures on late night TV in the late 1960s and early 1970s. I think they truly inspired me, especially the films of Roger Corman, who I later worked for in the 80s.

ID: Yeah, that Roger is one of a kind. The special FX have changed a lot, too. Now it's mostly CGI FX. I preferred the "hands-on" approach to FX myself. How about you?

JW: CGI — when it's done right — can be quite entertaining. Although I do agree with you that it's getting overused these days. But to be quite honest, computer-generated FX really leveled the playing field, allowing lower budget film producers to compete with the major studios.

ID: Do you ever write any of your own fiction? I think that could prove to be interesting.

JW: I've written a lot of scripts, but I never turned them into novels or short stories. I do enjoy the creative process however. Writing allows me complete freedom, but I always have to temper it by how much is in the actual budget.

ID: Did you ever get a chance to meet Forrest J. Ackerman?

JW: I knew Forry Ackerman since the early 1970s. The first time my name ever appeared in print was in his magazine, *Famous Monsters of Filmland*. He appeared in three of my films, *Hard to Die*, *Transylvania Twist* and *Vampirella* (the comic book heroine FJA created for Warren Publishers).

ID: That was mighty nice of him; then again, he was a very nice man. How's your film Fire From Below *coming along? Any exciting news?*

JW: It's due to air on The Sci Fi Channel sometime in the first part of 2009. I think it turned out quite well.

ID: Any advice to fledgling filmmakers?

JW: Please stay out of the business...I can't stand the competition.

ID: Any last words before you leave us?
JW: Stay Scared!

ID: With you on the loose, how could we not?

Director

Vampire in Vegas (2009)
Fire from Below (2009; as J.R. Mandish)
Road Raiders (2009)
Lost in the Woods (2009)
The Lusty Busty Babe-a-que (2008; TV)
Bone Eater (2007; TV)
House on Hooter Hill (2007; V; as H.R. Blueberry)
The Breastford Wives (2007; V; as H.R. Blueberry)
The Da Vinci Coed (2007; TV; as H.R. Blueberry; also as Harold Blueberry)
A.I. Assault (2006; TV; as Jay Andrews)
Busty Cops 2 (2006; V; as Harold Blueberry)
Cry of the Winged Serpent (2006; TV; as Jamie Wagner)
The Witches of Breastwick 2 (2005; V; as H.R. Blueberry)
The Witches of Breastwick (2005; V; as H.R. Blueberry)
Komodo vs. Cobra (2005; TV; as Jay Andrews)
Sub Zero (2005; V; as Jay Andrews)
Crash Landing (2005; as Jay Andrews)
Lust Connection (2005; TV; as H.R. Blueberry)
Bare WenCH: The Final Chapter (2005; TV)
Alabama Jones and the Busty Crusade (2005; V; as Harold Blueberry)
Gargoyle (2004; V; as Jay Andrews)
The Curse of the Komodo (2004; as Jay Andrews)
Busty Cops (2004; V; as Harold Blueberry)
The Thing Below (2004; V; as Jay Andrews)
Bare Wench Project: Uncensored (2003; V)
Lost Treasure (2003; as Jay Andrews)
Cheerleader Massacre (2003; V)
More Mercy (2003; V; as Bob E. Brown)
Treasure Hunt (2003; V)
Wolfhound (2002; V; uncredited)
Project Viper (2002; TV; as Jay Andrews)
Gale Force (2002; V; as Jay Andrews)
The Bare Wench Project 3: Nymphs of Mystery Mountain (2002; V)
Raptor (2001; V; as Jay Andrews)
Thy Neighbor's Wife (2001; as Jay Andrews)
Ablaze (2001; as Jay Andrews)
The Bare Wench Project 2: Scared Topless (2001; V)
Rangers (2000; V; as Jay Andrews)

Agent Red (2000; uncredited)
Militia (2000; as Jay Andrews)
The Bare Wench Project (2000)
Crash Point Zero (2000; as Jay Andrews)
Final Voyage (1999; as Jay Andrews)
Stealth Fighter (1999; as Jay Andrews)
The Escort III (1999; V; as Tom Popatopolous)
The Pandora Project (1998)
Desert Thunder (1998)
Storm Trooper (1998)
Against the Law (1997)
Demolition High (1996; V)
The Assault (1996)
Vampirella (1996; V)
Virtual Desire (1995; as Noble Henry)
Body Chemistry 4: Full Exposure (1995; V)
Victim of Desire (1995)
Sorceress (1995)
The Wasp Woman (1995; TV)
Hard Bounty (1995)
Joe Bob's Drive-In Theater (2 episodes, 1994)
Ghoulies IV (1994)
Point of Seduction: Body Chemistry III (1994; V)
Dinosaur Island (1994)
Munchie Strikes Back (1994)
Little Miss Millions (1993)
Sins of Desire (1993)
Munchie (1992)
976-Evil II (1992)
Scream Queen Hot Tub Party (1991; V; as Arch Stanton)
The Haunting of Morella (1990)
Sorority House Massacre II (1990; as Arch Stanton)
Hard to Die (1990; as Arch Stanton)
Transylvania Twist (1989)
The Return of Swamp Thing (1989)
Not of This Earth (1988)
Big Bad Mama II (1987)
Deathstalker II (1987; V)
Chopping Mall (1986)
The Lost Empire (1985)

Producer

The Da Vinci Coed (2007; TV; as H.R. Blueberry)
The Witches of Breastwick 2 (2005; V)
The Witches of Breastwick (2005; V; as Daniel Fast)
Lust Connection (2005; TV; as Daniel Fast)
Bare WenCH: The Final Chapter (2005; TV)
Gargoyle (2004; V)

Deep Evil (2004; TV; executive producer; as Noble Henry)
Busty Cops (2004; V)
The Thing Below (2004; V; executive producer; as Noble Henry)
Gale Force (2002; V; as Noble Henry)
The Bare Wench Project 3: Nymphs of Mystery Mountain (2002; V)
Venomous (2001; V; as Noble Henry)
Air Rage (2001; V)
The Bare Wench Project 2: Scared Topless (2001; V)
Kept (2001; as Noble Henry)
Vice Girls (2000; executive producer)
Submerged (2000; as Noble Henry)
Agent Red (2000; as Noble Henry)
Active Stealth (2000; V; as Noble Henry)
The Bare Wench Project (2000)
Intrepid (2000; as Noble Henry)
Jill Rips (2000; as Noble Henry)
Critical Mass (2000; as Noble Henry)
Final Voyage (1999; as Noble Henry)
Stealth Fighter (1999; as Jay Andrews)
Fugitive Mind (1999; V; executive producer; as Noble Henry)
Storm Catcher (1999; as Noble Henry)
Sonic Impact (1999; as Noble Henry)
Desert Thunder (1998)
Demolition University (1997; V)
Hybrid (1997; co-executive producer)
Friend of the Family II (1996; as Noble Henry)
Fugitive Rage (1996; V)
The Assault (1996)
Sorceress II: The Temptress (1996; executive producer)
Vampirella (1996; V)
Virtual Desire (1995; as Tom Popatopolous)
Bikini Drive-In (1995; executive producer)
Biohazard: The Alien Force (1995; V)
Hard Bounty (1995)
Midnight Tease II (1995; executive producer)
The Skateboard Kid II (1995; executive producer)
Dinosaur Island (1994)
Dark Universe (1993; co-executive producer)
Scream Queen Hot Tub Party (1991; V; as Arch Stanton)
Hard to Die (1990)
Not of This Earth (1988)
The Lost Empire (1985)

Writer

Fire from Below (2009; story and screenplay)
Lost in the Woods (2009; screenplay)
House on Hooter Hill (2007; V; writer; as Thaddeus Wickwire)
The Breastford Wives (2007; V; writer; as Thaddeus Wickwire)

The Da Vinci Coed (2007; TV; written by; as Thaddeus Wickwire)
A.I. Assault (2006; TV; writer; as Jay Andrews)
The Witches of Breastwick (2005; V; screenplay; as Thaddeus Wickwire)
Komodo vs. Cobra (2005; TV; writer; as Jay Andrews)
Sub Zero (2005; V; writer; as Jay Andrews)
Crash Landing (2005; writer)
Lust Connection (2005; TV; writer; as Thaddeus Wickwire)
Bare WenCH: The Final Chapter (2005; TV; writer)
Gargoyle (2004; V; screenplay; as Jay Andrews)
Treasure Hunt (2003; V; writer)
The Bare Wench Project 3: Nymphs of Mystery Mountain (2002; V; writer)
Raptor (2001; V; writer; as Jay Andrews)
Thy Neighbor's Wife (2001; story; as Noble Henry)
The Bare Wench Project 2: Scared Topless (2001; V; writer)
The Bare Wench Project (2000; written by; as Noble Henri)
The Pandora Project (1998; story)
Munchie Strikes Back (1994; writer)
Little Miss Millions (1993; writer)
Sins of Desire (1993; story)
Munchie (1992; writer)
Final Embrace (1992; writer)
House IV (1992; story)
Beastmaster 2: Through the Portal of Time (1991; screenplay; story)
Scream Queen Hot Tub Party (1991; V; writer; as Arch Stanton)
The Haunting of Morella (1990; writer)
Think Big (1989; story)
Transylvania Twist (1989; writer)
Not of This Earth (1988; screenplay)
Big Bad Mama II (1987; writer)
Deathstalker II (1987; V; story)
Chopping Mall (1986; writer)
Loose Screws (1985; screenplay "Screwballs")
The Lost Empire (1985; writer)
Screwballs (1983; writer)
Forbidden World (1982; story)
Sorceress (1982; writer)

Actor

Brain Dead (2007).... Sheriff Bodine
Sub Zero (2005; V; uncredited).... Tracking Station Scientist
Gargoyle (2004; V).... Bogdan
Lost Treasure (2003; as David Gibbs).... Police Helicopter Pilot
Treasure Hunt (2003; V).... Jim
Raptor (2001; V; uncredited).... Man in Sheriff's Station
Vice Girls (2000; uncredited).... Man with Top Popper
Desert Thunder (1998; uncredited).... Bartender
Storm Trooper (1998; uncredited).... Tannis Corporation Scientist
Alien Escape (1997).... Lester

Against the Law (1997; uncredited).... Action Film Director
Passion and Romance: Ocean of Dreams (1997; as Noble Henri).... Captain Rockford
Masseuse (1996).... Pig Truck Driver
Demolition High (1996; V; uncredited).... Police Sniper
Sorceress II: The Temptress (1996).... Agent in Car
Vampirella (1996; V; uncredited).... TV News Anchor
Bikini Drive-In (1995)
Body Chemistry 4: Full Exposure (1995; V).... Hanging Judge
Attack of the 60 Foot Centerfolds (1995).... Guy Who Can't Believe His Eyes
Midnight Tease II (1995).... Drunk at bar
The Skateboard Kid II (1995).... Drunk outside at the Bar
The Wasp Woman (1995; TV; uncredited).... Friendly Man at Bar
Dragon Fire (1993).... Night Club M.C
Little Miss Millions (1993; uncredited).... Man at Denver Bus Ticket Counter and Radio Voice
The Bikini Carwash Company (1992).... Ralph
Scream Queen Hot Tub Party (1991; V; uncredited).... Monster in basement
Hard to Die (1990; uncredited).... Porno Director
Hollywood Boulevard II (1989).... The Man Who Does Lunch
Deathstalker II (1987; V; as Arch Stanton).... Dying Soldier
Chopping Mall (1986; voice).... Killbots

Casting Director

Vice Girls (2000; as Noble Henry)
Scorned 2 (1997; as Noble Henry)
Night Eyes 4 (1996; TV; as Noble Henry)
Virtual Desire (1995; as Heny Henri)
Body Chemistry 4: Full Exposure (1995; V; as Noble Henry)
Hard Bounty (1995; as Noble Henry)

Echoes

Back in the 1950s, goggle-eyed lovers of werewolves, mummies and monsters were a disparate, lonely and voiceless community of movie geeks. Without videotapes, computers or easy access to any film archive, resources about their favorite creature-features or Boris Karloff frighteners were extremely limited.

Lovers of fantastic film were forced to make scrapbooks and write lists, treasuring each minute of every movie release at their local picture palace or fuzzy midnight TV screening introduced by *Vampira*.

But everything changed in 1958 when a magazine called *Famous Monsters of Filmland* was launched as a one-off special. Like an angry mob of villagers from a Universal horror movie, kids across America attacked newsstands for their first-ever chance to read about their favorite subject matter, uniting a group of monster-loving misfits and inspiring a generation of future filmmakers and writers.

A second printing followed to fulfill eager children's demands for more thrills, and the magazine quickly flourished in a monthly form.

Deep in the bloody heart of Horrorwood, Karloffornia, we find its creator, Forrest J Ackerman, also known as Dr. Acula, Mr. Science Fiction, or just plain Uncle Forry to his many famous friends and devotees, a man regarded as the world's number one fan of fantastic film.

So successful was his landmark release, that he wrote and edited *Famous Monsters* for two decades, its influence spawning spin-offs at Warren Publishing such as *Monster World, Famous Westerns of Filmland, Creepy, Eerie* and *Vampirella* (the sexy vampire from outer space, also created by Ackerman). A whole wave of writing for monster-movie fans had been unleashed.

"I sat with an old mechanical typewriter for 20 hours a day working on the first issue," explains Forry. "The publisher sent across a sign saying, 'I am 11-and-a-half years old and I am your reader. Forrest Ackerman make me laugh.'"

As a consequence, every single edition was filled with delightfully goofy puns that made gory guys and ghouls laugh all the way to the morgue. The magazine was dripping with salivating monster interviews, terror-ific articles on retrospective and contemporary genre flicks, creepy comic-strip adaptations of classic movies, petrifying picture galleries, a popular letters page called "Fang Mail" and regulars like "You Axed For It," where readers could request certain photos to appear and ask all sorts of questions of Forry.

Ackerman was the ideal choice to helm the monster mag, felt New York publisher James Warren. Forry had lived in the vicinity of the Hollywood 'nightmare' factory all his life, not only amassing a huge knowledge of these films but also his fanatical enthusiasm, which saw sympathetic studio workers giving him film stills previously destined for the dustbin. He also established good relationships with many of the stars of the day.

Forrest J Ackerman was the original super-fan. In 1954, he coined the phrase "Sci-Fi," now found in every modern dictionary. The flash of inspiration came one day while driving with his wife, when he heard some mention of "hi-fi" on the radio.

"Since science fiction had been on the tip of my tongue ever since 1929, I looked in the rearview mirror, stuck out my tongue and there tattooed on the end was 'sci-fi'," he recalled excitedly, his eyes squinting with delight as he began a trip down memory lane. "To her immortal embarrassment my dear wife said, 'Forget it, Forry — it'll never catch on.'"

The kindly Mr. Ackerman managed to acquire an astounding 300,000 science-fiction items, including those rare photographs (he had over 35,000 tempting terrors to offer the publisher when *Famous Monsters* was first published), props, books, artwork and memorabilia, a collection the Smithsonian once described as "one of the 10 best private collections in the country."

Originally, it was all housed in the "Ackermansion," an astounding 18-room giant cavern, jam-packed with all things fantastic, including stop-motion models from *King Kong*, a signed first edition of *Dracula*, and even a Martian spacecraft from *War of the Worlds*. It was a veritable treasure trove.

Sadly, after an extensive legal battle in the U.S. courts and a serious life-threatening illness, he had to strip down his collection to pay for all the expensive medical and legal costs.

Though frail, he remained as bright as a spark in Frankenstein's laboratory. At the mere mention of a photo opportunity with his original Bela Lugosi *Dracula* cape, he would jump from his chair like an excited schoolboy and toss the rare artifact around his shoulders, grabbing a pair of fake fangs and making childish horror expressions. It was no surprise that Forry continued to give tours around his down-sized bungalow, which has been dubbed the "mini-Ackermansion," and which boasted plenty of horrific delights to behold in the bastard mansion offspring and a treasure trove of tales to entrance from a man who befriended all the great horror-film icons of the sound era. His star connections in the genre world grew naturally from his career. As a literary agent, he represented more than 200 authors, including such illustrious SF names as Ray Bradbury, Isaac Asimov, L Ron Hubbard and Hugo Gernsback, but also a number of more infamous low-rent writers.

"I was Ed Wood's 'ill-literary' agent," he giggled, nonetheless terribly annoyed he binned one of the director of *Plan 9 From Outer Space's* ultra-schlocky manuscripts because it was so unbelievably awful. "Ed was talking about making a Bela Lugosi film, and I suggested he call him 'Dr Acula', and so he began giving me his short stories. I never saw him in drag, or he might have played 'Dragula'! To me, he was mainly a drunken voice at two o'clock in the morning, babbling incomprehensible things."

Over time, Forry was able to make strong connections with the horror glitterati, such as Boris Karloff, Vincent Price, Peter Cushing and the great Bela Lugosi. In Forry's home, one group of items on display was dedicated to the famous screen Count. Inside the display cabinet was a purple monotone photograph of Lugosi, an ornately carved ring marked with 'D' and an aged autograph in black ink.

"You are now looking at the only signature of Lugosi in the world as Count Dracula," exclaimed Forry with youthful delight. "His fifth and final wife turned out to be a witch with a capital 'B.'

"Once, they were at a party of mine; Bela was in the dining room and she was in the living room. Since he was deaf, he didn't realize how loud he was speaking and was singing the Hungarian blues to me about his wife.

"I thought, 'Oh God, she's hearing every word. Wait till he gets home.' After he died she once bragged to me, 'I married Dracula, and I frightened him!' Bela was very superstitious and believed you should sleep at night with a glass of water by your nightstand to keep away evil spirits. But she would terrify him by threatening daily, 'If you don't obey, I'll take the glass away.'"

Lon Chaney was originally signed to play *Dracula* onscreen but died before a frame was shot. Although Forry never met the silent-film star, he did meet Chaney's son, Lon Jr., most renowned for his lead in Universal's *The Wolfman* (1940), and another who hit the bottle in his later career.

"It was disappointing," sighed Ackerman. "One time the Count Dracula society gave a banquet for him and I sat opposite on the table. I ate my banquet and he drank his."

Forry's favorite movie of all time was well-represented in his Hollywood home, where tours and talks were conducted every Saturday.

Standing proudly in one corner was a full-size replica of the False Maria robot from Fritz Lang's *Metropolis* (1927), decked from top to bottom in fairy lights and wearing a bobble hat. There was, in fact, an entire room dedicated to the movie, with busts of the *Seven Deadly Sins* that appeared in the futuristic silent classic, numerous film posters and rare stills.

Forry sat through more screenings of *Metropolis* than he lived years. With wrinkly eyes wide open, he joyfully remembered some of his memorable screenings of the film:

"I was in Berlin and it occurred to me some of the hundreds of children in the film could still be alive. On a radio interview, I asked if any would come to my hotel and meet me. So a man and a lady came and introduced themselves. We watched the Giorgio Moroder version and I had the pleasure of sitting with two of the children of *Metropolis*. They had been too young to see it at the time. The man now saw his long-dead little sister because there was a close-up of her in the arms of Brigitte Helm.

"Another time, I was at a film festival in Rio with [*Metropolis* director] Fritz Lang. He was nearly blind. After the screening, the applauding audience wanted him to answer questions. It was very flattering, for he rose and said, 'Anything you want to know about *Metropolis*, ask my friend Forry Ackerman. He knows more about it than I do.'"

Forry's fascination with robots was equaled by his admiration of the real female form. Ackerman took delight in displaying a fully nude (and highly detailed) statuette of Hollywood legend Marlene Dietrich in his bedroom, and he housed a large collection of bondage erotica. He was an annual attendee of Hugh Hefner's (the other editor who changed the publishing world in the '50s) wild New Year's Eve parties: Ackerman reflected upon this fact as "very embarrassing. There are inevitably six young ladies so poor they can't afford to wear a single thing!"

Other famous fans included Steven Spielberg, George Lucas, Joe Dante, John Landis and Peter Jackson. A testament to Forry's influence and importance was his appearance in over 100 films — a record for a non-actor, though as Ackerman once wryly noted, "My film career has lasted over 50 years and my total time on film is probably less than an hour."

Still, he managed to show his face in everything from Michael Jackson's *Thriller* video to the recent remake of *King Kong*, even getting cast as the first lesbian President of the US in the spoof *Amazon Women On The Moon* (1987).

In the early 80s, *Famous Monsters* finally closed the lid on its publishing coffin after James Warren became ill, while Ackerman resigned in the face of the increasing disorganization and poor pay.

Though the magazine was revived in the 90s, Forry had no involvement. However, the legacy of Forrest J Ackerman and *Famous Monsters Of Filmland* stretches well into the 21st century.

As Stephen King once said about his huge contribution to fandom, "Forry was the first; he was best and he is the best. He stood up for a generation of kids who realized that if it was junk, it was *magic* junk."

Forrest James Ackerman was born on November 24, 1916, and died on December 4, 2008, at the age of 92.

Interview conducted by J.M. Sims

JMS: *As I understand it your collecting started with a fan letter to Carl Laemmle. Can you tell me about that?*

FJA: No, my collecting didn't start with that. It started with the October 1926 issue of *Amazing Stories*, which jumped off the newsstand, grabbed hold of little nine-year-old me. But the Carl Laemmle situation: in the 1930s there was a monthly magazine called *Photoplay*. He had a full page each issue, just publicizing the various Universal products that were coming out. And since my maternal grandparents were capable of taking me to as many as seven films in a single day, I obviously saw all the Universal pictures. And as fast as I saw one, I would write him with my comments on it. Well, I astonished myself a couple of years ago by running across 62 letters from Carl Laemmle, obviously responding to ones that I had sent. Eventually I guess he thought of me as the all-American, movie-going teenager, and on his President's stationery he wrote a little note that said, "Give this kid anything he wants." So what I wanted was, at that time, sound was still on huge discs. It was long before we ever had video cassettes. Once you saw a movie you thought it was gone forever. I thought, "Gosh! If I had those sound discs once they were through with it, I could put them on my phonograph and run the movie through my mind."

The problem was that these discs were in the new rhythm of 33 1/3, when my old-fashioned phonograph was 78. So I would rev up the phonograph, put the record on, which oddly enough started in the center and gradually worked its way out, and I used a cactus needle to preserve it. And I would have to, physically with my fingers, try to damp it down from 78 to 33 and a third, so I'd get some rather strange dialogue now and then. I'd hear Colin Clive exulting, "It's moving! It's elyve! It's urrlerve!"

JMS: *Do you still have those?*

FJA: Stolen. And about ten years after they were stolen, a voice on the phone says, "Oh, Mr Ackerman. I have something, I'm sure you're going to want to have these." And I said, "What's that?" He said, "I have the discs from *Frankenstein*, and I only want $8,000 for them." I said, "Oh really? Is that what my discs are worth?" "What do you mean, *your* discs?" I said, "Well, they were stolen from me about ten years ago." Click! Down goes the phone!

JMS: *It seems incredible having this open house that you have regularly. Other than the odd bad apple, do you find that people are mostly enthusiastic?*

FJA: There's a sort of sinister statistic. When there are 25 people or more in the house at once, then something seems to disappear. But as long as it's under 25…

JMS: *At what point did you start to realize that your collection was becoming extraordinary?*

FJA: When I had a 13-room home, and my wife, the university professor, came home one day and went to the refrigerator to get food, and found that I had replaced it with reels of film, we realized the end had come. I had finally filled up the bathtub with the collection, and under the bed, and every place in the kitchen where there wasn't a cup or a spoon. So we gave up and used the entire home and three-automobile garage for the collection, and we moved a couple of miles away to an apartment. Then realized even the 13 rooms wasn't going to do any more. Also I had accumulated so many friends that when I had a birthday, considering we could only pack about sixty people at most into the house at one time, I had to have five birthdays: Friday night, Saturday matinee, Saturday night, Sunday matinee, and Sunday night. So during her summer vacation, my wife looked around and she found a house that seemed like it would satisfy my needs as a collector. Well, she found two houses. I fancied one, and she really liked the other best, and I thought, "Whoever gives up will be forever complaining: we should have had that other house." But all of a sudden she calls, she says, "I think I've found the one that satisfies us both." It was the home of Jon Hall who was kind of a poor man's Tarzan called *Ramar of the Jungle*. Its 18 rooms looked so huge to me that I thought I could never fill them up, and now once again, they're bulging at the seams.

JMS: *How did you manage to move from one house to the other?*

FJA: It took 2,000 boxes, and one young lady who rented a truck and each weekend would drive things over. But when I think back 24 years ago, those 2,000 boxes seem rather trivial to what I have today.

JMS: How did Famous Monsters of Filmland *come about?*

FJA: In 1957, the World Science Fiction Convention was held in England, in London. There were 55 of us chartered a Dutch plane and flew over from New York. And after the convention we had a couple of weeks to spare before we all had to return, and I for one went to Paris and Germany. In Paris I spied a movie magazine that ordinarily was about everything under the sun, but this particular issue was all out on fantasy. It had Henry Hull on the cover as the *Werewolf of London,* and inside about a hundred pages of *Kong* and *Frankenstein* and the *Invisible Man* and so on. I bought a copy just for my collection. Then I got to New York and as an agent I had been selling to a magazine called *After Hours,* which was kind of a poor man's *Playboy.* I met up with its editor-publisher James Warren and in the course of a breakfast pulled out this magazine from France. Now, he was looking to publish what is called a one-shot; that is, he had no idea of subscriptions or carrying on beyond just once. And he wouldn't have cared if it was about Marilyn Monroe or Madonna or The Beatles or anybody of the time, as long as it would sell about 100,000 copies. So he looked at this French magazine — it was called *Cinema '57* I think — and in his mind's eye he could see all of the wordage turning into English. He thought all he had to do was write the publisher and borrow all the stills. Well, there were two things: he found that the stills didn't belong to any single individual, they came from about five different collectors; and also, as he began to translate, it didn't seem that an American audience would really care very much. I guess it was too dull and dry and didactic. He was going to give up on the idea and I said, "Wait a minute. You don't really know me but I have 35,000 stills, and I've been seeing these pictures ever since 1922. I'm sure I could put together a magazine to your satisfaction." Well, he didn't know whether I was full of hot air or not, so he came out to Hollywood and he saw it was all true. So the next thing I knew, we were sitting opposite each other at a dining room table. He was holding an imaginary sign in the air that sa*ID:* "Forrest Ackerman, I'm eleven and a half years old and I am your reader. Make me laugh."

Well, for twenty hours a day I was sitting at a smoking typewriter, afraid it was going to die of cancer, it was smoking so badly. We would get four hours rest, then back to the grind. It was right around the time of my birthday, November 24th, in 1957. I couldn't wait until February 4th when I held an issue in my hand. I didn't even think of it as an issue, I thought it would be a one-shot. It was quite different from what I had really imagined and hoped for. I wanted to call it *Wonderama,* and I thought of it as kind of an encyclopedia. There'd be one definitive still of *Dracula* and one great

King Kong and one *Frankenstein*, and there would be the cast of characters, what the world thought about it, what I thought about it and a synopsis of the plot. But there were 13 distributors of magazines at the time, and all of them turned down the idea of *Wonderama*.

It might never have appeared, but just about that time AIP brought out the first of their teenage films, *I was a Teenage Werewolf*, and that started a trend. *Life* magazine did an eight-page feature on the new teenage horror films, and one of the 13 potential distributors remembered this madman who had been around showing them all of these messed-up faces. They called him back and said, "Forget about *Wonderama*. Stick '*Monsters*' on the cover and I don't care what's inside." So that's the way it developed.

When it first appeared, it was not nationally distributed. It was just in New York and Philadelphia, just a trial balloon to see how it would sell. In New York there was a terrible snow storm on. The publisher was afraid nobody was going to go out and buy *Life* or *Look* or *Playboy*, let alone our curiosity, but at the end of four days he called all excited. He said, "My God, I've been getting 50 letters a day. I got 200 letters here and they all say 'More! More!' — do you think you could squeeze out one more issue?" And I said, "Well, you don't know me very well. I don't happen to believe in reincarnation, but in case I keep coming back for the next 5,000 years I think I could go on and on without repeating myself. The first 125,000 copies sold out and we went back to press for 75,000 more, and we were on our way, and here we are at issue 209.

JMS: What persuaded you to re-launch it?

FJA: Well, I never would have normally quit, but it was a time of rampant inflation in America and I was getting the same sum month after month after month for creating the magazine. I had a heart-to-heart talk with the publisher, I said, "You know, at the end of the year, the buying power has diminished. I'm not asking for a raise, I would just like to keep even with the economy." He said, "Oh yes, yes, absolutely." But four years went by and I just got the same salary. I figured I'd been chopped down by about one third in my purchasing power, and also I could see looming up was the 200th issue. I wrote him and said, "I know you won't pay me anything extra, but just out of pure pride I would like to give a 200-page issue to the readers. I'm willing to do it for the same amount of money." Didn't hear a boo out of him.

Finally, it was just too much for me financially: growing older and getting less, rather than being paid more for my efforts. So I gave up at issue 190. There was one more issue and that was the end of it. Promptly, another potential publisher got in the act, and I said, "I've got a lot of conditions. First of all, I gotta have my name on it. It's got to say: 'Forrest J Ackerman's' magazine, whatever it's called. And you have to let me alone, because the publisher was always saying to me, 'Well, you may be right, but I'm boss.'" And so we'd do it his way.

JMS: My publisher does the same.

FJA: So I said, "If I'm going to continue to do this, it's got to be under various conditions of mine." Every condition was met, and then the publisher went broke or whatever happened, went out of business. Once or twice through the years, other publishers have turned up and managed to make me miserable, so I thought, "Well, I think I've done with it once and for all." Two years ago, a young fellow who'd been an avid reader of the magazine, he woke up to a fact that had escaped my notice, namely that it was going to be the 35th year since the creation of the magazine. He felt there ought to be something done to recognize that. So he was ready, willing and able to put together a convention to which 7,000 people came from 13 countries in Crystal City, Virginia. And just for the occasion we brought back the magazine, but it was such a resounding success there was no point in stopping, and so on we go.

JMS: Can you explain what First Fandom is?

FJA: Well, in 1939 we had the first so-called World Science Fiction Convention, a pretty imposing name for 185 kids. I don't think anybody came from anywhere else in the world other than the United States. It took Ray Bradbury three and a half days and nights to get there with the $50 I lent him for a Greyhound bus ride. Out of the 185 attending, we had a banquet of 29 people, and I couldn't even afford to lend the money to Ray Bradbury, it was so expensive. It was one dollar a plate. But somebody, I don't know who, decided that anybody who could demonstrate that they had been a fan before the first World Science Fiction Convention — if they could show a letter they had in print in one of the magazines, or if they had their own fanzine or some way to demonstrate that they really existed as a fan — they would be called the First Fans.

JMS: Do you still consider yourself a fan?

FJA: Oh, absolutely, absolutely. Whatever I do, I'm *still* a fan.

JMS: You've met many great people — Karloff and Lugosi and HG Wells — but are there still people who can make you go gosh-wow-boy-o-boy?!

FJA: I'm sure there are. I don't know just who's left exactly that I would like to meet. I was very fortunate in meeting just about everybody that I ever wanted to.

JMS: People like Joe Dante were first published in Famous Monsters.

FJA: I took a little letter that he had written, complaining about the 50 worst monster movies ever made, and I saw the possibility of turning that into an actual article by bumping it up with stills and giving it subheads and so on. So I published what was called "Dante's Inferno," and most of the movies he was razzing were by Roger Corman, who eventually gave him his first job, I think, on *Piranha*!

JMS: There's a resurgence of monster mags nowadays, like MonsterScene, Psychotronic *and so on. Do you look on these and think, "I started all this"?*

FJA: Well, I don't know. I never think too much about it. Every once in a while at a convention like this, someone will say, "Boy, do you realize you're responsible for this? You started it." Something I sure know I started was I was the only person to turn up in a costume at the first convention. Now it's a standard part of the proceedings to have a masquerade. Finally, a couple of masquerades ago, they really took me by surprise. They called me up on the stage and had a nice, big plaque acknowledging that I was the inspiritor.

JMS: Has anybody ever entered a masquerade dressed as you?
FJA: No...!

JMS: Some of the items in your collection have reference numbers. Is the collection catalogued?

FJA: No. I think the reason for those reference numbers is because at one time they flew, I think, 250 pieces of my collection over to Japan. They had them on display in Tokyo in nine different department stores for three months. In conjunction with that, they put out a beautiful souvenir book, and I think these little numbers you notice are just related to the souvenir book.

JMS: So is there any definitive list of your collection? How do you know, when you see something, whether or not you've got it?

FJA: Well, I'll let you know my guilty secret — I don't always know! Sometimes I'll buy something and — oh, gosh! — the moment I get home, I had it all along!

JMS: It seems strange that you're still a humble fan. Do you feel an empathy with the attendees here? I saw that you were very good with kids.

FJA: I feel very fortunate, you know. I came from a time when I was the resident crazy at school. Everyone knew that Forry Ackerman was nuts. I thought people were going to the moon in rockets and there was going to be atomic power and color television: it'll never happen. I enjoy people, and having them come to my house, and I enjoy being interviewed. I feel very fortunate that the older I get, the further away it is from the death of Karloff and Lugosi and Price and Cushing and so on, the more the world will want of me. Not necessarily me *per se*, but the fact that I knew all of these people. I'm very happy to keep them all alive.

JMS: Do you see other collectors like Bob Burns?

FJA: Yes, there are three or four of us. Unfortunately, none of the other collectors seem to have the urge I do. One of them says, "When I'm gone, the heck with it. I've had the pleasure of it. Let my wife sell it or give it to charity or something." I wish the other collectors had the same feeling of preservation that I do.

JMS: Do you have any ambitions left?

FJA: The main ambition, which I've been working on for 15 years, is to try and get this collection solidified some place in the world. Of course, I would obviously prefer to have it in Los Angeles where I was born, where I'll probably die. But even if it has to go to Berlin or somewhere, as long as it's not all broken up, if it stays together.

Anonymous Posthumous Cheers from Forry's Fans...

"Growing up in the early '70s, a big part of my childhood revolved around Warren Publications. I was a gigantic fan of *FMoF* and, though I've read that horror had hit its peak earlier and was actually heading toward a decline, I sure did not notice it. Even in a small town in Alabama, a kid could buy a copy of *FMoF*, *Creepy, Eerie*, or *Vampirella*, watch a local TV horror show, and dream of all those cool Captain Company products in the back pages — and still grow up to be somewhat normal. Those were the best of times, and Forrest primarily made them possible. Thanks for it all. You will be greatly missed."

"*Famous Monsters* had a profound influence on my life. It didn't just inspire me to seek out vintage horror films: it also instilled within me the desire to write about movies. I discovered *FM* in the early Sixties, just as the magazine was entering a short-lived 'golden age' during which Forry largely abandoned atrocious puns and puerile jokes to lavish upon his favorite movies the serious and even scholarly treatment we felt they deserved. Around this time *FM* began covering horror-movie fanzines, and upon obtaining copies of such mimeographed journals as *Photon* and *Garden Ghouls Gazette*, some of my enthusiastic friends and fellow film buffs decided to publish their own zine (rather prosaically titled *Horrors*) and at age eleven I became a published author. A year later I began contributing to the aforementioned *Photon*, *House of Horros*, and several 'crud-zines' whose titles escape me. At fourteen, outfitted with a used mimeograph given to me as a Christmas present, I became the publisher of *Fantasy World*, branching beyond horror movies to cover science fiction, comic books, and movie serials. I never lost my enthusiasm for the stuff that thrilled me as a kid, and while still in college, after becoming an avid collector of 16mm prints, I became friendly with fellow hobbyists Sam Sherman and Bob Price, former Warren Publications employees who'd edited *FM*'s sister publications *Screen Thrills Illustrated* and *Wildest Westerns*. Sam put me in touch with Forry, and while I can't say I was a close friend of the Ackermonster, we conversed several times via phone. In 1992, shortly after I moved to LA, I visited him at the Ackermansion and got the nickel tour. That day I became reacquainted with another visitor, a guy named Ron Borst, a fellow *Photon* contributor I'd first met a quarter-century before at the 1967 World Science Fiction Convention in NYC. Ron had moved to LA and owned a movie-memorabilia store in Hollywood. (A world-class collector of horror/SF paper, he later turned out a book titled *Graven Images*, a treasure trove of poster reproductions.) Seeing him again at the Ackermansion was a real treat, and we kept in touch thereafter.

I moved back east in '94, but saw Forry several more times in the years that followed. He always retained his sense of wonder and his boundless enthusiasm for science fiction and horror — even during the bleak period that found him locked in battle with Ray Ferry.

To me, *Famous Monsters* wasn't just a magazine. It was a doorway to an entire world, a secret password that enabled me, and others like me, to network with an entire generation of people who shared my interests and passions. Forry made that possible."

"He had a bit part in the '80s movie *Future War*, which *Mystery Science Theater* did towards the end of the series. He got killed by a dinosaur. Or, as the bots put it, 'A man got snapped at by a forced perspective puppet today.' Before he is dispatched by the deadly puppet, he is shown reading *Famous Monsters of Filmland*. That's priceless."

"Oh, also, I remember reading an article, roughly five years ago, about Ackerman, written by a young female journalist. She visited the Ackermansion for the story, and related the fact that Ackerman lightly slapped her on the rear, which, given Ackerman's age and general personality, she found endearing, or at least excusable. And for that, I tip my hat to him."

"I first read *Famous Monsters* when I was a kid in the 1960s. From the late 1970s continuing through the present, I've been collecting *Vampirella* comics, having just received one of the books in the mail a few days ago. In the past few years, I've written two vampire novels that I'm trying to get published. Certainly, Forrest Ackerman's *Vampirella* character influenced many people, including me."

"Can still remember the joy I felt when the new issue of *Famous Monsters* would appear in the drug store magazine rack. Never got to meet him, but he was an important part of my young life and introduced me to wonder and imagination."

"I first learned about Ackerman in the back pages of the Perry Rhodan novels I devoured as a kid, where he often signed his essays with the moniker 'Forry Rhodan.' His affection for the material, hokey as it was, was infectious. He was living proof of the old saying, 'Find a way to make a living doing what you love, and you'll never work a day in your life.'

I'll raise a glass to him as well."

"I visited his house once, in the mid-1980s, and stared in awe at his collection. He and his wife were genuinely gracious and welcoming to all these strangers trooping through their home. It's still a lovely memory."

"*Famous Monsters of Filmland*. Gonna go dig out my old copies tonight, and walk down Nostalgia Boulevard.

Thanks for the memories, Mr. Ackerman."

"He was a one of a kind
Smart, funny and kind.
And a true pioneer in the sci-fi world.
And I mean sci-fi — Once upon a time, I encountered a stone science fiction fan who ridiculed me for using sci-fi. I replied 'If it is good enough for Forrest J Ackerman, it is good enough for me.' Then I had to explain to this dweeb that there was science fiction before *Star Wars* and who Forrest J. Ackerman is. I am sure Forry would have been kinder to the kid than I. But I could never claim to be a classy man like him.

He will be missed."

"For decades, Forrest J Ackerman opened his private home every week for public tours of his literally overwhelming collection of sci-fi and horror memorabilia. He had a practiced patter and plenty of horrid puns worthy of the founding editor of *Famous Monsters Magazine.*

A few years ago, Mr. Ackerman was hospitalized in serious condition. I had recently lost an inspirational college professor who I didn't even know was hospitalized, so I made a point of traveling to see Forrest to deliver a rocketship-featuring get-well card.

He looked bad. Really bad. He had spinal blocks in following a surgical procedure, a scar on his scalp.

And he was *smiling* at his visitors.

He was telling his trademark corny jokes.

He insisted I take a complimentary copy of *Cult Movies* magazine, an issue for which he recently wrote a column.

He was a gracious host even on what looked to be his deathbed.

That amount of grace in a person is stunning to experience.

You become very conscious of the air you walk through after such an encounter. He gave me proof of the possibility and ability of Human Grace first-hand. That's the kind of good man he is.

I am glad that in the subsequent years, and the last few weeks, he's had additional opportunity to receive well-wishers and tributes to him personally as well as his legacy to the unifying, not bickering, aspects of fandom.

I'm saddened he's gone, but I'm glad he existed, as Ray Bradbury said of our purpose, 'to witness and to celebrate.'

Amen."

Afterword

It's hard for me not to remember what my childhood would have been like without Forry's *Famous Monsters of Filmland.* As an avid reader of "scary" literature at a young age (I wrote my first scary story, "Bats," when I was only eight years old), Forry's magazine was like a dream come true for me. Each day after coming home from school, I would head to my room, put my homework on hold, and open the newest edition of *Famous Monsters* and relish every word and picture. He was, in all honesty, the King of Scifi, as well as a true pioneer in his own right, his magazine having paved the way for future publications such as *Fangoria* and *Gorezone,* just to name a couple.

His fan base was so vast, I knew of absolutely no one who didn't like or love Forry. His personality and warm heart touched so many lives during his 92-year stint on this earth, it would be impossible to ever catalogue the exact number of fans and friends he'd made while he was with us. But one thing remains certain: his very presence here, as well as his influence on future generations of Scifi and horror fans, to this day still remains unsurpassed.

When I first began compiling this collection of interviews — which took me a total of 13 months — one of the first things that came to mind was: *Who will I ask to be in this book?! He had so many fans, from all walks of life and many different industries, including fiction writers, filmmakers, FX artists, graphic artists, and beyond...*

I think I did a fair job of assembling a great group of people here to honor Forry, and I hope you enjoy reading this book as much as I enjoyed putting it together for you. As a matter of fact, now that you've read the book, I think it is only fitting to open a bottle of your favorite poison, pour a shot, light a cigar, and sit back and reflect back on not only how much you enjoyed the book (I hope!), but also on how much we all miss "Uncle Forry," and how much we wish him well, now that he's in a better place.

I think he would have really enjoyed this book, and I hope you all did, too. Rest in peace, Uncle Forry. We miss you!

Iron Dave, *February 5, 2010*

About the Author

David Byron literally BURST upon the horror community only two years ago, and his online magazine, *NVF Magazine* (now defunct) has boasted interviews with horror fiction legends Ramsey Campbell, Anne Rice, Philip Nutman, and Jack Ketchum, and has showcased fiction by Joe R. Lansdale, Roberta Lannes, and John Everson. Not bad for a guy who quit high school, and didn't earn his GED diploma until he was 39 years old.

Now 50, he has showed no signs of slowing down, having now edited three fiction anthologies, non-fiction memoir books, and has now signed on to be co-producer on three documentary films, to be released in 2010.

Dubbed by some of his friends as "the hardest working 'unknown' man in horror," he has accepted this honor with pride, but is now branching out into different genres and other projects that will not dwell within the horror genre.

"I have found the horror genre these days to be lacking in originality," he recently told someone in an interview. " It has started to become stale, clichéd. All I see when I look at the book store shelves is vampires, zombies, and serial killers. And horror films don't fare much better. The seemingly endless — and shameless — lame remakes and sequels to classic horror films almost borderlines on the ridiculous. Writers of horror films and fiction have seemed to have lost grasp on what key elements are necessary for a well-crafted horror film script or story."

Although he still reads some of his favorite horror authors — Stephen King and Clive Barker, to name a couple — he now wants to concentrate on other aspects of his life, one of which is re-connecting with his passion for screenwriting and crime fiction. His short-film screenplay, *Joan Crawford Has Risen From the Grave,* is right now being opted for film by Very Scary Productions, and his work in progress, *Dead Letter Office,* a book of interviews with celebrities within the TV, film, music, and fiction genre,s is in the works for 2011.

He lives in Southern Indiana with his cats, Toby, Sissy, and Buckwheat, who help him "edit" his manuscripts by jumping on his keyboard when he isn't looking. He may be contacted via his personal email here: *nvfmagazine@gmail.com*.

Bear Manor Media

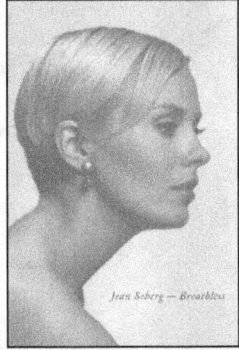

Classic Cinema.
Timeless TV.
Retro Radio.

WWW.BEARMANORMEDIA.COM

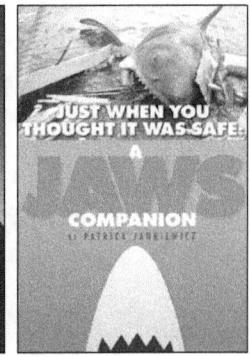

www.ingramcontent.com/pod-product-compliance
Lightning Source LLC
Chambersburg PA
CBHW062008220426
43662CB00010B/1274